THE PONY EXPRESS

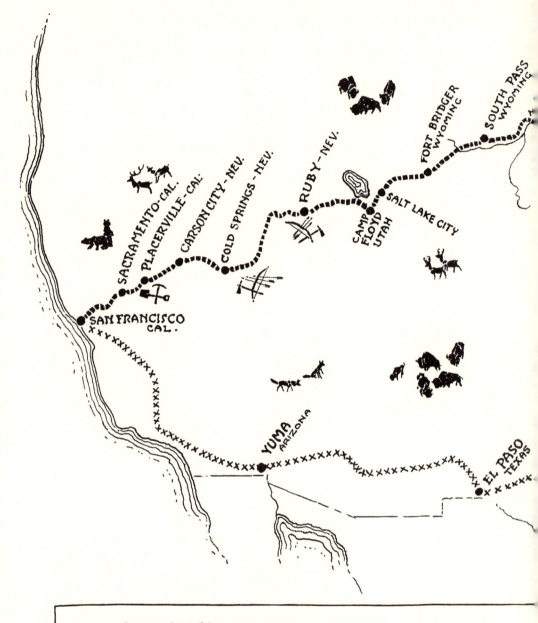

PONY EXPRESS AND CENTRAL OVERLAND STAGE ROUTE
BUTTERFIELD ROUTE

ROCK CREEK ~ Scene of Wild Bill's fight
JULESBURG ~ Slade's headquarters
COLD SPRINGS and RUBY ~ Center of the Pah Ute war
FORT LARAMIE ~ Where the Sioux made trouble for the riders

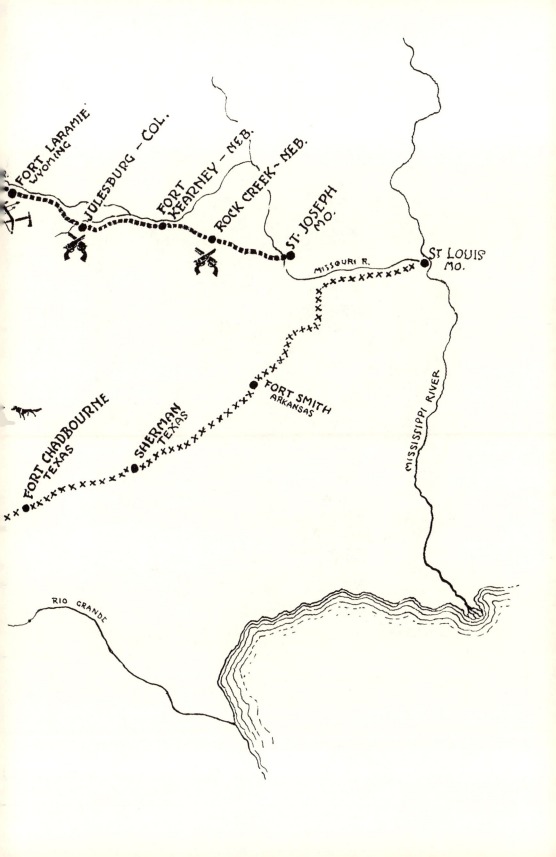

THE PONY EXPRESS RIDER

From *Hutchings' California Magazine* of July, 1860—The First Illustrated Magazine on the Pacific Coast.

THE PONY EXPRESS

The Record of a Romantic Adventure in Business

BY

ARTHUR CHAPMAN

ILLUSTRATED WITH
CONTEMPORARY PRINTS
AND PHOTOGRAPHS

COOPER SQUARE PUBLISHERS, INC.
New York
1971

Originally Published 1932
Copyright © 1932 and Renewed 1960 by Arthur Chapman
Reprinted by Permission of John Chapman
Published 1971 by Cooper Square Publishers, Inc.
59 Fourth Avenue, New York, N. Y. 10003
International Standard Book No. 0-8154-0391-7
Library of Congress Catalog Card No. 70-164522

Printed in the United States of America, by
Noble Offset Printers, Inc. New York, N.Y. 10003

TO

WILLIAM MacLEOD RAINE

CONTENTS

ILLUSTRATIONS

THE PONY EXPRESS

THE PONY EXPRESS

CHAPTER I

MEN AND HORSES

1

THE horseman displaced the man with the ax when the line of the Frontier West was extended beyond the lands of the Lower Missouri. Where walnut groves yielded to sagebrush, the man on horseback found free scope. Nature had attended to the problem of clearing the land. The chief question confronting those who were first on the scene was establishing communication in a country of such appalling distances.

The Indians, with their mustangs, had already provided the answer. They had developed mobility to a degree which later was to wring reluctant admiration from many a cavalry leader who opposed them.

The red men had their leaders in horsemanship. Tribal artists did their best to tell the world about the deeds of such riders. The lonely trapper, coming on an Indian pictograph on a smooth face of rock, could translate at least one symbol as he hooked his leg over his saddle-horn and tried to make out the entire story. That crudely drawn horse, with all four legs stiffly extended, represented speed. The rider was getting away from someone, or was going somewhere, *fast*. It was the horse *motif*, handed down in art through centuries. Nothing "belonged" more thoroughly in this Western upland, remote from the domain of steam and iron.

White men soon accustomed themselves to conditions which would have puzzled the tree-leveling pioneers of the Middle West in the days of Boone. Wild horses were caught and broken to saddle leather. Riders vied with the coyote and the antelope in speed. They pounded off great distances, timing themselves by the slant of the sun's rays. The primitive needs of the new frontier were mostly filled by horsemen. If there was a trail to be made, a red and agile enemy to be outmaneuvered, or a beleaguered force to be saved by the swift delivery of a message, man and horse stood ready to command.

Long before the arrival of the cowboy, the West had developed a school of riders, steeled against saddle fatigue. A wind-splitting crew, gaunt and hardy as the horses they bestrode, they were always eager for some new trial of their skill and endurance.

The most long-sustained and grueling test of the Western horseman's stamina was soon to come. Thousands of Californians, cut off from the East by a waste of sage and granite, were desperately homesick. They wanted letters from home and news of the world, without the delays attendant upon steamship delivery, plus re-handling at the Isthmus of Panama. These Californians had wrought good trails with their slow-moving ox-trains. Why could not the most direct of those trails be used as a lane of postal communication?

A green and poorly-supported Post Office Department staggered under the problem. Congress, doubtful of the experiment, grudgingly subsidized an infrequent service, scoffed at as the "jackass mail," between California and the Mormon settlement of Salt Lake City. The subsidy was as scanty as the trailside herbage on which the mules subsisted. From Salt Lake a few creaking wagons carried an occasional mail to Independence and return. Both contracts were soon annulled and a stage line, under more generous subsidy, was established. This mail route, chosen in the face of protests, extended through the Southwest, and was nearly a thousand miles too long. It saved little time as against steamer-Isthmian delivery.

California was more than impatient. The delay in getting mail was engendering suspicion and discontent. The main route of the pioneers was direct enough—why was it being neglected? The counter-plea was that it would be impossible to keep a more northerly route open winter and summer.

To refute this argument about closed passes in the mountains and insurmountable difficulties on the plains, the horseman was called upon. The Pony Express was formed, and nearly one hundred riders and hundreds of horses were pitted against Father Time in a race which is unique in modern history.

The Pony Express was not organized as a Government institution. Search the records of Congress for the years 1860 and 1861 and you will find only one or two brief references to the frontier's "fast mail," then functioning. Private enterprise backed the Pony Express and kept it going, though every month showed monetary loss. The "Pony," as it was soon affectionately called, was one of the outward expressions of a certain business audacity which was common at the time. Men in the whirl of frontier activities seldom stopped to figure costs. Mines were paying—the wealth of the new, raw West was inexhaustible. Fantastic schemes lost all aspect of distortion. Men plunged, and, if they lost, were game in defeat. The Pony Express could not have been born in any other era. When the last horse galloped into Sacramento, with a mechanized age close on its heels, a failure was posted on the record—one of those few financial failures which can be translated into terms of glory.

For upwards of two years the couriers of the Pony Express flitted back and forth between Missouri and California. Sometimes they carried messages on which hung the fate of the nation. Beyond the final westward lines of telegraph, they brought the first news of battles. Editors looked at their watches and wondered if the "Pony" would bring its supply of news in time for the next edition. California newspapers "played up" their columns of Pony Express dispatches. The *Tribune, Herald,* and other New York journals made front-page features of the news from California and the mines of Washoe "via Pony Express and Magnetic Telegraph."

The Pony Express seldom failed those who so anxiously awaited its arrival. Like a shuttle it wove back and forth across a 2,000-mile loom. If a horse faltered and fell dead, the rider seized the foam-covered *mochila* that contained the mail and staggered on afoot to the next relay station. Indians, outlaws, blizzards and cloudbursts were only a few of the dangers to be faced along the way, but the mail went through. The shuttle had to be kept moving. What it wove into the pattern of American life will be admired as long as we care for such things as adventure, romance and rugged devotion to duty.

Towns have sprung up where many a Pony Express rider bunked with scarcely more of shelter and comfort than a badger in its burrow. The trails along which the hoofs of the ponies shot fire have been lost in a maze of cultivated farms. Records have been destroyed and the names of riders have been forgotten. Yet it was only into yesterday's twilight that the Pony Express couriers disappeared.

2

The name of the Pony Express had never been heard in the West when F. X. Aubrey of Santa Fé performed a feat in long-distance riding which set men talking about the possibilities of quick communication by relay across the "great American desert."

Santa Fé was a meeting-place of great riders. The men who gathered about the sunlit plaza could appraise horseflesh at a glance. They watched the animals that were ridden in by the leaders of the dusty wagon trains which drew up at the Fonda. If an unusually good horse was brought in, the owner soon had offers. Whether he sold or not, the merits and demerits of the horse were good for an hour's discussion.

It was not that the men of Santa Fé were unduly curious. They were in a land where a man could not afford to be indifferent about the kind of horse he rode. A slight miscalculation as to the stamina of his mount might mean the death of the rider. Sometimes a trapper failed to come in from the "outside," just because he had made that little mistake.

Among those who passed many leisure hours about the plaza of the Southwest's great market center were the

"Taos men." They were hardy trappers who, with Kit Carson, made their chief rendezvous at Fernandez de Taos, an easy ride from Santa Fé. They liked to come in and talk over their adventures in the days of the previous decade, when beaver were plentiful. Every man had owed his life, not once but many times, to the fact that he could, and did, outride Indians who were in pursuit.

Carson himself had made notable rides, not only in forays against the Indians, but as a bearer of dispatches. From Bent's Fort on the Arkansas to the scene of his exploits in California with Frémont and Kearny, it was admitted that he was an ideal saddleman.

One of the most dangerous rides made by Kit Carson was for $300—plus the thrill of the adventure and the knowledge that he was on a mission of relief. Carson, starting East with Bent and St. Vrain from Bent's Fort, as hunter for the wagon train, found a command of United States dragoons camped at Walnut Creek. The captain said a train of several traders and one hundred Mexicans was close by on the trail. A large party of Texans was lying in wait at the crossing of the Arkansas, intending to kill or take prisoner as many of the Mexicans as they could. It was to be in revenge for the treatment of Texans at the hands of General Armijo in 1841. Carson was offered $300 if he would get word to Armijo at Santa Fé to send troops for the protection of the Mexicans.

Carson accepted the offer and started back along the trail, with a companion. At Bent's Fort he was told that Ute Indians were between him and Taos. Leaving his companion, Carson went on alone, riding a horse which was the pick of the animals at the fort. Discovering the Indian village, Carson waited till nightfall and went past it safely. Then he rode on at top speed to Taos, where his message was forwarded to Armijo, who sent a force to disperse the Texans but was defeated. Not until the dragoons had finally disarmed the Texans did the Mexicans venture to cross the Arkansas.

On his return trip to the wagon train, Carson was accompanied by a Mexican. A band of Indians approached, and the Mexican told Carson to escape. The horse which Carson was riding could not have been overtaken by the savages. But Carson refused to desert his companion. Both put on a determined front, and, after making a few hostile demonstrations and seeing that if they attacked they were certain to lose at least two of their number, the Indians went on.

Such affairs were incidents of the trail to Carson, who was willing to venture anywhere, as long as he could be assured of a good horse under him.

Frequently seen with Carson and the other men of Taos at Santa Fé was Lucien Maxwell, who lived in princely style on his enormous land grant, secured by a title that held after American occupation of New Mexico. Maxwell and Carson were close friends. While Maxwell made no pretensions as a rider, he was willing to back his judgment as to the ability of others in the saddle. Undoubtedly his gold figured in a wager which was made with Aubrey concerning the possibility of a lowered record along the trail from Santa Fé to Independence.

Aubrey was a French-Canadian trader at Santa Fé. His wagon trains were rumbling back and forth along the great trail. It would have been a pleasant and easy life for Aubrey if he had been content to watch the caravans

as they came in and to check over his own profits. But
Aubrey was a good deal like Carson, mentally as well as
physically. Each was of slight build, a little more than five
feet in height, and weighing not much over one hundred
pounds. Both were restless if they were long away from
the outdoors. With each of them being outdoors meant
being on horseback.

Aubrey, going back and forth along the trail, established records that surprised even the redoubtable Carson.
Gregg, in his book, *The Commerce of the Prairies*,
figures the trail distance between Independence and Santa
Fé as 780 miles. It took ox-teams from two to three
months to make the trip. Horsemen allowed themselves
three weeks or over. Aubrey completed the distance in
two weeks, and then set out to do better.

Aubrey knew every mile of the Santa Fé trail. Often,
on starting out with one of his ox-teams, he would push
on ahead, riding until far into the night and camping
at the trailside or "throwing in" for a meal and a few
hours' sleep under a wagon bed with some emigrant or
freight outfit. He knew the location of all the springs,
watercourses and quicksands, and could check off his
mileage by starlight from the natural landmarks along
the lonely way.

There was a buzz of interest at both ends of the trail
when Aubrey reduced his own record to eight days. Eight
consecutive days of travel at one hundred miles a day!
It was indeed something remarkable, when conditions of
travel on the Santa Fé trail were taken into consideration.

Then it became known that Aubrey was to make still
another attempt, and that he had wagered on his ability

to ride from Santa Fé to Independence in six days or less—with the proviso that he could use relays of horses.

3

Relays!

The horseback-riding West, as represented by the saddlemen of Santa Fé and Taos, was all attention when this feature of Aubrey's plan was discussed.

These horsemen, who ventured into the wilderness to outfight or outride other horsemen, never went on an expedition without their saddle reserves. Every trapping party had its extra horses, not only for pack purposes, but as the final resort in case of necessary flight. The reserve horses, in the event of a hurried retreat, could be driven ahead of the riders. Saddles could be quickly changed and the tired mounts abandoned, one by one.

Such a system was far from the relay. It was merely the best that could be followed in a wild country where relay stations could not be established, because of enemies. Not that the trail to Santa Fé was any too safe for lone riders, by any means. But if a man was lucky, he might get through without losing his scalp. And, if his relays of horses were not run off by Indians, this man Aubrey might establish something new in the way of a record for speed and endurance. The test, under such novel conditions, would be worth waiting for.

Aubrey was a man of vision and intelligence, as well as physical hardihood. It may be that he had caught his idea from some old history brought to Santa Fé in saddlebag or covered wagon. He may have read of the singular and amazing achievement of Genghis Khan,

Mongol conqueror of Northern China and Central Asia, in binding his huge empire together with a chain of thousands of relay riders.

A railroad through the Southwest was Aubrey's dream. The relay plan, whether original or borrowed from the thirteenth century, may have been part of his larger scheme—to speed the development of the frontier until the engineer crowded the bullwhacker off the trail.

At any rate, Aubrey was one of the parties to a wager of $1,000, which, if won, would bring Santa Fé and Independence closer together by two days.

4

Aubrey chose to travel by the Cimarron cut-off. The trail divided at Sand Creek, on the Arkansas River, about 350 miles from Independence. One branch of the trail continued up the Arkansas and across the Raton Mountains. The southern branch, which crossed the Cimarron, was more direct, but it was more difficult and the Indian menace was greater.

Aubrey started from Santa Fé on a September day in 1848. Between Santa Fé and Rio Gallinas (Las Vegas), ninety miles, were Pecos Village, San Miguel and Ojo de Bernal. Beyond Gallinas he was "on his own" in Indian country. The Apaches, Kiowas and Comanches had been taking many lives along the trail. There were countless places where it would be easy to ambush a lone rider.

Nearly every landmark past which Aubrey rode recalled a scene of tragedy. The Rio Colorado, which had been mistaken by the explorer, Stephen H. Long, for the source of the Red River, was the scene of a desperate fight in which twelve trappers had stood off two hundred Comanches. Beyond Point of Rocks and Round Mound was McNee's Creek, where a party of traders had been attacked, Captain John Means being killed and the others nearly starving before they were rescued. Near the crossing of the Cimarron the great pathfinder, trapper and fur trader, Jedediah S. Smith, had been killed by Indians.

Rock Creek, on the Dry Cimarron, was the scene of the massacre of a Mr. White and his family. White, with his wife and baby, had gone on ahead of one of Aubrey's wagon trains, with which he had been traveling. The Jicarilla Apaches who killed White and his child kidnaped Mrs. White. Kit Carson, Leroux and Fisher, of the "Taos men," started out as scouts, ahead of a rescuing party of dragoons. Disregarding Carson's advice to charge, when the Indians had been discovered, the commanding officer sought a parley. This gave the Indians a chance to escape. Mrs. White was found dead in a tent, an arrow through her heart.

Through such scenes of Indian massacre and surprise, Aubrey pounded on his way. His most desperate fight was against an almost overwhelming desire to sleep. Such food as he ate was snatched from the hands of the men he had stationed in charge of a few relay mounts along the trail, or hastily provided from the stores in some emigrant wagon.

Aubrey's slender system of relays had been established at great risk. The men who were stationed along the trail were in hourly danger of death at the hands of Indians who constantly roamed on both sides of the great highway, seeking scalps and loot. It soon became apparent that the relays were not sufficient in number. The horses

fagged easily in the sand. The experiment of driving
fresh mounts on ahead proved of little value. The horses
thus driven tired almost as soon as the animals he rode.

Two or three emigrant trains, outbound from Independence, were met. The emigrants were glad to "swap"
horses with Aubrey, whose feats of horsemanship were
familiar along the trail. The wayfarers looked on this
supreme attempt from a sporting angle. They would
have laid wagers on Aubrey's success had there been anyone else in the desert with whom they could bet.

Aubrey made the trip to Independence in five and one
half days and won his bet, but he was half-dead from
fatigue when he was dragged from the saddle. Flinging
himself on a bed, after giving the landlord instructions
to wake him in eight hours, Aubrey was lost to the world.
There is an Indian tradition to the effect that, after such
complete exhaustion, if a man is left to "sleep his sleep"
he will never awaken. Aubrey slept twenty hours and was
furious when he awakened. He threatened to kill the landlord for not arousing him, but the frightened host explained that he had done his best, to no avail.

Aubrey was not yet through with the saddle. He returned to Santa Fé and made several other long rides,
though none against time. In 1854 he rode from San
José, California, to Peralta, New Mexico, a short distance below Santa Fé, his object being to demonstrate
the feasibility of a railroad. Aubrey took copious notes
on this journey, which was to be his last.

When he arrived in Santa Fé, after completing his
California trip, Aubrey stepped into a general store and
saloon for refreshment. Friends gathered about to hear
the news of the journey. Among those who saw Aubrey

arrive was Major Richard Weightman. Getting up from his seat in the plaza, Weightman said: "I must see Aubrey," and entered the saloon.

Aubrey, according to the testimony of witnesses, asked Weightman to drink with him, but the invitation was refused. Aubrey accused Weightman of abusing him in a newspaper which he (Weightman) had published.

Weightman denied Aubrey's accusation. Getting off the counter where he had been sitting, Weightman seized a glass of liquor and threw the contents in Aubrey's face. Aubrey drew a gun and fired. In some way the weapon caught and the bullet went into the ceiling. Weightman closed with Aubrey, bowie knife in hand. Before spectators could interfere, Weightman had sunk the knife in Aubrey's body and the most intrepid rider in the Southwest was dead in ten minutes.

Weightman was acquitted in the inquiry which followed. It was the frontier code that the man who "drew" first was the aggressor, no matter what the provocation. Weightman had come to New Mexico with Kearny in 1846 and had taken part in the occupation of Santa Fé. He was the first delegate to Congress from New Mexico. At the outbreak of the Civil War he enlisted on the side of the Confederacy and was killed in action.

Though Aubrey was dead, his fame as a saddleman lived on. As the Oregon Trail and other great highways were extended across the country, speedier communication became the uppermost topic of conversation. Men talked over the achievements of Aubrey at camp-fires and in cabin councils. Nearly every locality had its champion rider, who was confident that he could better Aubrey's record.

Richard Burton, later to win fame and knighthood as a translator of the *Arabian Nights,* came upon the Aubrey tradition when he made his trip across the country on the Overland Trail. At Salt Lake, Burton found Porter Rockwell, whose feats of riding, mountaineering and man-hunting made him outstanding in a frontier company that was by no means composed of weaklings.

Rockwell, who was herding cattle at the time for the Overland stage outfit, fascinated Burton. Rockwell had been longing for years to have a try at Aubrey's record. He told Burton that, given relays, he could do even better than Aubrey had done. He had figured it out that he could ride nine hundred miles in 144 hours or less—and nobody familiar with the feats accomplished by Brigham Young's "man of iron" was skeptical enough to wager that he could not make good his boast.

Military commandants at the far-scattered Western posts talked over the possibilities of relay systems between the forts. If Aubrey's idea had been to set men talking, he had achieved his object. But it was not until several years after his death that the West was to echo to the sound of the galloping hoofs of the Pony Express.

CHAPTER II

CALIFORNIA'S PROBLEM

THE California of "the splendid, idle forties" posted and received its letters in a properly tranquil spirit. If there was delay of a week, or month, or if a letter never was delivered, it was all the will of Heaven.

California's first means of communication with the outside world was the *coreo*, or mounted courier, carrying messages to and from Old Mexico. Correspondence was mostly in behalf of the church. The delays consequent to such a long, arduous and dangerous trip seem to have been such that even a proper sense of resignation was violated. At any rate, in the early Spanish records, we find Father Garcia Diego addressing the Minister of Ecclesiastical Affairs at Mexico City in behalf of a better service to California.

Other *coreos* carried messages between presidios and missions in California. Relays were not established. News was not so important that unseemly haste need be manifested in its transmission, nor were letter writers unduly impatient. The vaqueros who acted as messengers, with their wide sombreros and leather chaparejos studded with silver ornaments, and their saddles and bridles heavy with the same metal, took a leisurely course amid California's forests of pine and oak and through the glades where their tapaderas sank deeply into the mustard and crackling grass at the trailside. Romantic postmen these, timing Spanish love songs to the lope of their horses. At night the *coreo* was always welcome at some rancheria along the way, where there was wine and dancing. If the messages were not delivered today, *mañana* was still in the offing.

In the first months of American occupation, just prior to the letting loose of Bedlam through the discovery of gold, something of this same spirit of leisureliness marked California's mail service. The chief difference was that it took on a touch of military formality.

Soldiers, instead of vaqueros, acted as mail carriers. Two troopers, one from San Francisco and one from San Diego, were dispatched once a week with mail sacks containing not only official communications but such letters as individuals might care to send. No charge was made for this service. At a half-way point the troopers exchanged mail sacks and returned to their respective posts. The schedule was drafted in most generous spirit. No trooper's horse ever broke down under the strain.

California, in those peaceful days, gave no hint of the struggle which was soon to follow—when the fight for better mail service was to bring tragedy in its wake, with carriers killed by Indians or frozen to death in mountain passes and contractors brought to ruin.

Americans who had settled in California under the Mexican flag received mail from the East because a few thousand Oregonians were getting an intermittent service by sailing vessels. The ships which carried mail to the Astorians put in at San Francisco, and eventual delivery was by grace of courier.

After he had taken formal possession of New Mexico, at the outbreak of the Mexican War in 1847, General Stephen W. Kearny was sent to California for the purpose of performing a like office there. He was met by General John C. Frémont with the information that the change in proprietorship had already been effected. Frémont had brought about the *coup* and had raised the American flag before he and his followers knew that war with Mexico had been declared.

There was no great rush to California in the wake of annexation. It looked as if the growth of the newly acquired territory would be due to a gradual filtration of agriculturists. In order to take care of this normal growth which was expected, some improvement was made in the mail service to the Pacific Coast. The Postmaster General, in 1848, reported as follows:

The ocean steamers California, Panama and Oregon, constructed under a contract with the Secretary of the Navy for service on the Pacific, have sailed from New York to Panama, and the California is expected to commence service for this department on the first of January next from Panama to Oregon.

The Secretary of the Navy has likewise employed the Falcon on the line between Havana and Chagres, and she is expected to sail from Havana to Chagres in time for the mails to reach Panama and be forwarded by the California to the territories on the Pacific Coast. This department has made a contract for the transportation of mails across the Isthmus from Chagres to Panama so that in the future there will be a regular monthly mail from Charleston, by Havana, Chagres and Panama to Oregon.

This service cost the government $600,000 in annual subsidies. The amount was increased to $725,000 when the service was made semi-monthly. The first charges were high—forty cents a letter to or from California or Oregon, thirty cents to Panama and twenty cents to Chagres, as against twenty-four cents to Europe. Protests induced the Postmaster General to recommend that a uniform price of fifteen cents be established, applying to Europe and the Western territories, but this seems to have gone unheeded until new and unlooked-for conditions forced a change.

John Augustus Sutter, a Swiss-American trader and settler, whose ideas ran along the line of agriculture, was the innocent cause of plunging the Government into postal problems which were to be subjects of bitter debate for many years. Sutter had possessed himself of several thousand acres of land in the Sacramento valley. He built a fort on the site of the present-day Sacramento. Several hundred settlers formed the nucleus of the enormous colony which he had in mind.

Sutter might as well have thrown away the title to his land when, in 1848, his carpenter, James Marshall, discovered gold while constructing a mill. The work on the mill was never completed. Gold seekers swarmed over Sutter's property. More came, and lost themselves in the wooded recesses of the Mother Lode. Within a year there were 100,000 new residents in California; in another year there were 300,000. Most of them had come overland by the covered wagon routes; the remainder had crossed the Isthmus. San Francisco and Sacramento became cities, with a constantly growing river traffic between.

These new Californians had mostly come from localities where the prompt arrival and departure of the mail was just a part of ordinary existence. They knew their rights and insisted on getting them. California newspapers wanted real news of the world to replace the poems, essays and stories with which they were compelled to fill their columns. The miners and settlers wanted word from home.

Congress took a remedial step in 1851. In that year the mail service to the Pacific Coast was changed from a monthly to a semi-monthly basis. There it was to remain for six years more. Postage was reduced from forty cents a letter to six cents. This was raised to ten cents in 1853. Even the ten-cent rate did not begin to pay the cost of handling mail via the steamer-Isthmian route. There was complaint from economically-inclined legislators, who seemed to believe that every Californian who received and answered a letter was putting a double burden upon his country.

The arrival of a mail steamer at San Francisco was an event which stirred the entire community. Telegraph Hill was closely scanned when it was known that a steamer was about due. A semaphore on the hilltop conveyed the intelligence that the anxiously-awaited vessel was in sight. Then there was a rush to the post office.

One of the classic stories of early-day California indicates how much a part of San Francisco life this signal on Telegraph Hill had become. An actor, taking part in a tragedy, stood against a curtained backdrop, with arms outstretched at his sides.

"What does this mean?" he asked.

A voice from the gallery replied:

"Sidewheel steamer," and the laugh that went up from the audience ruined any effect the playwright and actors might have sought to produce.

At the San Francisco post office, on the arrival of a steamer with mail, long lines were formed. Men waited for hours, sometimes in the rain, while the postmaster and his clerks struggled with the problem of distribution.

The people of San Francisco, in spite of these delays, were better off than those Californians who had turned to the gold fields. The situation was confessedly out of hand, so far as deliveries of mail were concerned. The Postmaster General, in his report for 1851, dismisses an unpleasant matter in the following words:

> The mail service in California and Oregon has been so irregular in its performance and so imperfectly reported that it is not included in this statement.

New settlements were springing up so rapidly in California that the Post Office Department could not keep pace. A special agent, who had been sent out to investigate, reported that he found several postmasters doing a thriving business, though they had never been appointed by the Government, nor were their post offices recognized officially!

Such a condition was made possible through the fact that private enterprise had stepped in and was seeking to remedy conditions which were admittedly beyond departmental control. Unofficial postmen were delivering letters, and it is not surprising that an occasional unofficial postmaster was heard of.

The appearance of private enterprise on the California scene was a natural outgrowth of the chaotic conditions which had arisen. Also it was a repetition of a little matter of history concerning postal affairs in the East. John Harnden, founder of the express business in this country, who traveled with his famous carpet bag between New York and Boston, had created a furor in the '40's when he had "cut in" on the Government's postal service. Rates of postage were excessively high, and Harnden agreed to carry letters for a fraction of the Government's charge. His messengers, in Western New York State, were arrested, at the behest of the outraged postmasters, whose receipts had been interfered with and whose compensation was accordingly reduced. Citizens were on hand to furnish bail to every messenger who was arrested, and the Government soon quit a losing fight by reducing its postal rates.

If so much could be accomplished in the East, where private express companies had started their promoters on the road to wealth, California could hardly fail to profit by the example. Only, instead of fighting the postmasters, Californians took them in as partners.

An express "company," for the delivery of letters to miners, might consist of one man and a mule. The first of these intermediary concerns was organized by Alexander H. Todd, in 1849. Todd had joined the gold rush, but his health was such that he could not stand the work in the "diggings." Like others in the placer fields, Todd had longed for letters which never came. They might be lying unclaimed in the post office at San Francisco or Sacramento. The Postmaster General reported that one of his chief problems was the dead letter mail—there was a matter of 2,400 pounds in 1851—accumulating in California. Why not get at least a portion of this dead letter mail into the proper hands and be rewarded by the grateful consignees?

Todd went at his new work systematically. He visited mining camps and made a list of those who were expecting to receive mail regularly. He charged one dollar for registration. Todd was sworn in as a postal clerk at San Francisco, and agreed to pay the postmaster twenty-five cents for each letter handed over to him for delivery. His charge for delivering a letter was $4. In addition to letters, Todd carried as many newspapers as he could gather. His charge for a New York newspaper of reasonably late date was $8.

Todd carried gold dust on his return trips. From Sacramento to San Francisco he traveled by steamer. On his first trip down the river he carried $250,000 in gold dust in a butter keg. His fee for such service to the gold-burdened miners was five per cent of the amount carried. Todd never had more than two pack mules in operating his express business, yet at the height of his affairs he often profited to the extent of $1,000 a day.

Of course such an enterprise could not be carried on long without competition. Mules were plentiful and express "companies" sprang up everywhere in the gold fields. No mining camp was too distant to be sought out by the enterprising individuals who operated the "jackass express" in all weathers. There were no complaints about non-delivery of mail or loss of gold dust. California road agents had not yet started the stand-and-deliver tactics which later on were to test the courage and marksmanship of messengers in charge of treasure boxes.

Hundreds of men found employment in thus establishing communication between the mining camps and the out-

side world. Enthusiasm for mining soon died in the breast
of the Forty-Niner who was not suited temperamentally or
physically for the work. Here was a job that had its difficult moments but was not a back-breaking grind. The
express rider was welcome in every camp. Not only was he
a bearer of individual messages, but he was a source of
general news. Men deserted gold pans, rockers and sluices,
and came blinking out of tunnels to hear what the courier
might have to say. Disappointment in not getting a personal message was often alleviated, at least in part, by a
few words of general gossip, or perhaps by the purchase
of a newspaper fresh from the press not more than six or
eight weeks before.

If the miner wanted to send a message back home, the
courier, who was also president, general manager and
hostler of his "company," provided stationery. The envelope corner usually bore the friendly nickname of the
Pooh-Bah of the saddle—also a pictorial design which had
to do with some feature of his calling. A favorite design
was a pony rider going at full speed, indicating the
celerity with which Bill's or Tom's Express put its lonely
customers in touch with a throbbing world. Zack, not to
be outdone, had his envelope corners decorated with a
mail carrier on skis. This appealed to the trade which
was located behind mountain barriers.

So many of these professional couriers took to the trail
that prices began to drop. The top charge of $4 a letter,
established by Todd, was not long maintained. There was
a sag, until the price reached the general level of $1. This
decline in the letter fee was not altogether due to competitive influences. As more miners flocked into the hills,
the messengers could afford to reduce rates.

Some letters were taken from the main post offices on a purely speculative basis. Perhaps a messenger dimly remembered that a certain Bill Jones had had a cabin near a certain camp some months before. The messenger would do his best to locate Bill. Somebody else was in Bill's cabin. Bill had taken his gold pan and pick and shovel, and had pushed along for a more promising location. He had not left a change of address—in fact he had no idea where he would be from one day to another.

Through all the gold camps on his route, the messenger would search for the miner. If success did not reward his efforts, he would turn the letter over to a messenger who had established a route somewhere else on the Mother Lode. By the time the miner was found, his letter might have been handled by half a dozen different express "companies." It might have traveled in saddlebags over hundreds of miles of mountain trails and across snow-filled passes. But, weather-worn and thumb-printed almost past deciphering, it was still word from "outside," and was well worth whatever fee was claimed by the messenger who made the final delivery. Through this system of interchange, many miners received letters which otherwise would have gone to swell California's accumulation of undelivered mail.

Joaquin Miller, who toiled in the California placer fields, in later years wrote an article for the San Francisco *Call* in which he said:

The Pony Express was a great feature in the gold mines of California long before anyone ever thought of putting it on the plains. Every creek, camp or "city" had its Pony Express which ran to and from the nearest post office. At Yreka we had the Humbug Creek Express, the Deadwood Camp Express, the Greenhorn, and so on.

The rider was always a bold, bright young fellow, who owned the line, horses and all, and had his "office" in some responsible store. He crowded an immense deal of personality into his work; would die in the saddle rather than delay ten minutes over the expected time. He was, of course, always a dashing rider, dressed gayly and blew a small bugle as he went up and down the creek at a plunging rate. "Three blasts, after the fashion of the London postman!" Whack and bang at the cabin door meant a letter for this or that "claim," as the rider dashed down the trail under the trees.

And then hats in the air! Hurrah, hurrah, hurrah! Whose is it—and which one of the half dozen or dozen men at the long sluice-boxes is to hear from his wife, mother or waiting sweetheart? This one starts to get it —that one, then the other. They look at one another hastily, and then one of them—strangely enough nearly always the right one!—springs up the ladder. Away, over the boulders with a bound, with pay for the letter clutched in his fist! He grasps the letter, away bounds the spirited pony, another blast of the horn!

The riders of the pony and the mule were not so popular in official Washington as they were on the trails of California. The Postmaster General, in his report for 1853, made this complaint:

For a single letter the Government receives six cents when prepaid and 10 cents when unpaid, and for each pound of printed matter 5 cents. Notwithstanding that the Government incurs a heavy loss in supplying the citizens of that state (California) with letters, newspapers and other mail matter, the citizen himself employs other facilities for the conveyance of his letters and pays thereon at a rate from twenty to forty fold greater than the Government charges for similar service.

Despite the fact that they were thus frowned upon in official circles, the private express companies continued to flourish. Theirs was a personal service which the Government either could not or would not perform. Between the larger towns the trails soon widened into roads traversed by stages. On these roads, well-organized express companies took up the messenger service in which the one-man outfits had been pioneers. But for years the chief communication with outlying districts was by horseback or pack mule courier. Wells, Fargo & Company, as late as 1864, conducted a Pony Express north from San Francisco and Sacramento to Marysville and south to San José.

California had solved its internal affairs of communication in its own way. It had given free rein to private enterprise and had received faithful and competent service in return. The pack mule and pony messengers had done their part well. The self-appointed couriers, without bond and with no semblance of Governmental authority in many instances, had established a record for integrity.

All this, however, was only a partial solution of California's problem, in which the Oregon country shared. Steamer transportation of mail would always be too slow. It was only two thousand miles overland to a rail connection. Why was it not possible to establish a land route which would cut days, and possibly weeks, from the cumbersome schedule which had been put in effect?

If Californians expected an offhand answer to the question, they were to find disappointment in store. Obstacles, political as well as physical, intervened. Congress, torn by sectionalism, was to seize upon this new subject for acrimonious debate. Ignorance and wilful misrepresentation were to have their say. Fantastic schemes were to be tried out. Men whose capabilities were as yet unknown were to achieve marvels in frontier transportation. The flames of Indian warfare were to be beaten back. Lead was to fly, blood was to flow, graves were to be filled—all because California, isolated but confident of its future, demanded that the last vestige of its remoteness be removed.

Men set themselves about the task of bringing speed to the trails which were still heavy with the dust from the ox-trains of the pioneers.

CHAPTER III

STEAMER VERSUS STAGE

1

PLACERVILLE, California, which had been descriptively christened Hangtown by the Forty-Niners, was more than usually interested in a string of pack mules which was lined up in the main street ready for departure early in May, 1851.

Pack mules were no novelty in Placerville, but this outfit was of special significance. It carried the first mail *bound East*. It represented the opening of overland competition with the steamer service which had been causing California so much discontent.

The mail had been brought, by river steamer, from San Francisco to Sacramento. It had been transferred to muleback, leaving Sacramento on May 1. Now it was at Placerville, the gateway to the El Dorado of which many thousands of pioneers had dreamed. The miners at Placerville scrawled messages which they saw added to the mail sacks. The total mail itself was not much—probably not over seventy-five pounds. One mule could carry it, with plenty of room to spare in the panniers. But Placerville cheered when the contractor himself gave the final tug to the diamond hitch and the mail was thereby officially closed.

It meant that from then on California was to be in direct communication with the "States," and that letters would come by "short-cut" instead of by way of that long loop around Panama. If the mail once got through, it meant that California had proved its point and that an overland service was feasible. Placerville, when the last mule disappeared on the trail, retired to its bars to celebrate.

The contractor in charge of this first overland mail from California was Major George Chorpenning, Jr., a trail-maker and Indian fighter, who was to become the center of controversy that involved Congress for years. Chorpenning and his partner, Absalom Woodward, had agreed to carry the mail from Sacramento City (as Sacramento was then called) via Carson's Valley to Salt Lake City and return. The term of this contract with the Government ended June 30, 1854. Service was to be performed monthly, each way, in thirty days, at an annual compensation of $14,000.

East of Placerville, over the trail so painfully traversed by the pioneers, there was a long, hard and dangerous grind to Salt Lake City. It was the worst part of the "Great American Desert" which figured conspicuously on all maps at the time. There were vast stretches of dusty sage. Where the soil showed through, it was leprous with alkali. In the whole immensity now known as Nevada there was not a white man's habitation. Indians were numerous and treacherous. The routes themselves were deceptive. A turn into the wrong canyon, or an inviting cut-off across some flat, might lead into difficulty. The Donner party, in 1846, had floundered into disaster because somebody had guessed wrong.

Chorpenning was not guessing. He had familiarized

himself with the country east of the Sierras before he had entered into the contract to carry the mails. The route that he chose was pretty generally followed by the surveyors and mail contractors who came afterward. His first mail train got through. So did the others that followed during the summer.

The contractors did not delay in putting up stations along the mail route. On May 22, 1851—which meant that Chorpenning had paused for this work on his first official trip to Salt Lake—ground was measured and a settlement begun at Carson Valley. This was the first settlement on the eastern slope of the Sierra Nevadas, where, within a few years, one of the richest mining regions in the world was to be opened.

The "jackass mail," more prophetic than practical, continued to function during the summer and early autumn. Chorpenning, far from any military post, had to furnish his own guard. His muleteers were required to be as handy with the rifle as with the pack rope. More than once Indians had been sighted, and occasionally it was necessary to beat them off. A job with the "jackass mail" was guaranteed to provide plenty of excitement, but the West was full of adventurous spirits who welcomed any such assignment.

The November train started from Sacramento City in charge of Woodward, with four men. There were heavy snows in the Sierras, but the party "broke trail" successfully and emerged into the open country on the eastern slope. At Willow Springs, hardly more than 150 miles from Salt Lake City, Woodward met the November westbound train. Woodward warned the mail carriers who were headed for California that he had encountered a large body of Indians the day before. Proceeding cautiously, the west-bound train went on, while Woodward's train headed for Salt Lake City.

Nothing was heard of Woodward and his party until the following spring. Then it was ascertained that Woodward and his men had been killed by Indians, and the mail, with all the property belonging to the party, had been stolen or destroyed.

In the meantime, with the fate of Woodward and his party still undetermined, an attempt was made to carry out the terms of the mail contract during the winter. In February, 1852, a party of five, including the supervisor, Edson Cody, left California with the mail. The mail carriers had with them ten mules and horses. They were fifty-three days on the road, and during that time all their animals froze to death. The men were compelled to travel on foot, through deep snow, some two hundred miles from Salt Lake City, with the mail packed upon their backs. They subsisted seven days on mule meat, and were four days without food of any kind. Starving and half frozen, they staggered into Salt Lake City—but with the mail intact.

Those in charge of the mule train which left California with the mail in April of the same year, went through experiences almost as trying. The train was forty-seven days in getting through, most of that time being spent in the deep snows of the mountains.

Chorpenning in May discovered the fate of his partner. Woodward's remains were found, and the means of his death established.

It was realized that the Indians would be more aggressive than ever, after the massacre of Woodward's party.

In spite of this, one of Chorpenning's assistants left Salt Lake City with the west-bound mail. His arrival in Sacramento was chronicled in the *Union* of June 4, 1852, as follows:

Mr. John Smith arrived in this city early on yesterday morning with the Salt Lake mails, having left the valley on the 13th May and Carson Valley on the 30th. By this arrival the melancholy intelligence of the murder of Capt. Woodward and his entire party is fully confirmed. He left the city on Nov. 1st last, with the Salt Lake mails, in company with John Hamilton, Harry Benson, —— Kennedy, and an Englishman named John Hawthorn. On the 28th of that month they were met by Samuel Hanson, carrier from Salt Lake, on the seventeen-mile stretch of Mary's River and ten miles this side of the Big Canyon. On the day previous they were attacked by seventy Indians on Mary's River, but at that time succeeded in beating them off. The former, however, passed them about the time they were met by Hanson, and continued on in advance of the company. By information obtained from Indians at Fort Hall, it appears that they were again attacked at Big Canyon by a party of Indians called the "Tosointches," a portion of the Pah-Utes. At first the four companions of Captain Woodward were killed and the Captain himself badly wounded. He succeeded, however, in escaping with two animals to Deep Creek, forty miles this side of the Salt Lake settlements, and upwards of 300 miles from the spot where he was wounded. It was here that his remains were found this spring. . . .

Mr. Smith left Salt Lake Valley in company with two others only, and was greatly annoyed by the Indians before he reached Carson Valley. On the north fork of

Mary's River, a party of "Diggers," who were armed, made a feint as if about to attack them for the purpose of getting in advance, but Mr. Smith and his companions were mounted on fine animals and thus thwarted their attempts. On the day before they arrived at Stony Point, they overtook a company of fifty-two men from Salt Lake, nine of whom came on with Mr. Smith's party. When they arrived at Stony Point they found a band of two hundred Indians, well armed and in a hostile attitude. They found it impossible to pass, and returned to the party they had left behind them. The train then advanced to Stony Point and camped there, the Indians firing during the night. . . . At Clay Banks, a few miles this side of Lawson's route, they were also annoyed.

The dangers of life on the California mail route, as proved by the death of Woodward and his men and the determined attacks on Smith's party, were now such that Chorpenning found it impossible to get anyone to accompany him out of Salt Lake City. But if the mail were not delivered the contract would be lost. So Chorpenning started out alone.

The details of Chorpenning's journey are not known. His story, as it stands, has been pieced out of official records. It is known that he started out of Salt Lake City without escort, in charge of the mail. It is known that he arrived in Sacramento, still without escort and still in charge of the mail. From Salt Lake City to Sacramento, over the trail as then laid out, was close to seven hundred miles. For more than six hundred miles of that distance, Chorpenning was on his own resources in a hostile Indian country. His danger would have been great enough if it had concerned only an accidental encounter with some roving band of savages. It was increased manifold through the certainty that the Indians were watching the trail.

One can only surmise such details as night travel, days spent hiding in *arroyos,* and detours made into the sagebrush at points where danger was particularly imminent. There is mention, in the records, of "successful conflicts," indicating that Chorpenning was put to actual combat. That he was not overwhelmed was due, no doubt, to the natural assumption of his foes that one man would never be bold enough to start out on such a journey alone and that reinforcements must be somewhere close at hand.

Whatever element of good luck had befriended him, George Chorpenning had saved his mail contract. The central overland route to California was still open.

2

Chorpenning's second contract with the Government was made in April, 1854. The terms of this contract put a temporary blight on California's hopes of seeing an adequate mail service built up on the emigrant route between Salt Lake City and Sacramento. The mail route was swung to the Southwest. From Salt Lake City it went through American Fork, Provo, Springfield, Payson, Summit Creek, Nephi City, Fillmore City, Red Creek, Parowan, Johnson's Springs, Cold Creek, Santa Clara (Calif.) and San Bernardino to San Diego (later changed to San Pedro). Over this route the mail was to be carried once a month each way, "with certainty, celerity and security," for $12,500 a year.

This arrangement left Carson Valley, the one hopeful

settlement between Salt Lake and California, without mail accommodations. As part of his contract, Chorpenning was called upon to supply the needs of Carson Valley, which was done for ten months. A messenger on snow-shoes carried the mail over the Sierras in winter. Snowshoe Thompson earned his name by his exploits in getting the mail across the mountains to Carson Valley.

Service over the new route was conducted generally by pack mule, though occasionally the mail from the east, by way of Independence and Salt Lake City, was so heavy that a wagon, drawn by six mules, was necessary. Indian hostility was in evidence all along the line, almost from the start. In San Bernardino County and the Tulare Valley there was open warfare. In August, 1854, a determined attack was made on a mail train. One of the men in charge was seriously wounded, several mules were killed, and the mail was seized. From then on the mail could proceed only under strong escort, which was provided by the contractor.

The populous mining districts of California seemed further than ever from direct overland connection with the East. For nearly a year their mail was carried from Sacramento, by river, to San Francisco; thence by ocean steamer to San Pedro; thence by pack mule through the counties of Los Angeles and San Bernardino to Salt Lake City. There was no saving of time in such a circuitous route; in addition there was the danger that the mail would fall into the hands of the Indians before it ever reached Salt Lake City.

The great bulk of mail to and from California continued to be sent by way of the Isthmus of Panama. It saved time, for one thing. It took from twenty-six to thirty days from New York to San Francisco, via the Isthmus. A record trip was made in twenty-one days. Nor were there any Indians to be encountered on the steamer route, whereas the letter poundage of the "jackass mail" was constantly being cut down by such sinister messages as this, to a special agent in California, from the postmaster at Salt Lake City, dated January 1, 1855:

In consequence of the Eastern mail arriving on the 1st of December at 4 p.m., bringing intelligence of the hostility of the Sioux Indians, killing the carriers and robbing the mail, I requested the mail carrier to San Diego to hold up for a day or two, to enable the merchants and others to forward duplicate drafts, letters, etc., by the Southern route, as the Eastern is becoming dangerous. Respectfully, your obedient servant, E. SMITH, P. M.

In the face of the obstacles that had arisen at the very outset of overland mail transportation, and in consideration of the fact that it had a safe and easy means of communication with the "States" by water, California, by all rules of logic, should have settled back and bothered no more with the problem.

No doubt this would have been the case had it not been for one or two inborn American characteristics. There was opposition to the Panama contract, which had ten years to run from 1847, on monopolistic grounds. Mail by the water route was costing patrons a great deal of money, and at that the government was losing on the contract. Not until the Panama Railroad was completed in 1855 was there any lowering of charges. Competitive lines, not sharing in mail subsidy, were frozen out. It was impossible to exist on passenger travel alone. Newspapers in California could not go wrong if they made the mail situation the subject of editorial themes. Public meetings were held, in favor of competitive service.

Another thing that kept California fighting for an overland mail, in spite of its apparent hopelessness, was a certain resentment against "trifling" legislation. Underneath, there was the feeling that official Washington was not trying to solve the problem in a serious way. Chorpenning's bids for carrying the mail were ridiculously low. His Salt Lake-San Pedro contract meant that he was to make two long, arduous and dangerous trips a month across desert country at practically $500 a trip; that he was to provide mules and subsistence for an escort of from four to ten men, and that he was to pay such escort out of his own proceeds. It was self-evident—at least to anyone acquainted with conditions in the West at the time—that the contractor would lose money if he gave adequate service, and that he would ask for, and be entitled to, extra compensation.

Scandals over "star route" contracts were coming up right along. Contractors were promising to deliver the mails with "safety, celerity and certainty" over routes that did not meet a fractional part of their subsidy.

California grew justly eloquent over the so-called Thirty-fifth Parallel route from Kansas City through Albuquerque to Stockton. This route was put in operation at a cost of $79,999, and operated nine months, during which time its receipts were $1,295. There were only four arrivals of through mail at Kansas City and two at Stockton. For several hundred miles the route ran parallel to another.

Such fiascos tended to injure, rather than help, the overland mail situation. Nor was any pack-mule service, however faithfully operated, sufficient for California's growing needs. What California wanted was printed matter—newspapers, magazines and books—as well as letters. It was impossible to burden a pack-mule express with hundreds of pounds of such material. And the occasional attempts to bring through the bulkier mail in light wagons were pathetic.

The pressure of public opinion was too much for the postal authorities, who had cut off all direct connection between Salt Lake City and Sacramento by routing the mail through the Southwest to San Pedro.

California rejoiced when it learned, in 1858, that the central overland route was to be re-established—this time between Placerville and Salt Lake City—and that stages were to succeed pack mules.

3

Twelve days, instead of thirty, from Placerville to Salt Lake!

Weekly stages leaving at either end of the line—not open wagons but real Concords, stout and roomy enough to carry printed matter as well as letters.

A subsidy of $190,000 a year for the new mail line!

The central overland route to be the main artery of communication with the East!

Such were some of the transportation excitements dangled before the eyes of Californians who, by this time, had become fairly skilled in picking out real gold from all else that glistens.

The schedule bristled with difficulties. Years afterward, when the trail had become a road, that roaring figure, Ben Holladay, swept through to the Missouri River in twelve days, to establish a record. But that was when a reserve of men, mules and coaches could be called upon every few miles.

Chorpenning, who had shouldered the new contract, seems to have gone about his task in good faith. A new road south of the Humboldt River was opened, graded and bridged, shortening the distance from Salt Lake City to Carson Valley by 150 miles. Stations were built every twenty to forty miles along the route. Chorpenning himself went to Concord to supervise the building of coaches and wagons.

In a later statement to Congress, explaining the expense incurred, Chorpenning claimed that it cost him nearly $300,000 to equip the line for service. At the end of the first year $60,000 was cut from the amount agreed upon, Chorpenning receiving $130,000. Then the service was reduced to semi-monthly trips and the pay to $80,000 a year. Chorpenning continued to run his stages weekly and to call for the mail, which was delivered to him only every other week. After many months of struggle between Chorpenning, his creditors and the Post Office Department, the contract was finally annulled, in May, 1860, "for repeated failures, for establishing an inferior grade of stock on said road." Chorpenning, the man who had fought Indians in establishing the first mail route in the wastes between Salt Lake and California, was definitely out as a carrier. He figured, thereafter, only as a claimant in one of the longest and most bitterly fought suits ever brought against the Government—a suit which attracted nation-wide attention and which exposed Congress and the Post Office Department to severe criticism.

4

While all these obstacles were accumulating on the western half of the central overland trail, conditions between Salt Lake and the Missouri River were quite as bad.

From Independence the mail route followed, in general, the Oregon Trail through a corner of Kansas, along the Platte in Nebraska, and to South Pass in Wyoming. From South Pass it followed the Mormon Trail to Fort Bridger and Salt Lake City.

The first mail contractor was Colonel Samuel H. Woodson of Independence, who, in 1850, agreed to carry a monthly mail for $19,500 a year for four years. Indian troubles and deep snows combined to keep Salt Lake City without mail from the East for as much as six months at a time. It sometimes happened that news sent by the steamer-Isthmian route to California beat the mules from Independence into Salt Lake City. Thus the news from Washington of the creation of Utah Territory in September, 1850, reached Salt Lake City in January, 1851, by messenger from California.

Other contractors on the Independence-Salt Lake City route, up to 1858, were W. M. F. McGraw, Hiram Kimball, S. B. Miles and Hockaday & Liggett, the last named operating from St. Joseph.

These early-day carriers of the mail struggled as best they could against such handicaps as hard winters, and summers that were marked by Indian raids. Considering the risks of the service, their contracts were almost invariably too low to allow any profit. McGraw had nearly $20,000 worth of property destroyed by Indians, for which he was fortunate enough to secure compensation.

In 1858 at the time of the "Mormon war," an attempt was made to maintain a weekly mail service on the central overland route. Hockaday & Liggett, in spite of a subsidy of $190,000 a year, were brought to ruin by Indian raids. The necessity for so frequent a service disappeared when the expected "war" failed to materialize. The Mormons burned General Albert Sidney Johnston's supply train and forced his command to spend an uncomfortable winter on short rations at Fort Bridger. After Johnston reached Salt Lake City, and a "Gentile" Governor had been appointed to succeed Brigham Young, any further thought of a weekly mail service was temporarily abandoned.

The actual carriers of mail under these first contracts on the central overland route suffered extreme hardships. Bill Hickman, who claimed to have been a Danite, or Mormon Avenging Angel, and who wrote a book entitled *The Confessions of Bill Hickman*, told, in that work, of his experiences during the winter in 1856–7. In that year Hickman and Porter Rockwell, who was said to be another Danite, between them covered the route. On one trip it took Hickman ten days from Salt Lake City to Fort Bridger, one hundred and ten miles, and fifteen days from Fort Bridger to South Pass. Hickman and the men with him camped where the wind had blown the snow off the hilltops. Their food supply ran low, but they killed a buffalo, on which they lived for several days. It took forty days to reach Fort Laramie and two months and three days to make the entire trip from Salt Lake City to Independence.

Maintaining schedules under such conditions was an impossibility. In winter, when there was no emigrant travel, men were regarded as lucky if they got through at all. One of Woodson's men froze to death in the mountains. Others were severely frostbitten in the blizzards that swept the uplands. When vehicles were put on the route, in response to departmental demand, they were light wagons which afforded little or no protection in bad weather.

To the very limit of human endurance, the carriers kept faithfully at their work—faithfully and honestly. Hickman tells of coming on a party of them at a lone station, nearly starving. In a storeroom there were supplies which the men would not touch, because, as they told Hickman, the food belonged to somebody else. Hickman convinced them that they were foolish. The storeroom was broken into and there was a feast.

Congress, in a wave of economy brought on by "star route" disclosures, trimmed postal expenditures by nearly one million dollars, the central overland route suffering with the rest. By 1859 the route from the Missouri River to California, by way of Salt Lake, was at its lowest ebb, so far as mail transportation was concerned. Emigrant trains and freight outfits, well protected against Indian attack and mostly traveling in seasonable weather, were getting through, but there was no certainty about mails.

Two things did much to save the day for the central overland route. One was "Old Pancake" Comstock's discovery of almost fabulous deposits of silver in Nevada. The other, happening almost simultaneously with the Nevada find, was the discovery of gold in Colorado by two prospectors, Gregory and Jackson.

The cries of "Ho, for Washoe!" and "Pike's Peak or

bust!" were to fill the central trail with fortune-seekers, who, like the Forty-Niners, must have their mail at any cost. But before the four-horse coach and the fleet pony came into the picture, the question of choosing the official mail route to California had to be settled in Congress. Ordinarily the question might have been decided readily enough, but the sectionalism which preceded the Civil War was at its height.

In case of war, the location of the post route to the Pacific Coast might be of considerable importance to North or South. A question which was normally commercial became the subject of bitter partisan debate.

CHAPTER IV

MAIL ROUTES IN DISPUTE

1

CALIFORNIA, from the time of the discovery of gold to the outbreak of the Civil War, afforded a fruitful subject for sectional argument in Congress.

True, there had been nothing of sectionalism in the rush to the California gold fields. Yanks and Southerners worked together, prospecting and mining. Arguments about slavery or its abolition were forgotten in the more personal and local issue of uncovering gold.

When the miners had time and opportunity to take stock of something besides nuggets and "dust," political issues began to take form. The Whigs made little impression. Democracy was soon in the saddle in California, as it was nationally. Such being the case, the slavery element in the party fell under certain delusions. Mexico, on ceding California at the end of the Mexican War, had requested that the territory be kept free from slavery. This feeble request from a beaten foe was ignored. California became a battleground for the slavery and anti-slavery forces.

The fact that California's constitutional convention, in 1849, was anti-slavery did not end the fight. Nor did California's admission as a "free" state on September 19, 1850. The battle of sectionalism, for a prize of gold, had just begun. As war clouds began to thicken, so did rumors overcast the political sky in California. There was talk of forming an independent republic—of making separate states of Northern and Southern California. The idea of a Pacific republic was prevalent even before the constitutional convention, and it came up in public discussion to the very outbreak of war. A "confederacy of coast states" was openly urged.

Even if some such bold stroke proved to be impossible, there remained the question of transportation to California. If it came to war between the North and South, the side which controlled the routes to the Golden State would be in an advantageous position. California's annual supply of unminted wealth would alone keep a considerable war going.

The transportation fight shifted to Congress. The thirty-sixth parallel—actually 36° 30', north of which lay the larger part of the wedge-shaped Louisiana Purchase—became the Mason's and Dixon's line of the West. Any proposal for a stage or railroad route north or south of that line brought out all the forces of argument on either side.

California furnished two Senators, Gwin and Latham, whose sympathies as after-events proved, were not in accord with the strong Union tendencies of the state.

Among all the men developed in California's rough political cradle, William M. Gwin seems the most extraordinary. His name will be mentioned frequently in these pages, as he was the man behind the scenes, politically, in the creation of the Pony Express, and, as a member of the Senate Committee on Post Offices and Post Roads, he had an important part in the debates on overland routes to the Pacific.

Gwin was easily the leader among the early-day Cali-

fornians who turned to political life. He was born in
Tennessee in 1805 and practiced medicine in that state
and Mississippi. He was appointed marshal of Mississippi by President Jackson, for whom Gwin always had
a profound admiration. In a biographical sketch, evidently prepared under his own direction in later years, he
denied the secessionist sympathies attributed to him, and
described himself as merely a "Jacksonian Democrat."

Gwin was elected to Congress from Tennessee, but emigrated to California, promising Stephen A. Douglas that
he would return with credentials as a Senator from the
new state that was in prospect. California, where anything might happen, was a fruitful field for Gwin, who
was another Burr when it came to schemes which had to
do with the changing of boundary lines and the placing
of new personalities in the seats of the mighty.

Gwin was a man of impressive mien, ready and eloquent of speech. Gertrude Atherton, in her book, *California*, ranks him as "the most intellectual, brilliant,
subtle, suave and unscrupulous leader California ever
had." She says further that Gwin had hoped to have
California admitted as ceded. This would have included
not only the present state of California, but Nevada,
Utah, a part of Colorado, and nearly all of New Mexico
and Arizona. Gwin figured, according to Mrs. Atherton,
that such a state would fall to pieces of its own weight
and the South, in case of war, would share liberally in the
inevitable dismemberment.

The polished and courtly Gwin was sent by San Francisco as a representative to the first General Assembly,
an organization of rough-and-ready character. Most of
the constitution-makers were from the mines, where life

was in the raw. Jeremiah Lynch, in his life of D. C. Broderick, entitled *A Senator of the Fifties*, says: "Of the thirty-six members of the Assembly, over two thirds never appeared without displaying knives or pistols, or both."

It was a time when duels were common in California. Gwin, the persuasive-tongued, only once felt himself put to the extremity of arms. He fought a duel with a former Member of Congress, McCorkle, in 1853. The weapons were rifles. The men stood back to back at forty paces and wheeled and fired when the word was given. Three shots were exchanged. Gwin's opponent was a small man, and, perhaps by reason of that saving physical gift, was not hit. Gwin's size seems to have had an overpowering effect on McCorkle, for all three of the latter's shots went wild. Honor having been satisfied, the men shook hands and their enmity was declared at an end.

Gwin and General John C. Frémont were chosen Senators by the First General Assembly. Frémont drew the short term, and served only a few months, being succeeded by Weller, who afterward became Governor. In 1857, Gwin was re-elected for four years. At the same time D. C. Broderick was chosen Senator for the six-year term.

Broderick, hard-fisted, self-educated and blunt of speech, had received his political training in a school vastly different from that of Gwin—still, not a bad school from a practical standpoint. Broderick had learned the rudiments of politics in Tammany Hall. He was the son of an Irish bricklayer and had fought his way up in New York politics until he had been sent to Congress. When he emigrated to California, Broderick said, like Gwin, that he would come back to Washington as a Senator.

Between mining ventures and real estate deals in Sacramento, Broderick was soon on the road to wealth and meanwhile was building up a political following which menaced the supremacy of Gwin.

It was not long before the two Senators from California were open, bitter enemies. Broderick found that the senior Senator, secure in the confidence of President Buchanan, had· "blanketed" him in the matter of political appointments. Broderick, helpless as to the distribution of patronage, made himself felt as a critic of Buchanan's administration. For one thing, he aligned himself solidly and unmistakably with the anti-slavery forces. For another, he came out openly in favor of direct stage and railroad communication with California by a central route—north of the line of controversy, 36° 30'.

Broderick fell in a duel with David S. Terry, Justice of the Supreme Court of California. Terry was a strong supporter of Gwin. Broderick had made a light remark, reflecting on Terry's probity in office. The remark had been overheard by one of Terry's friends, and was carried to the Judge. Terry resigned from the bench. Then he sent a challenge to Broderick, which was accepted. The men fought with pistols, before a "gallery" of some fifty or sixty spectators who looked on in the California dawn much as if they had assembled to witness a banned prize-fight.

Broderick, who was reputed to be a dead shot, accidentally discharged his pistol into the ground when he raised it to fire. He fell, mortally wounded, with a bullet through his breast. His words, constantly repeated in the delirium which followed, were: "They have killed me because I opposed the extension of slavery."

LEADERS IN OVERLAND MAIL STRUGGLE

Upper, left to right, W. H. Russell and Alexander Majors, founders of the Pony Express. Lower left, Senator W. M. Gwin, who claimed to have originated the "Pony" idea. Lower right, John Butterfield, stage and express magnate, from a family portrait in possession of Clare Dana Mumford, mother of Daniel Butterfield II.

M. S. Latham succeeded Broderick in the United States Senate. Of him Bancroft says in his *Chronicles of the Builders:*

> Latham entered the United States Senate to share in the most momentous of congressional struggles, and California herself became the scene of strife between the factions of two great parties. . . . The Lecomptonites nominated for their candidate J. C. Breckenridge of Kentucky, while the anti-Lecomptonites chose for their standard bearer S. A. Douglas of Illinois, the sole associate of Broderick in the Senate, with the principle that slavery in any territory was to be optional with the people, not with Congress. Gwin and Latham, though at variance, decided for the former and persuaded the entire Democratic delegation to join them, despite instructions. Gwin hinted at a Pacific republic, bounded by the Rocky Mountains, and declared that, in case of secession, California would side with the South. . . . Latham drifted into pronounced slavery ideas.

One last picture of Gwin. After war had been declared, and California had gone definitely for the Union, Gwin, whose term expired in 1861, was retired from politics in his adopted state. He traveled extensively, and met Napoleon III in Paris. Maximilian had been put on the throne in Mexico. Napoleon, impressed as most men were by the Californian, installed Gwin as colonization adviser to the doomed court.

Gwin, once more in an atmosphere suited to scheming, entered upon his new duties with characteristic enthusiasm. He soon found that he was with a cause that was marked for early death. Maximilian, though he had made

Gwin "Duke of Sonora," soon refused him audience, perhaps because the brilliant schemes of the new Colonization Minister bored rather than dazzled him. Maximilian's chiefs, more intent on affairs with women than affairs of state, were likewise indifferent. Gwin asked for and received personal escort to the United States boundary line. Thus he escaped personal disaster in the fall of Maximilian's government, but even years after, when he was a broken man in San Francisco, he could not escape from the title, "Duke of Sonora."

These men have been placed in review because they were political leaders at a time when the question of overland transportation had become something more than a mere matter of public service. War issues had crept in. Men took the judgment of the military strategist, rather than the engineer, in studying the map.

California's future transportation connection with the "States" depended on the comparative strength of the parties massed on both sides of the divisional line of 36° 30'.

2

The prevalence of the "Great American Desert" idea did much to retard the establishing of lines of communication to the Pacific Coast. It was a catch phrase often heard in Congress. In the minds of the uninformed, the phrase conjured up a picture of the entire West as a wilderness, peopled by a few settlers who, in time, would be overwhelmed by Indians. It reflected the attitude of those legislators who had grudgingly given their votes in favor of the Louisiana Purchase on the theory that the Rocky Mountains might, at any rate, prove a barrier against the encroachments of an invading enemy from the Far East.

The desert stretches that actually existed were magnified manifold in popular imagination. Death Valley had claimed its toll of the Jayhawkers and other insufficiently equipped and badly guided parties that had attempted to cross its wastes. In the public mind the whole Southwest was little better than an extension of Death Valley.

Just how little information had been secured, as late as 1853, regarding actual conditions beyond the frontier, was shown when Congress voted an appropriation for the introduction of camels in the Southwest, to solve forever the problems of swift and adequate transportation.

The idea of using camels as carriers came up officially through Jefferson Davis, then Secretary of War in the Cabinet of President Franklin Pierce.

It is not difficult to understand how, in that day, serious attention was paid to a notion which nowadays seems worthy of nobody more practical than Colonel Sellers. The public prints were full of stories about the suffering of pioneers who had themselves succumbed to the desert heat, after their mules and oxen had died of thirst. If camels could be used successfully in traveling across the sands of the Sahara, why could they not be propagated in the southwestern United States for all transportation purposes that demanded swiftness and strength? Fleeter than the horse, stronger than the mule, and able to go for days without water, what animals could be more ideal for closing that terrifying gap which Nature had imposed between California and the "States"?

The first offices of these Americanized camels, according to the sponsors of the plan, were to be more or less

Governmental until a sufficient number of the animals had been bred to make them general servitors to the migrating public. Camels at the outset would be used to carry mail and express, and to maintain speedy communication between military posts. In case of war with the Indians, a camel corps of scouts could do effective service in the matter of reconnoissance. It was even possible to train and equip a light artillery camel corps. From the humps of these useful animals, cannoneers would pour a deadly fire into the ranks of Apaches or Comanches, who, quite obviously, would quit scalp-hunting rather than have such a fearsomely mounted foe set upon their trail.

Official records show that Congress defeated a camel bill in 1853. The year following, another bill was introduced and defeated. But in 1855 Congress either became camel-conscious or figured that there was no use trying to resist such a camel enthusiast as the Secretary of War proved to be. An appropriation of $30,000 was voted, the Secretary of the Navy furnished a ship for transportation, and Major Henry C. Wayne and David D. Porter, U. S. Navy attaché, were delegated to make the necessary purchases of camels.

After the leaders had studied camel lore at the London Zoo, with enthusiasm growing day by day, the expedition departed for Arabia, where seventy-five camels were bought. Two camels, which were presented to the Government by some minor ruler, were curtly rejected as not being good specimens and were promptly replaced with better animals and apologies.

The camels, which were to solve future questions of transportation in the Southwest, were finally landed in

Texas. Major Wayne, in a report from the camel camp near San Antonio on August 12, 1856, set forth that:

> the experiment should show that the dromedaries may be sent anywhere along the frontier or within the settlements. . . . One or more may be mounted with a small gun, throwing shrapnel. These experiments would not only show the absolute value of the animals for burden and the saddle, but also its relative usefulness in comparison with the horse, the mule and waggoning.

The first experiment was in charge of Lieut. Edward F. Beale—the survey of a wagon road from Fort Defiance, Ariz., to the Grand Canyon. Difficulties presented themselves at the start. The camels caused many runaways among horses and mules. Nor was it long before the camels developed sore feet on the rough trails of the desert, so unlike the soft, shifting sands of the Sahara. The animals were provided with leather boots, but such makeshifts did not seem to be satisfactory. When it came to bearing burdens, there were no indications that the camels would supplant the mules and ox-teams which were going about the business of hauling heavily loaded freight wagons. Nor in the matter of speed did any camel seem able to outdo a swift horse—perhaps owing to the handicap of the boots, or lack of sand, or both.

The camels were taken around the Southwest on various experimental trips, in charge of native cameleers who had been dragged from a happy existence as Bedouins in Arabia to see that Uncle Sam's new charges did not die of nostalgia. The camels ambled into Southern California and across the reaches of Nevada. Their real mission seemed to be lost in the public's idea that a kindly Government was providing a free circus for the Southwest—an idea that persisted in spite of ringing editorials like this in a San Francisco newspaper:

> The camel is the last institution necessary—before the advent of the Pacific railroad—to bend the uninhabitable portions of the continent into contact and annihilate the wilderness that separates the new from the old world.

But the camels which the Government had bought did not annihilate the wilderness. They did not appear as swift couriers on mail routes. They were taken to a ranch near Bakersfield. Official interest in them seems to have died. Such camels as were not sold into circus bondage wandered into the desert.

For years the tradition has maintained in the Southwest that camels have been seen by lone prospectors. Every time this story reappears it recalls a pleasant interlude in the long and grim fight for overland transportation.

3

For nearly ten years following Chorpenning's first trip across the Sierras with the pack mule, and Woodson's daring excursions into the snows between Salt Lake and Independence, conditions on the Central Overland route showed little improvement. One contractor after another had either quit in disgust or had been brought to ruin by trying to give adequate mail service under an impossibly low subsidy.

Salt Lake City considered itself lucky if a mail from Sacramento or the Missouri struggled through once a month. All efforts to improve the service on this route met with disfavor in Congress and the Post Office Department. The administration seemed convinced that the Southwest was the only portal through which mail could be carried to and from the Pacific Coast. Among the various experimental lines which had been established in the Southwest was one from San Antonio to San Diego, thence to San Francisco. It was roundabout and irregular, but the desert conditions and the Indian menace along this line did not seem as great a handicap, in the opinion of the postal authorities, as the severe winters on the plains farther north.

Postmaster General Aaron V. Brown said in his annual report for 1857: "The route through the South Pass is as much closed by snow from four to six months in the year as if barred by a gate of adamant."

In further explanation of the position of his department, he said, in the same report:

The United States had a mail carried for years between Independence and Salt Lake, and the records of the Department show the following facts: The mails for November, December and January, 1850–51, did not arrive until March, 1851. The winter months of 1851–52 were very severe. The carrier and postmaster reported that they started in time but had to turn back. The mails of February, March and December, 1853, were impeded by deep snow. Those of January and February, 1854, on account of deep snow, did not arrive until April. There was no improvement of the service, even down to the November mail of 1856, which left Independence November 1 and on account of deep snow was obliged to winter in the mountains. The snow caused an almost entire failure for four months of the year. These actual experiments, made from 1850 to the present time, without referring to the concurring testimony of explorers and travelers, put this route entirely out of the question.

Military protection throughout the West was inadequate, but neither side, under the tense conditions then prevailing, would yield additional posts along any route in its opponents' territory. Senator Gwin, in January, 1855, introduced a joint resolution for the establishment of an express mail weekly between St. Louis and San Francisco. The resolution called for building a military road to California at a cost of $1,000,000, the establishing of five military posts for protection, and a soldier guard to accompany the mail along the most exposed portions of the route. The proposal had too much of a military angle, and was smothered in committee.

Something had to be done, in one way or another, and in 1857 Congress took a step by which the administration believed it had solved the overland mail problem, not only to its own satisfaction but to the satisfaction of the public. The Butterfield overland route was established through the Southwest.

The contract, which was let to John Butterfield, provided for a semi-weekly mail, to be carried in coaches, from St. Louis to San Francisco and return, at an annual subsidy of $600,000.

The Butterfield route extended from St. Louis to Fort Smith, Ark., where it was met by a branch route from Memphis, Tenn. From Fort Smith the route continued southwest through what is now Oklahoma, into Texas to El Paso, where it joined the previously established route from San Antonio to San Diego. Near Yuma the Butterfield line branched off to Los Angeles and San Francisco.

This route apparently gave great satisfaction to the administration. In his annual report, following the letting of the Butterfield contract, the Postmaster General wrote, with an enthusiasm unusual to official documents:

> Instead of projecting this route and its attendant benefits from the frontier of Missouri, to buffet with winds and snows upon the plains of Kansas in Winter and drag over monotonous, waterless, treeless wastes in Summer, it was located through the center of Missouri and Arkansas and throughout the Western frontier of Texas. It will thus develop hitherto unknown resources in those states. It will open a vast agricultural and mineral region in Missouri, lend a helping hand to the young, growing and unappreciated state of Arkansas, and conduct the hardy pioneer to the delightful woodlands and prairies of Texas. For nearly a thousand miles the traveler will be traversing a country abounding in beauty and healthfulness, possessing a salubrious climate and a fruitful soil.

Legislators who had voted for the Butterfield contract were quick to resent any criticism that the route was too long. Senator Toombs of Georgia said: "If we are to do away with any route, let us cut off the routes from St. Joseph [the central route] and Kansas City [the route to Albuquerque and Stockton]."

Senator Iverson of Georgia took a frankly sectional view of the matter when it was proposed to make the Butterfield contract operative on the Central Overland route instead of the one which had been chosen. He said:

> They want to take this away from the Southern states and put it upon their own region, for the purpose of

depriving the South of the poor benefit of having a mail
route in the Southern states. The object is to operate
upon the construction line of the Pacific railroad. That
is the ultimate design, and is another one of those circumstances in which the Northern numerical majority
of the Government intends to absorb all the benefits of
the Government. I hope that Southern Senators will put
their foot down on this proposition, and that this amend-
mènt, which is nothing less than an attempt to monopolize
the benefits of this Government for the North, will be
voted down.

This impassioned appeal had its effect, and the Butterfield route, described by its critics, from its appearance
on the map, as "the great ox-bow route," remained at
least temporarily intact.

4

St. Louis, which in 1830 had witnessed the departure
of the fur traders, Jedediah S. Smith, David E. Jackson
and William L. Sublette, in the first wagon to mark the
course of the Oregon Trail, was given one of its old-time
thrills when, on October 9, 1858, the first stage coach from
San Francisco over the Butterfield route rolled into town.

Reporters questioned a determined looking man who
had held the "ribbons" during a part of the long journey.
He was John Butterfield, president of the company which
bore his name, and destined to become the most powerful
figure in Western transportation.

What the reporters learned was succinctly contained in
the following dispatch from Washington, printed in the
next day's newspapers:

WASHINGTON, Oct. 9.

The President has received a telegraphic dispatch from John Butterfield, President of the Overland Mail Company, dated St. Louis, Oct. 9, informing him that the great overland mail arrived there today from San Francisco in twenty-three days and four hours, and that the stage brought through six passengers.

The President replied by telegraph as follows:

"JOHN BUTTERFIELD, President, etc.,

"SIR—Your dispatch has been received. I cordially congratulate you upon the result. It is a glorious triumph for civilization and the Union. Settlements will soon follow the course of the road, and the East and West will be bound together by a chain of living Americans, which never can be broken.

"JAMES BUCHANAN."

The mail was to have left San Francisco on the 16th of September. Our previous advices were of the 6th of that month. Consequently the news from California is eleven days later and it ought to be here tonight. This is the first trip of the overland mail from the Pacific, and its arrival in St. Louis at this early date shows what can be done. It was not expected to reach Fort Smith until the 16th inst.

One can imagine a saturnine smile curling Butterfield's lips as he read the enthusiastic message from the President. Butterfield, probably the most practical of all the early-day transportation leaders, knew that the route which he had established was nearly a thousand miles too long. He knew that it could not best serve the needs of East and West, and that it was wide open to Indian attack. No choice had been given him, or he would have selected the shortest, most direct way to the Pacific Coast.

Some idea of the tremendous scope of the Butterfield route can be obtained from the following official description:

From San Francisco across the Sierras by Carrada de las Uvas, skirting the desert and crossing the San Bernardino range through San Francisquito Canyon, thence by San Fernando Pass to Los Angeles; southwest from there to Warren's Pass, and connecting with the old San Diego Trail, which it follows to Fort Yuma. From Fort Belknap along Captain Marcy's trail; through Gainesville and Sherman, Texas, across the Red River and thence to Fort Smith, Arkansas, and thence to St. Louis.

There were only four military posts on the entire route. The first special agent of the Post Office Department to make the trip wrote, no doubt thankfully feeling his scalp as he finished this comment: "The stations in Arizona are at the mercy of the Apache, and the Comanche may, at his pleasure, bar the passage of stages in Texas."

No one questioned the efficiency with which Butterfield had fulfilled his contract. In less than a year he had built stations along this route, had put on a complete stock of mules and coaches, hired station keepers and stock tenders and assistants, selected drivers who could fight Indians as well as guard four-mule teams, and had set wheels grinding and brakes squealing along a road that was such in name only.

Butterfield had been put to tremendous expense. A man less resourceful financially would have been overwhelmed when Congress failed to pass the appropriation bill for the support of the Post Office Department. Butterfield merely dug deeper into his own pocket and kept the stages running until he could collect the entire amount due him. For more than two years his stages ran on schedule—a performance unsurpassed in the history of early-day transportation.

Only a man of the most forceful character could have succeeded under such circumstances. John Butterfield [1] was all of that. He had climbed from the stage driver's seat to control of thousands of miles of stage lines and the management of many large business enterprises. Yet there was nothing of the spectacular in his make-up. He shunned publicity where others courted it. A man of

[1] John Butterfield was born at Berne, N. Y., in 1801. He began his career as a stage driver for an Albany firm, his education having been limited to a few winter periods in country schools. He bought a horse and conveyance and built up the leading livery business in Utica, afterward establishing stage lines of his own. He became interested in packet boats on the Erie Canal and steamboats on Lake Ontario, the construction of plank roads to Utica and the development of the first street railway system in that city. He was largely instrumental in the promotion and construction of the Black River and the Southern railroads. Among the first to recognize the possibilities of the telegraph, he joined Faxton, Wells, Livingston and others in establishing the New York, Albany and Buffalo Telegraph Company.

In 1849 he formed the express company of Butterfield, Wasson & Co. He successfully engaged in transporting freight across the Isthmus of Panama during the gold rush to California, and became impressed with the future of the Pacific Coast. He brought about the merger, in 1850, of the firms of Wells & Co., Livingston & Fargo and the Butterfield & Wasson Company, under the title of the American Express Company. As superintendent, Butterfield had much to do with the success of Wells-Fargo in the West and the American Express Company in the East. After a temporary breakdown in health, Butterfield returned to the direction of his multifarious projects, but was stricken with paralysis in 1867 and died November 14, 1869. His son Daniel Butterfield, who drew up the schedule for the first overland stage line between St. Louis and San Francisco, was a Brigadier General on the Federal side in the Civil War, and later was general superintendent of the Eastern division of the American Express Company.

limited education, he carried most of the details of his business affairs in his head, as he "put little faith in bookkeepers," to use his own words. For any further reference that was necessary, he carried a few papers in his hat.

Various "Napoleons" were to rise in Western transportation before the era of the railroad. This silent man was to survive them all, and the records of their achievements were to make just a few more figures in the sheaf of papers in John Butterfield's beaver hat.

CHAPTER V

THE PONY EXPRESS

1

THE Oregon Trail, which had been flattened into a broad ribbon of dust across the northeastern corner of Kansas and along the Platte and the Sweetwater in Nebraska and Wyoming, as we know them today, showed an astounding new activity at the close of the winter of 1858–59.

The trek to Oregon was practically over. The Mormons, who had branched off at South Pass, with their wagons and handcarts, were past the peak of their emigration. The California-bound were few in number. Travel on the great trail had sunk to a discouraging low, when suddenly the rumble of wagons was again heard and dust clouds once more challenged the gaze of the Indians.

Fifty thousand gold seekers started for the new "diggings" in the Pike's Peak region. The sagebrush which had begun to hide the wagon ruts and to provide a kindly covering for the unmarked graves of those who had died in the rush to Oregon and California, was again beaten into the earth. Hopeful "Peakers" filled the trail, their wagon-tops decorated with the sign: "Pike's Peak or Bust."

Along the western part of the trail there was the same activity, with Washoe as the goal. Placerville was busy equipping pack outfits. Miners, with their sole possessions on their backs, trudged through the late snows in the inhospitable Sierras toward Virginia City. Wagons, many of which were survivors of the long pull to California in '49, were headed east again, for the Nevada silver fields. As fast as one mining camp after another developed at either end of the treasure trail, there came the old cry of the California miners:

"Give us letters, newspapers—mail!"

Among the most interested observers of these new conditions along the trail was Alexander Majors, whose freight wagons for several years had been plying between the Missouri River and various isolated military posts in the frontier West.

Majors controlled an enormous business in freighting. His bullwhackers, heading west from Independence, Atchison, Leavenworth or Nebraska City, had made his name familiar in every outpost. Since 1848, when he started from Independence with his first train of six wagons, drawn by oxen, Majors had steadily built up his enterprise, his principal returns coming from hauling supplies to military garrisons. In 1855, according to his autobiography, *Seventy Years on the Frontier*, Majors went into partnership with Russell and Waddell of Lexington, Mo., and did business for three years under the name of Majors & Russell, changing the name of the firm to Russell, Majors & Waddell in 1858.

In that year the partners secured a contract from the Government for hauling supplies to Johnston's army, which had been sent West on the threat of trouble with the Mormons. Some idea of the enormous business conducted by the firm can be obtained from the fact that this one contract called for 3,500 large wagons and teams.

It necessitated the establishment of a new base of supplies at Nebraska City as well as at Leavenworth. Sixteen million pounds of freight were sent out to Utah. Not all of it reached its destination, as the Mormons burned three of Johnston's supply trains. In the hard winter during which the Government forces were cut off at Fort Bridger on short rations, only 200 oxen were saved out of 3,500— a monetary loss of $150,000. After Johnston had gone through to Utah and had settled at Camp Floyd, with the war flurry over, freight wagons which had cost $175 apiece were sold to the Mormons at $10, and horses, oxen and equipment at proportionate prices, the Government footing all the loss.

Russell and Majors, whose names are indissolubly connected with the Pony Express, and with Western transportation in general, were different in temperament. William H. Russell was a man of many enterprises, whereas Majors was inclined to stick to freighting. Russell plunged deeply in mining ventures; his name figured among the incorporators of the town of Denver; he was a familiar figure in the national capital, where he had a large acquaintanceship among political leaders.

In Washington, in the winter of 1858, soon after the discovery of gold in the Pike's Peak region, Russell broached the idea of starting a daily stage coach line between Leavenworth and Denver. Majors was skeptical, and concluded to stay out. Russell, in partnership with John S. Jones, of Pettis County, Missouri, started his line of coaches to the new gold district. The line was lavishly equipped, and carried passengers as well as mail and express. General William Larimer, a Colorado pioneer, says in his *Reminiscences*:

The coaches in this service were large, strongly built vehicles, known as Concord coaches. Each one cost about $800 and was especially fitted for the heavy work required of it. Nine passengers could be accommodated with ease inside of each. They were softly cushioned, and in winter were warm and comfortable. They were altogether the finest stages run in the West. Each coach was drawn by four fine, strong Kentucky mules, which were changed every twelve to twenty miles. The drivers were well paid, intelligent, experienced and fearless. An accident was a rarity. The stage fare between the Missouri River and Denver was at first $150 but later $100 each way. There were said to be 52 coaches running on the Leavenworth–Denver line.

The equipment for the Leavenworth & Pike's Peak Express, or Jones & Russell's Pike's Peak Express Company, as it was sometimes called, was secured on credit. At the end of ninety days, when notes fell due, Alexander Majors' prophecy was borne out. The new stage line was heavily in debt, the chief creditor being Russell, Majors & Waddell. The stage line was taken over, in order to save at least part of the money that had been advanced, and thus Majors found himself part owner of the enterprise which he had refused to embark upon voluntarily.

The stage line continued to run daily, but was losing heavily. Hockaday & Liggett, who had the mail contract between the Missouri River and Salt Lake City, were in financial difficulties. With the idea of effecting a combination that might pay, Russell, Majors & Waddell bought out the Hockaday & Liggett line, and moved the Denver stages to the Central Overland route, by way of Fort Kearney, Julesburg, Fort Laramie, South Pass,

Fort Bridger and Salt Lake City. Hockaday & Liggett had only a few stations along the route. They had insufficient live stock and their stages were light and unsuited to rough travel.

Russell, Majors & Waddell established new stations between St. Joseph and Salt Lake City. They put on nearly 1,500 mules, and added new coaches to those which they had transferred from the Denver route, Denver being given a semi-weekly service from Julesburg. The schedule time was cut from twenty-two days to ten days, an average of one hundred and twenty miles every twenty-four hours. This time was made possible through the fact that stations were numerous. Each station had an experienced man in charge, with stock tenders and other assistants. Supplies for the men and feed for the stock were hauled at great expense.

Russell, Majors & Waddell in May, 1860, secured a charter from the state of Kansas under the name of the Central Overland California & Pike's Peak Express Company. It was a bulky title for a closely knit, efficiently working organization. For the first time there was something approaching adequate passenger service between Salt Lake City and the Missouri River. Travelers who were whirled westward at a rate of speed hitherto unknown, began to write home about it.

In spite of its general effectiveness, the Overland line, as it was known, did not pay. In fact, it would have been impossible for any stage line, at the time, to have paid without the aid of Government bounty. The Butterfield line could not have existed without its subsidy for carrying the mails. The subsidy which Hockaday & Liggett had been receiving for carrying the mail to Salt Lake had

been comparatively small. Something more was required
if Russell, Majors & Waddell were to bring their expensive, highly organized line to a profit-making basis.

The only hope, apparently, lay in convincing official
Washington that the Central Overland route should receive first consideration in the letting of mail contracts.
The aid of Senator Gwin was counted on. His position
as senior Senator from California, his influence as a member of the Committee on Post Offices and Post Roads, and
his close connection with the administration generally,
from President Buchanan down, made him the one man
who could turn the balance in favor of the central route.

Russell, at Washington, seems to have secured the
necessary Senatorial pledges of support. But political
promises did not fill Russell's mind so much as a suddenly
developed plan for a swift courier service between the
Missouri River and California. Men and horses were to
form a veritable telegraph line of flesh and blood between
the muddy Missouri and the bright Pacific. It was to be
a super-service of speed, kept going day and night at all
seasons of the year and demonstrating that the objections
to a northern mail route were based on prejudice or
misinformation.

This courier service was to be known as the Pony
Express.

2

Again Alexander Majors was dubious of one of Russell's enthusiasms. Majors had seen Russell guess wrong
in the case of the daily stage line to Denver. It seemed
to the veteran freighter that a Pony Express mail service,
entirely without Government subsidy, was even more

chimerical than a de luxe passenger service to a mining district that might or might not live.

Majors stated his objections. He was given the same assurance that had been received by Russell—that this brilliant demonstration of the possibilities of the central route would lead to substantial contracts for the future carrying of mail. Under the circumstances, with the overland stage line going in arrears, Majors gave his consent.

There is still some doubt as to the originator of the Overland Pony Express idea. It is claimed that B. F. Ficklin, manager for Russell, Majors & Waddell, made the suggestion to Senator Gwin in the course of an overland trip from California. Gwin, in a public speech after the "Pony" was running, claimed that the enterprise was due to his efforts. An article in the *Alta California,* dated March 23, 1860, would indicate that John Butterfield was about to establish a "Horse Express" on the route from St. Louis to San Francisco, and that Russell, having the advantage of a shorter route, "beat him to it" by establishing the Pony Express. The article says:

> The announcement of Russell, Majors & Co., the well known contractors on the Salt Lake route, that they intend in April to start a Horse Express to Placerville, via the Great Salt Lake, has caused a fluttering among the friends of the Butterfield route. It appears the scheme originated with Mr. Butterfield himself in this city about three months ago. At that time Charles M. Stebbins and his Great Overland Mail chief were in consultation on the subject of a regular Horse Express to California, running from the terminus of the telegraph line on this end to the commencement of the Street line on the other, in ten days, carrying important dispatches and packages

at the rate of about $50 per pound, and news dispatches for the press at a high figure.

They estimated upon the expense of the enterprise and were resolved upon its execution but it was deemed advisable first to extend the telegraph line about fifty miles beyond its present limit. The proprietor backed out, and when Stebbins, a month later, went to Washington to arrange matters he was surprised by the news that Russell, Majors & Co. contemplated a Horse Express upon the same basis, carrying valuable packages by the Pike's Peak and Salt Lake route, which they calculated to run in ten days, or two days less than the lowest calculation of the Butterfield Company. The latter have since changed their plan somewhat, and from all that can be gleaned here [Washington] Stebbins and the telegraph company have withdrawn from the undertaking, but Mr. Butterfield is not so easily discouraged. According to the popular statement he goes so far as to swear that Russell, Majors & Co. shall not carry off the laurels heretofore gained by quick time on the El Paso route. It is hard to decide in advance which will win. Butterfield's rivals are rich, able and energetic people, plenty of cash, plenty of stock and ample credit along the route to defy competition. They are playing a bold game for a fat contract to carry a tri-weekly mail to Placerville, and are not the set of persons to give up without a sharp contest. If their Horse Express enterprise is successful, the contract is sure; if the Southern route is proved the quickest, they lose it. But Butterfield understands all this, and will do all in his power to prevent success in the first case and defeat in the last.

It is certain that there was intense rivalry between the two stage companies. Butterfield, had the matter been left to his own judgment, would have selected the central, rather than the "ox-bow" route on which he now found himself threatened with serious disadvantages. If his rivals, now established on the central route, could demonstrate a quicker all-the-year-round service to California, the argument would be unanswerable. California newspapers, at the time of the starting of the new service, said that Butterfield had actually started a pony service in competition, but this statement cannot be verified. It is extremely unlikely that a man of John Butterfield's shrewdness would have started a race which he was bound to lose. The quickest time possible on the Butterfield route would have been days later than a feasible schedule on the central route.

If any contest was contemplated, it was soon abandoned, and the promoters of the Pony Express were left to work out their plans without competition.

3

Once committed to the cause of the Pony Express, Russell, Majors & Waddell went at the work of organization and carried out the details so promptly and quietly that the general public had little idea of what was going on.

Russell assumed managerial charge of the eastern division at St. Joseph. W. W. Finney was appointed agent. Sacramento was made the western terminus of the line, the mail to be carried from there to San Francisco by boat. Alexander Majors' experience was drawn on in the matter of general detail, such as hiring men, buying livestock, and establishing stations.

From St. Joseph to Salt Lake City the company had

its stage stations, but they were too far apart for Pony
Express purposes. At first the Pony Express stations
were established twenty-five miles apart. This was found
too great a distance for a horse to travel at top speed.
Intermediate stations were established, between the
"home" stations, so that no rider had to go more than
from ten to twelve miles before changing horses.

The company had to build stations all the way beyond
Salt Lake City. The total expense at the outset, before
the express had been put in operation, was heavy. In
summing up these preliminary arrangements and their
cost, Greene Majors, son of Alexander Majors, now Judge
of the Municipal Court at Piedmont, California, has given
the following information:

> To establish the Pony Express required five hundred
> of the best blooded American horses; one hundred and
> ninety stock stations for changing the riding stock; two
> hundred station tenders to care for the horses and have
> them ready, saddled and bridled, for the incoming rider
> to mount and be off like the wind; eighty of the keenest,
> toughest, bravest of western youths for the riders, with
> stations all supplied with hay, grain and other needed
> materials. It required $100,000 in gold coin to establish
> and equip the line.

The company was strict in its choice of riders. One
hundred and twenty-five pounds was the outside limit of
weight, though this rule was broken occasionally rather
than lose exceptionally good riders who might touch one
hundred and forty pounds. The rule was that no one
under twenty years of age was to be accepted, but some
of the eager applicants who had just turned eighteen or

nineteen did not scruple to add a year or two in order
to secure enlistment.

Many young fellows along the trail, from St. Joseph
to Sacramento, who were confident of their saddle prowess,
besieged the stage company's offices when it became known
that there were to be opportunities in the Pony Express
service. They were looked over by keen-eyed men who had
fought their way to the top in the hurly-burly of the
trail, and who could pick out a real horseman almost at
a glance. To illustrate the difficulty of getting into the
Pony Express service, Major Luther C. North, veteran
plainsman now living at Columbus, Nebraska, writes to
the author of this book as follows:

> I was at Fort Kearney, Nebraska, in 1860 when the
> Pony Express was started. I asked my brother [the late
> Major Frank North] to go with me to the station to see
> if I could get a job as a rider. I had ridden a mail route
> for a year—from 1859 to 1860. The agent, or manager,
> at Kearney said they would not hire any rider under 20
> years of age.

Seventy-five to one hundred miles a day, which meant at
least seven changes of mounts, was to be a rider's "stint."
At the "home" station which marked the end of his run
he could rest awhile and then ride back with the return
mail. Few of the applicants realized what it meant to keep
up such a terrific pounding day after day. Not many of
the eighty riders signed for the start, carried through
the ensuing nineteen months of the existence of the Pony
Express. Some dropped out after a few weeks in the
saddle. One or two went into quick consumption. Many a
rider finished his "run" bleeding at the mouth and nose.

Yet these youths from the western frontier had not even the protection afforded the riders of Genghis Khan's *yam*, or Pony Express, the saddlemen who carried messages for the Tartar ruler being tightly bound about the head, chest and stomach to withstand the terrific strain.

The saddles and mail-carrying equipment of the Pony Express riders afford excellent examples of the care with which every detail was planned in advance.

In order to save weight, saddles of a special design were made. These were mostly turned out at Israel Landis' famous saddlery in St. Joseph. They were a modified design of the regular stock saddle generally in use in the West. The "California tree" was lighter than the heavy model which has come down from the vaqueros and which has been found most comfortable for man and horse in roundup work or in day-to-day riding on the ranch. The leather "skirt" was cut down to a minimum, and the stirrups, used with or without tapaderas, or leather coverings, were lighter than those ordinarily used. The saddle horn—a necessary part of the equipment, as will be shown —was short and broad. The cantle was low and sloping. The finished product was something between a jockey saddle and a stock saddle. It did not weigh more than a third as much as any of the types of saddles in ordinary use in the frontier West, yet it was strong and roomy enough to afford the rider some necessary degree of comfort in the course of a long ride at top speed.

Mail pouches were never in use on the Overland Pony Express. On account of their size and shape, they would be difficult to attach to the saddle, and would cause undue delay in changing mounts. To get around this difficulty, a

REPLICA OF PONY EXPRESS SADDLE

This saddle, which shows the leather covering, or *mochila*, and the mail pockets, was designed under direction of W. A. Cates, Pony Express rider. Drawings show "stripped" saddle, and *mochila*.

Photograph by the author.

mochila, or covering of leather, was thrown over the saddle. The saddle horn and cantle projected through holes which were cut in the *mochila.* Attached to the broad leather skirt of the *mochila* were four *cantinas,* or boxes of hard leather. When the rider was in the saddle, his legs came between these boxes. The mail was put in these *cantinas,* which were locked with small padlocks. Station keepers at either end of the line, or at designated way stations, had keys to these boxes.

Through the use of the *mochila,* it was not necessary to change saddles at all, properly speaking. When a rider arrived at a relay station, a fresh horse, saddled and bridled, was waiting for him. The rider changed the *mochila* from one saddle to another and was away, inside the two-minute limit allowed for changing horses. If a horse fell and was killed or injured, the rider could strip the *mochila* from the saddle and walk to the next station with the mail.

Israel Landis, who turned out the Pony Express saddles, was a well-known character, not alone in St. Joe, but along the trail. He started business "at the sign of the Big Saddle," in 1844. When the rush of '49ers began, he rented three buildings, to keep up with the expansion of his business, and hired some of the emigrants who were compelled to winter in St. Joe. In front of his shop was a large wooden frame in which he inserted each week a "poem" advertising his wares. These bits of doggerel became famous all the way to California and were sung or chanted along the trail. Everyone stopped to see what there was new in "Big Saddle Poetry" in St. Joe. The verses usually started off something like this:

If a good saddle you would find,
One that's just suited to your mind,
You need not to St. Louis go,
For you can get one in St. Joe.

Then would follow local allusions, perhaps to Landis' part in the fight to remove the county seat from Sparta to St. Joe, or other local and political activities in which the saddle-maker was prominent.

The selection of horses was made with great care. Stamina, as well as speed, was a requirement. At the eastern end of the line, the cavalry was heavily drawn upon for suitable mounts. The *Missouri Free Democrat*, late in March, 1860, printed the following news item:

"The stables of the Pony Express company are being rapidly filled with horses bought from Captain McKissack at Leavenworth."

At the western end of the route, California mustangs were purchased. In tribute to the prowess of these animals, Jeremiah Lynch in his book, *A Senator of the Fifties*, says:

Only a year prior to the gold discovery, Colonel Frémont was hastily summoned from Los Angeles to Monterey. Leaving the former place at early dawn with two companions, he rode 125 miles before halting for the night. They had nine horses as a *cabadalla*, driving six ahead of them, running loose on the trail, and changing every twenty miles. The second day they made 125 miles. On the third they did not start until eleven o'clock, yet traveled eighty miles, and on the fourth day they dashed into Monterey at 3 o'clock, having ridden ninety miles since morning and four hundred and twenty miles in four days. Fremont and his party left on their return the next day at four of the afternoon, galloping forty miles that afternoon, one hundred and twenty miles the next day and one hundred and thirty miles on the two succeeding days, arriving in Los Angeles on the ninth day from their departure. They traveled a rough and unpeopled trail. Their actual time in the saddle was seventy-six hours, and their average was eleven miles an hour. Frémont rode one hundred and thirty miles in twenty-four hours on one horse. The California horses are small, but with deep withers and broad flanks. Except in weight and color they much resemble the Arabian stallions to be seen in the streets of Cairo.

Horses of the quality demanded for Pony Express use were bringing from $150 to $200 each at this time in the West, whereas the ordinary, range-bred horse could be had for $50. Many a Pony Express rider, later on, owed his life to the fact that the horses which had been so carefully selected for his use, and which were always kept in the best of condition, could outrun even the swift ponies of the Indians.

The Pony Express riders and other employees, who received from $40 to $100 a month, were housed and fed at the company's expense. The cost of food on the frontier was very high, as most of it had to be freighted for great distances. Hay and grain, besides being expensive at point of shipment, cost as high as twenty-five cents a pound for transportation alone, when delivered at outlying Pony Express stations by ox-team. But for the enormous transportation business built up by that pioneer freighter, Alexander Majors, the Pony Express would have been foredoomed to failure at the outset, on account of the difficulty of securing supplies.

The multifarious details, relating to flesh and blood and saddle leather, having been attended to, in the space of a few weeks, advertisements were put in the prominent newspapers, East and West. It was announced that beginning April 3, 1860, a Pony Express service, running weekly between St. Joseph, Mo., and Sacramento, Cal., would cut the time between New York and San Francisco, for telegraphic dispatches, to ten days. The time for letters, between those two cities, was thirteen days. Charges, for carrying telegraphic dispatches and letters, would be $5 a half ounce.

The schedule, it transpired, was subject to fluctuations, depending chiefly on weather conditions along the trail. But the weekly service, as at first projected, was soon changed to semi-weekly. When the mettle of horses and riders had been tried out, and special occasions demanded extra-rapid service, schedule limits were to be cut by hours.

The first advertisements, which were enlivened by tiny figures of jockey-like riders in full tilt, were sufficient to stir public interest to a high pitch. A saving of twelve days in the coast-to-coast mail service! If it could be done, it meant that the age of speed had arrived.

CHAPTER VI

GOOD-BYE AT ST. JOSEPH

1

ST. JOSEPH, the starting point of the Pony Express, had flung open the door to the West for many a hopeful emigrant.

Joseph Robidoux, one of three brothers who were prominent in fur trading and settlement in various parts of the West, chose the site of "Robidoux's Landing" with a frontiersman's eye to security. The writhing Missouri, seeking what it might destroy, could burrow in vain against that high eastern bank. On the other side, where the whole West stretched in prospect, the river could riot as it pleased. Many a night, snug on the property which he had bought from the Indians, old Joe Robidoux could hear the crash and hiss of earth falling into water, as the playful Missouri kept up its work of making new channels.

Trappers from St. Louis, a lot of them *bateaux* men from the Canadian wilds, used to pole their craft up to "Robidoux's Landing" for a last to-do of entertainment before they vanished into the reaches of the Upper Missouri. Such as came down with their peltries would stop, too—usually not as many as had made the upstream venture.

When the gold rush of 1849 was on, "Robidoux's Landing," now the town of St. Joseph, played host to fifty thousand gold-seekers. A nice town St. Joseph was, too. A thousand population, lacking a hundred or two—not bad, when one considers what a constant temptation it was to break away through that magic Western gateway oneself. Robidoux had named a street for each member of his family—Angelique Street for his wife, Sylvanie for his daughter, and Francis, Jules, Felix, Edmond and Charles for his sons. There was even a lane named "Poulite," for his old Negro servant who spoke only French. The business of selling supplies to the California-bound put St. Joe on its feet. Wagons, saddles, provisions, oxen, mules —they were all to be had at St. Joe. It is even said that one St. Joseph merchant laid in a large supply of Bibles, only to find that the emigrants who were inclined to Bible reading had brought their own from "back East."

The claim is made for St. Joseph that she started more emigrants along the Oregon Trail than were sent from Westport. It is certain that their wagons filled the bottom lands where walnut groves had been cut down to make room for hemp fields—hemp being one of the chief products of that part of Missouri.

One reason for St. Joseph's prominence in the "trail trade" lay in the matter of its accessibility. When he was once ferried across the river from St. Joe, the emigrant's course was easily followed. Diagonally across the northeast corner of what is now Kansas, the trail led by easy stages to the watercourse of the Platte.

When the Pike's Peak gold fever broke out, St. Joseph once more became an outfitting point. By this time the remote landing where Joseph Robidoux used to deal out entertainment for the *voyageurs* on the Missouri, had

become a real city. It was the final western railroad stop
in the "States." Furthermore, it was the final eastern
stop of the Central Overland, California and Pike's Peak
Express Company—the meeting place of stage and railroad.

The completion of the Hannibal & St. Joseph railroad
had marked an era in the advancement of the city. Much
of the credit for building the railroad line was due to M.
Jeff Thompson, Mayor of St. Joseph—a man who was
to be the central figure in many a stormy episode in
succeeding months. Jeff Thompson was highly respected,
even by those who differed with him politically. He was a
familiar figure about the streets of St. Joseph—lathlike
and over six feet tall and always wearing the broadest of
broad hats, in order, he said, to make up in some way for
his slenderness of build. He was much given to whittling
with a knife which he said had been given him at a church
fair for being the homeliest man present. His moods of
quaint humor could change, under the pressure of political
argument, and he was known as one of the most forceful
speakers of the day in behalf of the Southern cause.

Thompson, in surveying the line of the Hannibal & St.
Joseph railroad, had made the acquaintance of a fifteen-
year-old boy, over on the Mississippi side of the state.
Sam Clemens, a bushy-headed youth from Hannibal, was
fascinated with the work of the surveyors. At every opportunity, Clemens was out on the line of survey, carrying
water, lugging a chain, or doing whatever else he could
to help. A deep liking had sprung up between Jeff Thompson and the boy. Sometimes, however, Sam's presence
became somewhat of a handicap, and it was necessary for
him to be sent home. But he always showed up again at

the first opportunity and Jeff Thompson good-naturedly allowed him to "trail along." A few years later, when the Hannibal & St. Joseph was completed, Clemens was to go over the stage trail which stretched beyond the end of the tracks, and was to give the world an unforgettable picture of the frontier West in *Roughing It*.

It was Mayor Jeff Thompson who built the fire under the engine that was first to speed across the state of Missouri on the new line. The initial trip was something joyfully celebrated, both in Hannibal and St. Joseph. A jug of Mississippi River water was emptied into the Missouri at St. Joe. Local writers for the press were spurred to their best efforts. It was a time when poets did not care to have their names bandied about as such —witness the following tribute to the Missouri and Mississippi, from the St. Joseph *Gazette*, "written by a gentleman who has achieved a widespread reputation at the bar":

Two Ancient Misses

I know two ancient misses
  Who ever onward go
From a cold and rigid northern clime
Through a land of wheat and corn and wine,
To the southern sea, where the fig and vine
  And the golden orange glow.

In graceful curves they wind about,
Upon their long and lonely route
  Among the beauteous hills;
They never cease their onward step,
Through day and night they're dripping wet,
And oft with snow and sleet beset,
  And sometimes with the chills.

The one is a romping, dark brunette,
As fickle and gay as any coquette;
She glides along by the Western plains
And changes her bed every time it rains,
Witching as any dark-eyed houri,
This romping, wild brunette Missouri.

The other is placid, mild and fair,
With a gentle, sylph-like, quiet air,
And a voice as sweet as a soft guitar;
She moves along the meadows and parks,
Where naiads play Æolian harps,
Nor ever goes by fits and starts.
No fickle coquette of the city,
But gentle, constant Mississippi.

I love the wild and dark brunette,
Because she is a gay coquette;
Her, too, I love, of quiet air,
Because she's gentle, true and fair.
The land of my birth, on the East and West
Embraced by these is doubly blest.
'Tis hard to tell which I love the best.

In keeping with its dignity as the chief way-point
between East and West, St. Joseph had provided itself
with a hotel which was one of the marvels of the time. John
Patee, in 1856, began the construction of what was to be
the finest hotel in the West. The Patee House cost
$200,000, but, unfortunately for its promoter, its location
was such that the project could not be made to pay. Stage
coaches ran special excursions when the hotel was opened.
Guests came from Liberty, and Weston and all the way
from Hannibal. The long hitching rack in front of the

hotel was lined with the "rigs" of the young bloods from
St. Joseph and vicinity. But the railroad terminal, instead
of being located on Penn Street, as Patee had been
assured, was built several blocks away, at Eighth and
Olive streets, and St. Joseph's marvel among hotels was
a financial failure from the start.

Many distinguished guests of stage-coach days put up
at the Patee House, notwithstanding. For the east-bound
it afforded the first glorious plunge into the luxuries which
the "States" possessed and the frontier lacked. For those
bound west, it afforded a farewell revelry in such luxuries.
William H. Russell and Alexander Majors were familiar
figures about the Patee House when they were establishing their stage line and later the Pony Express. Richard
F. Burton, keen to penetrate the mysteries of Mormon-
dom; Horace Greeley and the correspondent Albert D.
Richardson, intent on "writing up" the Colorado gold
camps; adventurers headed for the distant excitements
of Washoe; sportsmen who wanted to shoot buffaloes and
perhaps have a not-too-dangerous brush with Indians—
such figures gave the corridors of the Patee House something more than local swank.

The town which Trapper Joe Robidoux had started so
conservatively and whose narrow streets he had named
with such domestic fidelity, had become a part of both
East and West. It could outfit a wagon party, down to
home-made hempen rope for making repairs or hanging
horse-thieves, or it could provide the aristocrats of stage
travel with a wine dinner not to be outdone even at the
Planter's in St. Louis.

St. Joe, conscious of the gaze of the world, forgot all
else in the preparations that were made for establishing

the Pony Express during those busy spring days of 1860. The town feverishly awaited the day when it could speed the mail couriers away from the rail ends into that void on the other side of the Missouri.

2

For several weeks before the date set for the opening of the Pony Express, youths who had "signed articles" as riders were drifting in and out of St. Joseph to receive instructions and to be looked over at headquarters.

Upwards of thirty riders, a large proportion of those selected to ride the eastern half of the trail, had been quartered at the Patee House, at company expense. The boys found that nothing in St. Joe was too good for them. Dances were given at the big hotel, and the "Pony" riders were privileged to dance in the costumes which they were to wear in the saddle, even spurs being permitted.

A hint of showmanship was evident at the St. Joe end of the route—probably the work of the astute Russell, who knew the value of little touches of advertising. Each rider who left St. Joe and the neighboring "home" stations, where there was some population to which appeal could be made, wore a red shirt, blue trousers, fancy boots and, to be donned in case of cold weather, a buckskin jacket. Later on, as the grind developed, the thought of special costuming was dropped. All the riders were provided with horns, which they were supposed to sound before they arrived at a relay station to announce their coming. Usually the sound of galloping hoofs was all the advance notice necessary.

Every rider along the two-thousand-mile route was required to sign the unique pledge Alexander Majors for

years had required of every one of his employees in his
freighting business:

> I do hereby swear before the great and living God that
> during my engagement, and while I am an employee of
> Russell, Majors and Waddell, I will under no circum-
> stances use profane language; that I will drink no intoxi-
> cating liquors; that I will not quarrel or fight with other
> employees of the firm, and that in every respect I will
> conduct myself honestly, be faithful to my duties, and so
> direct all my acts as to win the confidence of my em-
> ployers. So help me God.

Each Pony rider, after he had signed this pledge, was
presented with a small, leather-bound Bible. This, also,
was an idea faithfully carried out by Alexander Majors.

Just how far Majors' efforts went toward stemming the
tide of profanity and intemperance in a country where
civilization was getting its first hold is problematical. The
cynical Burton, whose ears were not easily shocked, says
in his book, *The City of the Saints:*

> At St. Joseph I was introduced to Mr. Alexander
> Majors, formerly one of the contractors for supplying
> the army in Utah—a veteran mountaineer, familiar with
> life on the plains. His meritorious efforts to reform the
> morals of the land have not yet put forth even the bud
> of promise. He forbade his drivers and employees to drink,
> gamble, curse, and travel on Sundays; he desired them
> to peruse Bibles distributed to them gratis; and, though
> he refrained from a lengthy proclamation, commanding
> his lieges to be good boys and girls, he expected it of
> them. Results: I scarcely ever saw a sober driver; as
> for the profanity,—the Western equivalent for hard

swearing,—they would make the flush of shame crimson the cheek of the old Isis bargee.

It is more than probable that so shrewd a judge of human nature as Alexander Majors was not seeking any widespread reform—that he closed his ears more than once when he heard his own bullwhackers talking to his own oxen—but his real object was to make some slight impression on the frontier's younger element. And it is certain that no man could find a more effective way of being dropped from a "Majors outfit" than by abusing the livestock in his charge.

The youths who had received their Bibles and their general instructions were soon back along the trail, waiting at the various "home" stations for the race to start. Most of these riders on the eastern division were young fellows from the ranches that thickly dotted the trail as it approached the Missouri but thinned to a few scattered homesteads out toward Kearney. The riders were not cowboys, as the term was accepted later. The cattle industry had not started. The mavericks which were to found that industry were still running wild in Texas, not to be rounded up and trailed North until after the Civil War. Yet every young fellow of sound limb was a rider. There were wild horses to be caught and broken to saddle. There were buffaloes to be hunted. By the time they were fourteen, these boys along the big trail in Kansas and Nebraska feared nothing that needed to be shod with iron. At twenty they resisted saddle fatigue as if they were so much whipcord.

Among the riders who were best known in St. Joseph —some of them having been brought up on ranches near the city—were Johnny Frey, Billy Richardson, Charley and Gus Cliff, Alex Carlisle, Henry Wallace, Don C. Rising and J. H. (Jack) Keetley. Frey was the most celebrated of all the riders at the eastern end of the route. He was brought up near Wathena, Kansas, and had already achieved a reputation as a daredevil rider when he entered the Pony Express service. Frey was kept for the ride in and out of St. Joseph—a "key" man who could give the mail a quick start on its outgoing trip and make up lost time if the incoming mail was late. Frey was small, weighing less than one hundred and twenty pounds, but, like Aubrey, Carson and other great riders, was all muscle and determination, plus the intuition which is the gift of the real horseman—seeming to know by instinct just how much he could get out of a horse without overtaxing the animal.

Some doubt exists as to the riders who were quartered at the Patee House in St. Joseph, ready to carry the first Pony Express mail Westward. It is certain that Johnnie Frey was in St. Joseph on that date, as old residents of the city who were present at the celebration, have testified to seeing him just previous to the arrival of the train with the mail. Carlisle, Richardson and Gus Cliff—all these are said by one authority or another to have been present. It is not unlikely that the company had grouped several riders at the eastern starting place in order to have a substitute in case of accident, though such precaution does not seem to have been taken at Sacramento. Nor is it unlikely, in the ovent of more than one rider being present, the men drew lots, as claimed, for the honor of being first in the saddle.

These were details about which St. Joseph was not too

particular. The main thing in mind was that here lay a two-thousand-mile line of communication, stretched tight as a bowstring, waiting the hour of release.

3

When the general agent of the Central Overland, California and Pike's Peak Express Company announced, in his Pony Express advertisements, a schedule of thirteen days for letter delivery between New York and San Francisco, there were many who said it simply could not be done. There would be delays, it was claimed, on the long trail between St. Joseph and Sacramento, where delivery depended on the speed and stamina of horses.

No one figured that the only delay in this initial trip of the country's overland fast mail would be met in the region of steam and iron. Yet that is what happened. A train connection was missed at Detroit. Word was flashed to St. Joseph that the train bearing the first through mail of the Pony Express would be two—perhaps three hours late at Hannibal.

A crowd had assembled early in the afternoon at St. Joseph. The train was not due until 5 o'clock. This delay meant that it might be dark before the "Pony" service was set in motion. Mayor Jeff Thompson and others had tried to ease the growing impatience of the crowd, between "pieces" by a famous brass band which had been hired for the occasion. But a rumor about railroad delays had run through the crowd, to be met by the confident assertion:

"Ad Clark's the engineer on the run from Hannibal. Ad'll be sure to make up any lost time."

Years later a correspondent of the New York *Sun*

checked up among grizzled railroad men to get the inside
story of what happened on this run of the pioneer fast
mail across the state of Missouri. From the *Sun's* graphic
article the following is quoted:

The Government had not yet closed a mail contract
with any railroad. Until 1860 the mail had been going
up to St. Joseph by boat. So it became necessary for
the management of the new railroad to show Uncle Sam
what could be done.

Every man on the line considered himself an important
part in the event. George H. Davis, the roadmaster,
issued orders for every switch to be spiked and all trains
kept off the main line. He was selected to make the run,
with a nervy engineer, "Ad" Clark, at the throttle.

Clark was a fine specimen of the early-day engineer.
He was absolutely fearless. His fame rested mainly on
his ability to get his train over the line without mishap.
In those days that was a great achievement if running
at a high rate of speed. The light rails were easily thrown
out of line by heavy rains and the roadbed was no firmer
than a country highway.

The mail car used on the run of the Pony Express
was the first car constructed for mail purposes in the
United States. The engine, named the Missouri, was a
wood burner. From an artistic standpoint it was a much
handsomer machine than the big black Moguls of today.
There was scroll-work about the headlight, bell and
drivers, and all the steel and brass parts were polished
till they resembled a looking glass.

Fuel agents all along the line were notified to be on
hand with an adequate force to load the tender in less
than no time. The orders given to Engineer Clark were

simple. He was to make a speed record to stand for fifty years.

The train pulled out of Hannibal amid the waving of hats and the cheering of a big crowd. All the way across the state, at every station and cross-road, it was greeted by enthusiasts, many of whom had journeyed miles to see it. Nothing in Northern Missouri had ever excited greater interest.

The first seventy miles of the journey were comparatively level and straight. Through Monroe and Shelby Counties the eager railway officials figured that the little train was making over sixty miles an hour. At Macon it began to strike the rough country, where hills and curves were numerous.

It stopped at Macon for wood. The fuel agent, L. S. Coleman, had erected a platform, just the height of the tender. On this spot he put every man that could find room, each bearing an armful of selected wood. As the train slowed up, the men emptied their arms. The fuel agent, watch in hand, counted the seconds. Just fifteen seconds passed while the train was at a standstill. Then it was off again, like the wind. The spectators saw the occupants of the car clutching their seats with both hands as it rocked to and fro and threatened to toss them all in a heap on the floor.

Out at Macon at that time was a steep grade running down to the Chariton River. If Clark shut off his steam ever so little on that stretch, none of those on board recollect anything about it. If the man at the throttle were alive today he could look with grim satisfaction at the record he made down that hill. That part of the run, at least, has never been beaten by any engineer who has been in the company's employ.

It was like an avalanche. If there had been a tender-foot on board, a more than reasonable doubt would have arisen in his mind as to whether all the wheels of the train were on the track or not. The furnace was drawing magnificently. A streak of fire shot out of the stack, and the wood sparks flew through the air like snowflakes.

Across the Chariton River came the New Cambria Hill, a still greater grade than that down from Macon. The momentum attained served to drive the train half-way up with scarcely any perceptible reduction of speed, but the exhausts became slower before the peak of the grade was approached. The fireman piled his dry cotton-wood, and the safety valve sent a column of steam heavenward.

The white-faced passengers breathed easier, but the relief did not last long. The summit of the hill was reached and the little engine snorted as something alive, took the bit in its teeth, and was soon rushing along at top speed.

When the train pulled in and stopped, amid the waiting thousands at the St. Joseph station, Engineer Clark stepped majestically from his iron horse, looking mussed up, grimy and grand. For the present, he was the hero of the hour. He had made the run from Hannibal to St. Joseph, two hundred and six miles, in four hours and fifty-one minutes—a feat hitherto regarded as impossible. Everybody wanted to shake hands with the keen-eyed man who had done this great thing. It was up to blood, nerve and muscle to take up the burden where fire, steam and mechanical skill had left off.

Thanks to the record-breaking run of the special train, the Pony Express mail, which had left New York the preceding Saturday, was only two and one half hours late in arriving in St. Joseph on this eventful Tuesday. The speeches had all been made. In its telegraphic account of the proceedings the next day, the New York *Tribune* said:

> Before the departure of the Express, the assembly were addressed by Mayor Thompson and Messrs. Majors and Russell, of the Express Company, who, in brief and appropriate remarks set forth the benefits to the country from this undertaking and the prospects of its future and undoubted success, which were received with applause.

Both Alexander Majors and Mayor Thompson prophesied that the Pony Express was only the predecessor of a railroad to the Pacific Coast. Mayor Thompson declared:

> Hardly will the cloud of dust which envelops the rider die away before the puff of steam will be seen on the horizon. Citizens of St. Joseph, I bid you give three cheers for the Pony Express, three cheers for the first overland passage of the United States Mail!

There were no speeches at the stable of the Central Overland, California and Pike's Peak Express Company where the rider stood ready to make the start. The bay mare, which had been led about while the crowd was waiting, had been put back in the stable for the reason that the crowd had been eagerly plucking hairs from her sweeping tail and mane. Watch chains and rings made of hair from the first pony on the overland run, were to be at a premium in St. Joseph for many months.

The mail stowed in the *cantinas* on the *mochila* which had been thrown over the saddle, consisted of forty-nine letters, five private telegrams, and some newspapers— special editions for Salt Lake City, Sacramento and San Francisco. President Buchanan had sent a telegram of congratulation to the sponsors of the "Pony," which message was to be relayed to the Pacific Coast.

Despite the fact that a large part of the population of St. Joseph had gathered to witness the start of the "Pony," there is doubt with regard to the identity of the rider who departed with the first mail. Many St. Joseph residents have testified that they saw Johnny Frey riding up and down during the wait for the train, and that it was Frey who made the actual start. Claims have been put in for Henry Wallace and Gus Cliff and Alex Carlyle, though such claims apparently have little justification.

So far as the testimony of eye-witnesses is concerned, there seems to be plenty of room for error. If the rider was finally chosen by lot, it would have been easy for an onlooker to make a mistake in identity, in the gathering twilight and during the excitement of the last moments at the Pike's Peak stable.

The files of the local newspapers no doubt would have settled the matter, had they been available. But during riots which followed the outbreak of the Civil War, the files of the principal newspapers of St. Joseph were destroyed. In a systematic search for some printed record with regard to the first rider out of St. Joseph, Mrs. Louis Platt Hauck of that city, a valued contributor of matters relating to Missouri history, discovered a file of the St. Joseph *Weekly West*. In its issue of April 7, 1860, the *Weekly West* printed the following:

From our Daily of Wednesday Morning

St. Joseph Still in Advance!
Departure of the San Francisco Express!!
The Missouri and Pacific United!
The Greatest Enterprise of Modern Times!!

At a quarter past seven o'clock last evening, the mail was placed by M. Jeff Thompson on the back of the animal, a fine bay mare, who is to run the first stage of the great through express from St. Joseph to her sister cities of the Pacific shore. Horse and rider started off amid the loud and continuous cheers of the assembled multitude, all anxious to witness every particular of the inauguration of this, the greatest enterprise it has yet become our pleasant duty, as a public journalist, to chronicle.

The rider is a Mr. Richardson, formerly a sailor, and a man accustomed to every degree of hardship, having sailed for years amid the snow and icebergs of the Northern ocean. He was to ride last night the first stage of forty miles, changing horses once, in five hours; and before this paragraph meets the eyes of our readers, the various dispatches in the saddlebags which left here at dark last evening will have reached the town of Marysville on the Big Blue, one hundred and twelve miles distant, an enterprise never before accomplished, even in this proverbially fast portion of a fast country.

The editor concludes his article with a general account of the celebration, the arrival of the special train and other details of the eventful day.

The records of the Pony Express, as kept by the Central Overland, California and Pike's Peak Express Com-

pany were long ago either lost or destroyed. The fact that
the Pony Express was not a Government institution, but
was privately owned and controlled, absolved postmasters
from the duty of making official records of arrivals and
departures. Old letters and diaries, which have been sub-
mitted, have only tended to make the confusion greater,
as they, too, have been conflicting in the names of riders.

Whether it was the sailor boy, Johnson William
Richardson, or the ranch boy, Johnny Frey, who swung
into the saddle in front of the express office where Russell
and Majors had been anxiously awaiting a reply to a
telegram of inquiry as to the expected arrival of the train,
the crowd had little chance to figure out.

The mail was hastily stowed away in the *cantinas*, which
were then locked. The St. Joseph *Gazette* had hastily run
off a special edition, the first column of page one being
made over and containing a brief account of the celebration. The rider tucked away a few copies, to be left at
Salt Lake City, Sacramento and San Francisco.

A cannon in front of the Patee House boomed forth a
signal which told the town and the ferry boat captain
that the Pony Express was about to start. Russell, Majors
and Mayor Thompson shook hands with the rider. Then
the bay pony was edged through the crowd. Once past
the shouting throng, the rider urged his horse to Jule
Street, at the foot of which lay the ferry boat *Denver*,
Captain Blackinstone in charge.

Directly across the river was the little town of Elwood,
where a crowd roared its welcome. Once more through the
hands that clutched at his pony's mane and tail, and then
the rider was following the winding creek road, past Cold
Springs, Troy, Lancaster, and Kennekuk to Granada,

where Don Rising was waiting with his pony. In this distance the rider out of St. Joseph had made four changes of horses.

Ahead of Don Rising, as he shot out of Granada into pitch darkness, were Log Station, Seneca, Guittard Station and Marysville. Here everybody in town was awake, ready to watch the first fast mail go through. Jack Keetley was on hand, and his nervous steed was eager to go, sensing the excitement of the moment. Slap!—and the *mochila* was on Keetley's saddle. A leap, without touching stirrup, and the rider was in the leather and away from the old Cottrell livery barn, out across the Blue and its encompassing prairies to Hollenberg, where Henry Wallace made the next transfer and galloped up the Little Blue.

It was well into an April morning now. There was good going between the big welts that marked the emigrants' Trail of Scars. That trail had never before heard hoofbeats in such rapid, staccato measure.

The Pony Express was well on its way.

CHAPTER VII

CALIFORNIA SPEEDS THE "PONY"

1

FOR several weeks prior to the date of April 3, 1860, which was to witness the starting of the east-bound Pony Express to meet the mail from St. Joseph, California had been assailed with doubts as to the feasibility of the entire project.

The newspapers carried accounts of the activities of the agents of Russell, Majors & Waddell in establishing stations and distributing live stock along the trail from Salt Lake City. California wanted to see the project succeed, but a majority of residents of the state knew, from hard experience, the difficulties that were to be met.

California emigrants had encountered most of their troubles after they had trailed past Great Salt Lake. The same dangers and difficulties now faced the Pony Express. The freighting activities of Russell, Majors & Waddell had not extended beyond Camp Floyd, near Salt Lake City. Their mail contract, acquired from Hockaday & Liggett, was effective only between the Mormon capital and the Missouri River. This meant that, between Salt Lake City and California, a complete new line of Pony Express stations must be established, through the wildest and most desolate part of the West.

Mormon settlement had tended more toward southern Utah than directly west of the capital which Brigham Young had founded. There were few settlers along the plateaus and lonely canyons which the Pony Express riders would have to traverse in Utah. The rush to Washoe had put one or two splashes of civilization on the map of Nevada, around the silver mining region. The old Mormon Station settlement, renamed Genoa, boasted a few ranchers who sold their products in and around Virginia City. Chorpenning's old station at Carson showed some small evidence of life, but for the most part Nevada was still a waste, where one could easily wander from any trail and be lost in the sagebrush, or among marshes which were white with alkali.

Toward the extreme western end of the trail, the Sierras were the main problem. The wagon trains and pack outfits which struggled toward Washoe had made the trail from Placerville worse, if anything, than it had been before. Each heavy snowfall halted this traffic, and the stage coaches as well. It seemed impossible that any regular means of communication could be maintained, with such a barrier raised against it.

Another question which caused much concern among the well-wishers of the Pony Express was: How will the Indians accept this new invasion of their hunting grounds? The Mormons, thanks to diplomats like Jacob Hamlin, had demonstrated a peculiar knack of getting along with the red men. Hamlin and his followers had established settlements in southern Utah, among the war-like Pah-Utes, with a minimum of trouble. But Nevada was now outside of Mormon jurisdiction. To establish a chain of lonely stations through the Pah-Ute country, and to ex-

pect them to remain without being attacked, was daring
to the point of foolhardiness. Unless the "Pony" could
secure military protection, which did not seem likely, in
view of the fact that it was a private enterprise and none
too high in the favor of the administration, it seemed like
suicide for riders to attempt any regular trips through
Nevada.

In spite of the prophecies of disaster, the projectors of
the Pony Express went ahead with their work of prepara-
tion. On March 23, nearly two weeks before the date set
for the start, the Sacramento *Union* published the following summary of achievements:

Overland Pony Express—The agent of the proprie-
tors, W. W. Finney, has completed his arrangements
for stocking that portion of the line assigned to him, and
has detailed his men and secured his stock for distribution along the route. For express and other purposes
he has purchased 129 mules and horses—about 100 of
the latter. They are California stock and well adapted
for riding and packing purposes. The necessary saddles
for riding and packing, with bridles, blankets, etc., were
purchased here and in San Francisco. A certain number
of tents and tent poles were also provided for the men
stationed beyond Carson Valley.

Twenty-one men, as express riders and packers, started
with the train. The men and animals will be distributed
between this city and Eagle Valley; the line to that point
is to be stocked from Salt Lake. Finney goes to Ruby
Valley with the train to fix upon the points for the
stations and make a proper distribution of men and
horses for the service. Provisions and grain for the present
have to be packed from Placerville to the points along
the route where they will be needed. It is the intention

of the agent to run the express from Carson Valley along the route surveyed last summer by Captain Simpson. By that route the distance from this city to Salt Lake is not far from 700 miles. At the rate of 200 miles in 24 hours, the time between the two points will be three and one-half days.

The stations will be from 20 to 25 miles apart, so that each horse will have to travel from one station to another twice a week. Each expressman will ride from 35 to 75 miles, using three horses. The average traveling schedule, night and day, will be nine miles an hour. Two minutes will be allowed for changing saddles at each station.

At this time, preceding the starting of the Pony Express, it seems to have been commonly understood in California that the promoters had been pledged mail contracts in the future, if they made their enterprise a success. Commenting editorially on the Pony Express, the *Union* says:

> If encouraged as it should be by business men, it will be the forerunner of a line of daily mail coaches, and they will be put on *with a mail contract.*

San Francisco was not less keenly interested than Sacramento in the progress of preparations for the new overland mail service. The *Alta California* of April 3, the day of starting, said:

> The mail to be carried by the "Horse Express" will be made up at the Alta Telegraph Office and dispatched to Sacramento by the 4 o'clock boat. Stations as far as Carson Valley are at short distances, from twelve to fifteen miles [indicating that the relay distances had been

shortened at the Western end of the route just before the start] and beyond that somewhat longer. W. W. Finney, the agent of Russell, Majors & Co., has placed his stations 300 miles from Sacramento towards Salt Lake. Another division extends from Salt Lake to meet him, and from the latter station eastward, the stations of the mail from St. Joseph to Salt Lake will be used.

In this same issue, the editor of the *Alta*, doing his manifest duty by a public enterprise, calls upon citizens to give the "Horse Express" a good send-off. San Francisco, always ready for a celebration, was willing to respond, but bets were being laid at the Mining Exchange and elsewhere that the first mail would never get beyond the barrier of the Sierras.

2

Between San Francisco and the golden interior of California, in early days, most of the travel was by water.

Leading directly to the gold fields, the Sacramento River and its tributaries saved the prospector a long, hard trip overland, through rough country, from the coast city. Stern-wheel steamers carried freight and passengers to Sacramento. The town which had sprung up almost under the walls of Sutter's Fort became the chief base where miners from the interior "diggings" could secure their supplies.

It was customary to dispose of such supplies at auction. Great loads of provisions, picks, shovels and general equipment would be piled on the bank of the river at Sacramento and sold to the highest bidders.

It was only natural that this waterway should become the mail route between California's chief cities. When the

Eastern overland mail arrived at Sacramento, whether by pack mule as in Chorpenning's day, or by stage, much of it had reached the end of the route, in so far as land trails were concerned. The mail addressed to San Francisco was put on swift steamers and in a few hours had reached its destination.

When the Pony Express was organized, the river played its part in getting letters to and from San Francisco. So far as actual "Pony" arrivals and departures were concerned, San Francisco saw just one of each. These were for the purpose of arousing the interest of San Francisco residents in the new enterprise.

On April 3, 1860, the San Francisco *Bulletin* reported:

> From 1 o'clock till the hour of our going to press, a clean-limbed, hardy little nankeen-colored pony stood at the door of the Alta Telegraph Company's office—the pioneer pony of the famous express which today begins its first trip across the continent. . . . Personally he will make short work, and probably be back tonight, but by proxy he will put the West behind his heels like a very Puck, and be in New York thirteen days from this writing.

It is evident that the little yellow pony which staged this "first and only appearance" at San Francisco, was not of the regular relay "string" and the fact was known, else the writer would not have made his reference to the animal being "back tonight."

It has been claimed—evidently in error, if the newspaper records of the time are to be accepted—that the first bearer of the "Pony" mail out of San Francisco took the trail after he landed from the boat at Sacramento and made the ride to Placerville. Harry Roff is said, in contradiction of newspaper testimony, to have been the rider who made the boat trip to Sacramento. It was assumed, perhaps naturally enough by some of the writers who took up the Pony Express subject later on, that the courier who came up the river from San Francisco with the first "Pony" mail would carry on from Sacramento to Placerville.

Roff was a "Pony" rider, according to such records as are available. But if he went to Sacramento on this first boat trip with the mail, it would seem that he did so as a passenger. It does not appear that he had any part in the demonstration at the Alta Telegraph Company's office when the "little nankeen-colored pony" left for the boat. The San Francisco *Alta California*, of April 4, 1860, describes the preceding day's celebration as follows:

> *The Pony Express*—The first "Pony Express" started yesterday afternoon, from the office of the Alta Telegraph Company, on Montgomery Street. The saddle bags were duly lettered "Overland Pony Express," and the horse (a wiry little animal) was dressed with miniature flags. He proceeded, just before 4 o'clock, to the Sacramento boat, and was loudly cheered by the crowd as he started. We had forgotten to say that the rider's name was James Randall—an old hand at this business—and evidently quite at home as a rider, though he did get up on the wrong side in his excitement. The express matter amounted to eighty-five letters, which, at $5 per letter, gave a total receipt of $425. In nine days the news by this express is expected to be in New York.

Among all the eighty riders selected for the Pony Express service, chosen as they were from the hundreds of saddlemen who made application, it is difficult to imagine one who would mount from the wrong side of his horse under the stress of any sort of excitement. Not only was it as natural as breathing for a western saddleman to mount from the left side of his horse, but it is hard to visualize the wiry little "nankeen-colored pony" or any other western horse submitting to such a "tenderfoot" performance as an attempt to mount from the right side. Indian horsemen mount from the right, but Indian ponies and riders were not in use in the Pony Express service.

It would appear, therefore, that James Randall, like the little, yellow pony which, according to the *Bulletin* editor would be back in San Francisco that same night, was part of a show. Having a horse and rider go to the boat with the mail was more impressive than dispatching the letters from the Alta Telegraph Company's office by ordinary messenger. It would be a useless expense to send one of the regular relay riders from Sacramento to make this gesture at San Francisco. Any horse would do, and any rider—even one who tried to mount from the wrong side!

Such are the conclusions to be drawn from the celebration at San Francisco marking the start of the Pony Express mail for the East. The affair seems to have been successful. A friendly press gave it a "hand." It paved the way for a larger jubilation, a few days later, when the first "Pony" mail arrived from the East.

3

It was after two o'clock in the morning of April 4 when the steamer from San Francisco warped up at the dock at Sacramento. For days it had been raining in the low-

land region. Reports from Placerville were that snow had
been falling steadily in the Sierras.

There was no send-off for the "Pony" in Sacramento
on that soggy morning. The local letters, scheduled for
the dedicatory trip overland, were added to those which had
been picked up in San Francisco. The rider who splashed
out of town, into the inky blackness, was not the man who
had received the cheers of the crowd at the coast city, a
few hours before. He was William Hamilton, a sturdy
young Californian, who had been chosen not only on account of his ability as a rider, but for his knowledge of
roads and trails in the vicinity of Sacramento.

Ahead of Hamilton, as he galloped out of town without
escort, was the long road eastward, out of the flat valley
of the Sacramento, along the American Fork. Then the
foothill country and a steady up-grade to Placerville. The
schedule to Placerville, forty-five miles, called for four and
one-half hours—ten miles an hour, with three relays in between.

Schedules—and none realized this better than the riders
who were called upon to fulfill the demands of these early-
day timetables—were generally made out on a basis of
good going underfoot, daylight and fair weather. Two
minutes was the outside time allowed for changing horses
at each relay station. That meant six minutes added to the
actual traveling time, unless Hamilton could save a few
seconds at each station.

The big bosses would be checking up on this initial run
in particular. Finney would be having his eye peeled for
any lapses in time that could not be satisfactorily explained—Finney and his lieutenant, Bolivar Roberts.
There was a man who couldn't be fooled when it came to

horses and riders—Bolivar Roberts! He had picked the men and ponies for this far western end of the route. He knew every horse, and could tell just what it could do under quirt and spur. And he knew every foot of the trail from Sacramento to Salt Lake. No use to tell him there was sand where there wasn't sand, or mud where there wasn't mud. If this first overland mail was behind schedule time in St. Joe, and particularly if the "key" man at the end of the line hadn't given it a good start, Bolivar Roberts would be raging. There was a rumor around that Russell had posted a big bet that the first run of the "Pony" would be made on schedule time or better, but such things didn't mean so much as a word of approval from a man like Bolivar Roberts.

With the padlocks on the *cantinas* jingling, Hamilton breezed through the dark of early morning. There was no chance to look at a watch when it was hard to see so much as a glimmer of water when his pony splashed through a puddle. The rider had to time himself by the rhythm of those hoofs. If any time was to be stolen from the schedule, it must be along these first miles of valley going. Hamilton could tell that he was cutting under the schedule figures. He checked the pony slightly. No need of the horse's being "winded" at the start and then losing what he had gained.

The boys at the Five Mile House must be hearing that clatter by now. There was nothing else in the California night that might blur the sound. But, just to make certain that there would be no delay at the relay station, Hamilton sounded his horn.

There they were, waiting! Lights! Out of the saddle and into another, and up the road to Fifteen Mile House.

A few seconds saved there in making the change. Then Mormon Tavern, with things distinguishable now and a faint glow of pink on the snow-caps of the Sierras.

Placerville, which had cheered the departure of Chorpenning and his first pack train to carry the mail across the mountains, was awake when Hamilton clattered into town. It was 6:45, a full half hour ahead of the schedule. In less than two minutes, Hamilton was dashing out of town, on his way to Sportsman's Hall, twelve miles beyond. Another hour in the saddle and Hamilton drew up his panting pony for the final stop. Leaping to the ground, Hamilton stripped the leather covering from his saddle and threw it across the back of a rearing, plunging pony. Then he stood and watched while another rider spurred his way up the trail toward the white barrier to the East.

The California mail had been carried as far as the snowy range. Would the bettors at San Francisco win their wager that the "Pony" would not get beyond the Sierras?

CHAPTER VIII

THE MAIL MUST GET THROUGH

1

THE young fellow who took the mail from Bill Hamilton and headed toward the steeps of the Sierras had been picked for this particular job by Bolivar Roberts at Carson when the "Pony" service was being organized.

Sixty of the hardest riding, most devil-may-care youths in Nevada and California were considered as candidates for berths in the new organization. Out of the sixty, Roberts chose his men, knowing when he had finished that if the far western division of the Pony Express "fell down" it would not be through any fault in personnel.

Roberts selected his men with the care of a general, picking each one for his fitness as applied to the "run" that was to be allotted to him.

Bob Haslam, muscular and square-jawed, was assigned to the worst of the Indian district through Nevada. Little did Roberts think, as he made the selection, that "Pony Bob" was to face emergencies on the express trail which any man would have been excused for refusing to meet.

For the "run" across the Sierras, Bolivar Roberts chose a mere youngster from California—Warren Upson. Like many another California youth, Upson had joined the rush to Washoe. But mining did not interest him, when once he had arrived on the ground. He preferred a life in the open, rather than inside some dark tunnel.

Upson came of one of the best families in California. His father, Lauren Upson, was editor of the Sacramento *Union*. But journalism, and the certainty of an important post on one of the most powerful newspapers in the state, did not appeal to young Upson. He had lived an outdoor life. He had learned to ride, not at any riding school, but among the vaqueros on some of the biggest *rancherias* in California. He learned to outdo his teachers at the *rodeos* which were the forerunners of the cowboy exhibitions of today. Besides acquiring more than local fame as a rider, young Upson was a wonderful shot. He had roamed the Sierras from foothills to peaks, and Bolivar Roberts knew, when Upson had taken the oath and accepted his little leather-bound Bible, that the right man had been found for getting the "Pony" mail over the toughest spot in the entire route.

The schedule had been made out with a view to giving the rider all possible daylight in crossing the Sierras. But even the experts who had planned the schedule could not allow for the vagaries of weather conditions in the Sierras. Heavy snows had fallen, all along the range. The Marysville stage, which had not missed a trip in three years, was held up. Attempting the crossing from the Nevada side, the stages from Carson were snowed in near Strawberry Valley. The Placerville *Mountain Democrat* reported:

> No feed can be had on the road from Placerville to Genoa. The Pony Express and stage company are well provided, but will not sell at any price.

In this connection it is interesting to note that Ben Holladay, who was later to acquire the eastern divisions of the Pony Express, saved the young institution from serious complications at the very outset of its career. Holladay had been a co-bidder with Chorpenning in mail route transactions. He was operating local stage lines of his own and was recognized as a coming figure in transportation, though none realized that he would rise to the Napoleonic heights which he afterward attained.

Finney, in establishing Pony Express stations east of Placerville, had found himself confronted with conditions that seemed impossible. The cost of feed and provisions along the western divisions had risen enormously, owing to the late snows which had virtually stopped all traffic. In order to stock the "Pony" stations it would be necessary to pack all supplies on mule back in the Sierra region.

There had been a heavy drain on the treasury of the company, owing to these and other unexpected conditions which had to be met. It meant a long delay if the preliminary work had to wait until Finney could get in touch with headquarters at St. Joseph. Holladay came to the rescue and promptly cashed the drafts of the company. Teams of pack mules were purchased and the work of stocking the stations went ahead, enabling the "Pony" to open on schedule.

Even though the station keepers were ready with their remounts, it remained to be seen if the first rider could get through the snow blockade which had stalled the stages.

Upson, thoroughly accustomed to travel in the California hills, had selected a stocky, trail-wise pony, rather than an animal that promised speed. It was going to be just a scramble getting across the mountain range, and, if time was to be made up, it must be on the Nevada side.

From Sportsman's Hall to Strawberry the trail grew worse at every step. Heavy snow was beating down from the range. Wagon tracks were covered and the rider had to break his own trail. In some places Upson had to dismount and lead his pony. He was familiar with the road, but the snow had blotted out landmarks. There was danger of going over the trailside into a canyon. The pass seemed to act as a funnel, through which the cold wind roared. Loose snow on the mountainside was swept up and added to the stinging particles which were coming down from the low-hanging clouds.

At Hope Valley there was a change of horses. Then more battling with the storm on a hazardous trail. Twenty-one miles of fighting, and Upson arrived at Woodbridge. From there to the old Mormon settlement at Genoa it was easy going—twenty miles, with the snowbanks gone and the pony hitting a faster pace. From Genoa to Carson City it was fourteen miles, and Upson clicked it off in fast time.

It was late at night when Upson arrived at the Carson City "home" station and turned the mail over to the next rider. He had done eighty-five miles under conditions which none but a born mountaineer, as well as a born saddleman, could have met.

The blizzard was still howling, back there in the mountain. There was a return trip to be made, as soon as the first mail from St. Joe arrived. Roberts had some men and mules out, trying to keep the trail clear. Upson was not greatly worried about their success or failure, as he turned in for a little sleep at Carson City. He had fought

LE PONEY-POST

An early-day poster, popular in Paris, showing a French artist's conception of the Pony Express. From the Alfred F. Lichtenstein collection.

his way through twenty-foot drifts and had successfully run the snow blockade.

The rider who had justified the faith of Bolivar Roberts, and who had kept the "Pony" chain from snapping at its weakest link, knew that he could turn the trick again.

2

Nevada and Utah, all the way from Carson City, near the California border, to Camp Floyd, south of Salt Lake City, constituted a mystic maze in which many an emigrant wandered to death.

The Mormons, who had made the first settlement in Nevada, were bitterly disappointed when territorial lines were established in present-day form. At the time of the "Mormon war," in 1857–8, there was a general exodus of Brigham Young's followers from Nevada. They were needed for possible resistance to the "enemy" in the form of Brevet-Brigadier General Albert Sidney Johnston and his Federal soldiery.

The threatened trouble over, Johnston settled down at Camp Floyd, not far from the fresh and inviting waters of Lake Utah. Johnston was soon to follow the example of Lee and Jackson and follow the standard of the Confederacy. Among his men at Camp Floyd, in the humble capacity of cook, was Quantrell, later of guerrilla fame. And, in the warfare which was to come, guerrillas were to "get" Johnny Frey after he had quit the Pony Express saddle for the McClellan saddle of a Federal cavalryman.

With no Mormon "war" on their hands, Secretary of War Floyd and General Johnston made a commendable effort to solve the wagon route problem between Salt

Lake and California. Captain J. H. Simpson, U. S. Topographical Engineers, in charge of the survey, struck west
from Camp Floyd. In general his route followed the mail
route established by Chorpenning and previously traveled,
in great part, by Major Howard Egan, a Mormon
pioneer. This route lay south of the emigrant trail generally followed in the California gold rush. On his return
trip, Simpson surveyed a road still farther south, but it
was his outward route that was followed by the Pony Express.

The difficulties of choosing a "best" route through
Great Salt Lake Basin were numerous. Some routes were
better than others at certain seasons of the year. There
was little opportunity to follow natural watercourses, as
had been done between the Missouri River and Salt Lake
City. More than one hundred separate mountain ranges,
extending north and south, make the Great Basin region
a series of ridges. These ridges are without form or se-
quence. Few extend, unbroken, for more than twenty miles.
Low and without verdure, their sameness baffles the individual who is lost in their endless maze.

Not one of the principal streams of Nevada flows to the
sea. The Humboldt, the Carson, the Truckee and Walker
River converge and either evaporate or lose themselves
in "sinks" within a radius of fifty miles. To be sure, some
of the valleys through which these streams flow have
proved wonderfully rich in agriculture, and the barren
hills have contributed much to the world's wealth of min-
erals and phosphates, but the emigrants knew nothing of
these possibilities. To them it was a confusing land where
water holes existed today and were gone tomorrow; where
mirages shimmered fitfully and vanished; where mountain

ranges were maddening in similarity and where streams began in obscurity and ended nowhere. The best road through such a country was the road that proved the shortest way out, either east or west.

From Carson City to Camp Floyd, when the "Pony" stations were established, there were only a few habitations where white folk dwelt. "Carson City" was a name that "sounded big," but its impressiveness was limited strictly to its name. It was not laid out until 1858, and then through the accident of one man's stubbornness. Abram Curry had not intended to found a city—all he wanted was a corner lot in the "ancient" Mormon settlement of Genoa, all of ten years old when the news of the Washoe silver discoveries was first heard.

The Mormon settlers at Genoa wanted $1,000 for a corner lot of the sort Curry had in mind. Not a cent less would they take, and Curry became "riled."

"I'll found a town of my own," declared Curry. He went a little farther along the Eagle Valley and paid a few hundred dollars for a ranch which belonged to one "bad hombre" named Mankin, who was said to have killed fifty Pah-Utes and a considerable number of white settlers with whom he had differed on matters which ranged from finance to politics. Mankin took the money and his children and a stallion with feet of fire, and disappeared. Curry went ahead and laid out Carson City, where the whole population had a dance as late as 1859 and could muster only three sets for a quadrille!

Between Carson City and Camp Floyd, after the express was running, three adobe buildings were built which might, in case of emergency, afford some slight degree of protection to harassed riders of the "Pony." One of these adobe structures was at the sink of the Carson; another was at Sand Springs, twenty miles east of the sink, and the third was at Cold Springs, thirty-seven miles farther east. Bob Haslam, Jay Kelley and some of the other riders had helped Bolivar Roberts put up these "forts." The mud was so strongly impregnated with alkali that it peeled the hands and feet of the men who worked in it!

The " 'dobeys" were palaces compared with the other refuges along the route. The stations varied from tents to flimsy shacks. Occasionally, when the lumber ran out, the back part of the station was a dugout, in the side of a hill.

Let us hope that the shade of that princely ruler, Genghis Khan, whose *yam* riders rested on silken cushions and ate of the best in the land, never wandered along the Chorpenning-Egan-Simpson route of the Overland Pony Express!

3

The route of the "Pony" was no sooner announced than it was subjected to sharp criticism from individuals who thought they knew of better ways through the mystic maze of primitive Utah and Nevada.

The whole nation was interested. The New York *Herald*, which, with the *Tribune*, the *Evening Post* and other metropolitan newspapers, had made arrangements to secure complete reports from California and Washoe, printed the following from a Salt Lake City correspondent:

The Government has not been asked for any money in behalf of the Pony Express, nor has it offered any. The

motive for the enterprise is purely and simply business
—an eye on the future. . . . In the Eastern papers I
notice that the contemplated Pony Express is to pass
over the new Simpson route to California. This is not
correct. The Simpson route reads fine on paper, but that
is all. The present route to California is over the route
explored by Major Chorpenning's agents, the chief of
whom is the indefatigable mountaineer, Major Egan. To
lift the veil from an official report, and to the undeceived
emigrant who might follow the "itinerary," I should say
that the route is universally condemned. Instead of the
mail following the Captain's route, the Captain followed
the Chorpenning mail route for 300 miles out, and only
left it ten miles west of the Ruby Valley. He then took
a southerly direction for the sink of the Carson River.
On his return he took a more southerly route and struck
Chorpenning's mail route thirty miles west of Camp
Floyd. Many of the places marked in the itinerary as
springs, and which probably looked so at that season of
the year, have been found to be nothing else but streams
created by melting snow and dry at the season of the
year when emigrants would require the assuaging bever-
age for themselves and cattle. This little rectification may
save much uncomfortable traveling and life itself. "Wells
without water" are horrible revelations in the desert
places.

Captain Simpson himself, from Washington, took occasion to answer this criticism in the *Herald* of April 23,
as follows:

My attention has been called to a letter in your paper,
from Great Salt Lake City, which represents that the
Pony Express is not running on my route from Camp

Floyd to California, but Major Chorpenning's. I have just called at the office, in this city, of the President of the company, Mr. William H. Russell, and learn that the Express is running as follows: From Camp Floyd to Short-Cut Pass, 64 miles on my route of the fall of 1858, thence to Hastings Pass, 170 miles, on Chorpenning's extension of my route, made that winter, and thence to Genoa, 300 miles, on my outward route of 1859—that is, for more than two-thirds of the way from Camp Floyd to California the Express is running on my more northern route.

Chorpenning's route is about 140 miles longer than mine, and hence the reason why the mail company, as well as the Express, have preferred mine. . . . In regard to the sneer of the writer about "wells without water," on my route, I have the gratification to know that the mail company, as well as the Express, have been running successfully on my more northern route.

J. H. SIMPSON, Capt. Topographical Engineers.

As officially given out, at the time of the start of the Pony Express, the route made excessive demands on horse and rider. The stations were widely spaced, the distances between them averaging more than twenty-five miles. Many intermediate stations, for relay purposes, were added after the Pony Express had been started and a semi-weekly, instead of weekly, service made it necessary to shorten the relays and "speed up" all along the line.

4

Salt Lake City was the pivotal point on the Pony Express route. It was the one big settlement between the Missouri River and California and it was within two hundred miles of being in the geographical center of the over-land mail route.

If both the east- and west-bound couriers of the "Pony" arrived at Salt Lake City within schedule time with the first mail, it meant the virtual success of an enterprise which had been greeted with considerable doubt in its formative stages.

There was one newspaper in Salt Lake City—*The Deseret News*, founded by the leaders of the Mormon Church. The editor of the *News* was dependent largely upon the arrival of outside newspaper mail by stage, in order that his readers might be informed of world affairs. If the stage happened to be delayed, or if, as often happened, the newspaper mail was soaked into a pulpy mass owing to high water in the streams that were forded, world news had to be postponed to the next edition or brought out in the form of an "extra."

The Pony Express service promised some relief from this condition. The Salt Lake division was in charge of Major Howard Egan, working in coöperation with Bolivar Roberts. Egan, whose knowledge of trail conditions west of Salt Lake was a great asset, was prepared to carry the first mail out of the Mormon capital. He was probably the oldest rider in the Pony Express service. He had been among the first arrivals in Utah in the great Mormon trek and was one of Brigham Young's "Captains of Ten," a semi-military organization affording protection to the new settlements that were organized at points distant from Salt Lake City. Egan's son, " 'Ras," a daring horseman, was also one of the Pony Express riders.

Pony Express headquarters had been located on State

Street, not far from the Mormon Tabernacle, on the site now occupied by the Salt Lake *Tribune,* which newspaper was not then in existence. *The Deseret News* thus succinctly reports the arrivals of both east and west couriers, in its issue of April 11:

The Pony Express: The first Pony Express from the West left Sacramento City at 12 P.M., on the night of the 3d inst., and arrived in this city at 11:45 P.M., of the 7th, inside of prospectus time. The roads were heavy and the weather stormy. The last 75 miles was made in 5 hours and 15 minutes in a heavy rain.

The Express from the East left St. Joseph, Mo., at 6:30 P.M., on the evening of the 3d and arrived in this city at 6:25 P.M., on the evening of the 9th. The difference in time between this city and St. Joseph is something near one hour and fifteen minutes, bringing us within six days' communication with the frontier, and seven days from Washington—a result which we Utahians, accustomed to receive news three months after date, can well appreciate.

Much credit is due the enterprising and persevering originators of this enterprise, and, although a telegraph is very desirable, we feel well satisfied with this achievement for the present.

The weather has been disagreeable and stormy for the past week and in every way calculated to retard the operations of the company, and we are informed that the Express eastward from this place was five hours in going to Snyder's Mill, a distance of 25 miles.

We are indebted to Mr. W. H. Russell for a copy of the St. Joseph *Daily Gazette,* with dates from Washington and New York to the evening of the 2d, and from St. Joseph to 6 P.M. of the 3d inst.

The probability is that the Express will be a little behind time in reaching Sacramento this trip, but when the weather becomes settled and the roads good, we have no doubt that they will be able to make the trip in less than ten days.

The prophecy of the Salt Lake City editor that the Pony Express would fall behind schedule on its first trip seemed to be justified by the weather conditions that prevailed in California and across the Great Salt Lake Basin to Salt Lake City and beyond. But, after the east-bound mail had crossed South Pass, conditions became better. Across Wyoming the riders made better than schedule time, in compensation for the precious minutes lost in the heavy weather between Salt Lake City and Fort Bridger.

Down the Sweetwater, toward the valley of the Platte, the riders raced, with time still to be made up when Fort Laramie was reached. At Julesburg there was a narrow escape from disaster. The waters of the Platte were high at the crossing which had trapped many a California-bound emigrant. The rider, whose name is not known, spurred his horse into the stream. The animal was swept off its feet, and horse and rider drifted downstream into some quicksands. Seizing the *mochila*, with the mail, the rider swam and crawled to safety. Leaving his horse to be rescued by the onlookers who had gathered to speed the mail, the rider commandeered a mount and rode to the relay station, where the *mochila* was passed on to the next courier.

On across Nebraska the riders sped—past Kearney and then making the turn to the south and east that meant the home stretch leading to St. Joseph. It was Johnny

Frey who covered the last sixty miles, with a fresh horse awaiting him at the end of every ten miles. There was a crowd at the foot of Jule Street to welcome the rider who spurred his horse from the ferry boat and delivered the San Francisco mail at the Overland office at 3:55 o'clock in the afternoon of April 13.

The race eastward had attracted the attention of the "States" in general. The New York newspapers printed the story of its successful outcome, and the *Herald* gave special prominence to the time made by the riders in the final spurts, saying that "the last 120 miles was covered in eight and one-half hours."

On April 17, four days later, the first Pony Express mail was delivered in New York, the letters bearing the handstamps, "Pony Express, San Francisco, April 3" and "Central Overland California and Pike's Peak Express Company, St. Joseph, Mo., April 13"—proof that the seemingly impossible had been accomplished and the "Great American desert" had been bridged in ten days.

CHAPTER IX

WELCOME TO CALIFORNIA

1

FROM Salt Lake City to Carson City is five hundred and eighty-five miles—not as the crow flies, but as the Pony Express trail was patterned. Streams, springs, water holes—these, as well as grades and short cuts, had to be considered by the men who looped the trail around the ends of mountain ranges and swung it away from alkaline marshes.

The first mail from St. Joseph, by Pony Express, which arrived in Salt Lake City on April 9 at 6:25 in the evening, left Carson City at 3:30 o'clock in the afternoon of the 12th, on the last lap to California. This meant that the boys between Salt Lake City and Carson City had covered a trifle less than six hundred miles in a little less than three days. They had kept to the required speed of two hundred miles a day on the initial trip. Night and day they had galloped on, threading canyons and speeding across valleys—their horses sometimes literally skating across adobe stretches which the rain had made as slippery as ice.

Upson was waiting at Carson City. He headed back toward Placerville, to run into problems which were different from those which he had encountered during his battle with the snow on the out-trip.

135

The snow had stopped falling in the mountains, and the Washoe rush was on again. Pack trains, loaded with provisions which could be sold at high prices at the mines, now that the blockade was lifted, had fought their way through the drifts. Wagons were coming through, and stragglers on foot. Before the rider reached Strawberry Valley along towards dawn, he had been compelled to leave the trail many times, breaking his way into the deep snow, in order to get past some pack train or wagon outfit.

It was doubly dangerous going through the mountains under such conditions. Upson put his superb horsemanship to the test in making up time between the constantly increasing numbers of freight wagons and pack trains. There was a possibility of running into some outfit at any sharp turn in the mountain road. No one had ever set such a pace before on a wintry trail in the high country. Upson was cursed for a fool or a lunatic by many a wagon boss, or sworn at in Spanish by dark-skinned muleteers who refused to yield an inch of the trail.

It was 1 o'clock in the afternoon of April 13—the tenth day of travel for the mud-spattered *mochila* which enclosed the St. Joe mail—when Upson arrived at Sportsman's Hall.

Bill Hamilton made a quick transfer of the mail to his own pony and started for Placerville, where a surprise awaited him. The rider found himself the center of an official reception, which impeded his progress for a few precious minutes, and which was described as follows in the *Union* the next day:

The reception of the Pony Express here was most enthusiastic. Flags were suspended, bands of music played, guns firing, and the entire populace cheering. Our Mayor, Swan, escorted the rider, Hamilton, into and out of the city.

Hamilton, intent only on maintaining his schedule, spurred his way through the mining camp, unaware of the fact that California was preparing to "cut loose" and celebrate in characteristically Western fashion.

2

For several days prior to the arrival of the "Pony," Californians admitted to a growing conviction that the experiment, at first regarded with doubt, was going to be a success.

It was known that Hamilton and Upson had given the Pony Express mail a good start eastward from the Sierras, and that the long chain of riders past Carson City was carrying on, with what measure of success time alone could tell.

Such a situation of mingled expectancy and doubt seems to have been too much for some of the eminent jesters at Carson City to resist. Carson had more than its share of such humorists, their ranks (soon to be augmented by Mark Twain) being headed by the inimitable William Wright, who, in the *Territorial Enterprise* under the name of Dan DeQuille, "put over" some hoaxes which set the whole country laughing. One can trace the influence of Carson City's rough-and-ready school of humor in the following in the Sacramento *Union* of April 2:

The *Bee* printed an April Fool story to the effect that, just at the time of going to press the postmaster rushed in to inform the editor that he had secured dispatches from Carson Valley informing him that the Pony Express had arrived in seven days from St. Joseph and that it would reach Sacramento by tomorrow morning.

We learn that some persons were misled by the article and really expected that the Overland Pony Express had arrived from the East. Others correctly looked upon it as an April fool sell, knowing that the Pony Express would not leave the East until April 3. By express yesterday we received the following dispatch from Carson City, April 1:

"The Pony Express arrived last night at half past six o'clock at Carson City in three days, twenty-one hours from Salt Lake. It is an experimental trip. Signed G."

Coming to the conclusion that the dispatch was an experimental trip upon our disposition to take a joke, we returned an answer roughly to the effect that any real Pony news was to be sent along. As it was beyond the capacity of the operator to manufacture any that would pass current, this rather brought him to an end and he accordingly dried up.

Sacramento, when it had passed the "April Fool" stage, and had learned that the "Pony" was really on the last lap of the overland journey, lost no time in its preparations for celebration.

The Sacramento of 1860 was "ready for anything that came along." No city in the state partook more of the varied characteristics that made California unique. The steamers that came up from the Bay brought along some of San Francisco's touch of cosmopolitanism. The miners who flocked in from the "green hills" for supplies and entertainment added their touch of the frontier. Men like D. O. Mills who had started banking and other institutions under canvas, had moved into small but substantial brick structures and were making Sacramento a center of finance. Big warehouses now lined the river bank where supplies had been auctioned in the open. Soon, within a few feet of the spot selected for the Pony Express terminal, the first shovelful of earth in the construction of the Southern Pacific railway would be turned.

Politically, Sacramento was the state's battleground. Its newspapers, the *Bee* and the *Union* (the latter founded by four printers) were impressive in size and well-edited as to contents. Part mining camp, though miles removed from the golden gravel; a port many miles from the sea; the financial hub of a wheel set with gold; a trading center where men bartered with legal tender unminted, Sacramento teemed with life. None could look ahead and see the day when old John Sutter's ideas would be proved right—when Sacramento, beneath its spreading palm trees, would count its agricultural surroundings as its greatest and most enduring asset.

3

Sacramento, in common with the rest of California, had been hoping for telegraphic and railroad connection with the "States." Anything that led toward these magic gifts was to be regarded as a public benefaction. Here was the Pony Express, cutting eleven days from the quickest delivery of mail by the "great ox-bow route." And how long would it be ere the rails were being laid over the pony tracks? No wonder the "Kossuths" went in the air!

The lone rider who was hurtling on toward Sacramento was not a mere carrier of the mail; he was the *avant courier* of singing wires and hissing steam. Behind him and the gallant little mustang, coming nearer and nearer along the American Fork, the excited residents of Sacramento could vision all the powers and blessings of civilization.

The reception to the "Pony" was thus chronicled in the *Union* of April 14:

Arrival of the Pony Express—Great Enthusiasm!— Upon the hint dropped in our columns yesterday, on the propriety of receiving the first rider of the Pony Express with all the honors, our townspeople acted as well as spoke. Yesterday's proceedings, impromptu though they were, will long be remembered in Sacramento. . . . Inquirers at the telegraph office elicited the fact that the Express was behind time between Genoa and Placerville —in fact had not reached the latter place at ten o'clock in the morning, owing to the heavy state of the road over the mountains. When this fact became known to the agent of the California Navigation Company in this city, he at once generously proposed to detain the San Francisco boat mail to an hour sufficiently late in the afternoon to allow for the arrival of the "Pony," in case he reached Placerville by noon or shortly after.

The reporter then goes on to tell of the arrival of the Pony Express rider in Placerville, in time to allow for the holding of the boat to San Francisco.

The superintendent of the Sacramento Valley railroad came forward with the offer of a special engine to carry the mail from Folsom to Sacramento. This offer was declined by the agents of the Pony Express.

When it became known to a certainty that the courier would arrive, late in the afternoon, flags were run up on all the public buildings in Sacramento, from awning posts along J Street and across the intersection of J and Third Streets. Merchants rigged up appropriate window displays, with such signs as "Hurrah for the Central Route!" and "Pike County *vs* Butterfield & Co.," this latter sign being inspired by the rumor that a rival Pony Express service had been started to San Francisco over the Butterfield route.

Continuing his account, the *Union* reporter says:

> The more earnest part of the "Pony" welcome had been arranged early in the day. This was a cavalcade of citizens to meet the little traveler a short distance from the city and escort him into town. Accordingly, late in the day, a deputation of about eighty persons, together with a detachment of fifteen of the Sacramento Hussars assembled at the old fort, and stretched out their lines on either side of the road along which the Express was to come. . . . Meantime the excitement had increased all over the city, and J Street was lined with watchers from Tenth Street to the levee. The balconies of the stores were occupied by ladies, and the roofs and sheds were taken possession of by the more agile of the opposite sex, straining to catch the first glimpse of the "Pony."
>
> At length—5:25—all this preparation was rewarded. First a cloud of rolling dust in the direction of the Fort, then a horseman, bearing a small flag, riding furiously down J Street, and then a straggling, charging band of horsemen flying after him, heralding the coming of the Express.

No outdoor celebration in California in early days was complete without the participation of the fire department. There was great rivalry in Sacramento and San Francisco between local companies. After telling of the simultaneous pealing of bells from fire engine houses and churches when the rider arrived in town, the reporter goes on:

A cannon, placed on the square at Tenth Street, and served by the boys of Young America No. 6, sent forth its noisy welcome. It was answered by the anvil chorus from one of those implements placed at the corner of Ninth and J, and fired by No. 2's boys, and another, managed also as a piece of ordnance, by Holmes and Andrews, on Sixth Street, near J. The latter fired nine, then thirteen, guns. Each of the other pieces mentioned gave nine guns as a salute.

Amidst the firing and shouting, and waving of hats and ladies' handkerchiefs, the pony was seen coming at a rattling pace down J Street, surrounded by about thirty of the citizen deputation. The little fellow stretched his neck well to the race and came at a fast pace down the street, which was wild with excitement. Out of this confusion emerged the Pony Express, trotting up to the door of the agency and depositing its mail in ten days from St. Joseph to Sacramento. Hip, hip, hurrah for the Pony Carrier!

Our pioneer rider at this end of the line, Hamilton, informs us that he left Sportsman's Hall at 1:25 P.M.; left Placerville at 1:55; had the first relay at Mud Springs, the second at the Mormon Tavern, the third at the Fifteen Mile House, and the fourth and last at the Five Mile House. The last five miles was made in twenty minutes, notwithstanding the obstructions of which we make special mention. He complains that the cavalcade which met him at the Fort to escort him into town, soon after starting generally put spurs to their fresh animals and took the lead, creating a great dust, which was not only annoying to him but exceedingly injurious to his pony—possibly simply for the purpose of being able to say that they had beaten the Pony Express.

Hamilton states that the Express can be carried through in much less time, by several days, in a more favorable season. In consequence of the late rains the road was in very bad condition, compelling him to ride zig-zag as though traveling a snake fence. Hamilton is the rider who carried the first Express to Placerville on the 4th inst., in four hours, three minutes. . . . The Express brought through about eighty letters for this city and San Francisco.

The *Union*, in its issue following the arrival of the Pony Express, called attention to its "extended details of the news," which as it explained, had been especially prepared by the newspaper's special correspondent at St. Louis and telegraphed to St. Joseph and subsequently telegraphed from Carson City. In this same issue, the *Union* carried the latest news received from St. Louis by the regular overland mail, under date of March 22—a difference of twelve days in favor of the Pony Express.

Commenting editorially on the achievement of the Pony Express the *Union* further said:

The ability of the Express Company to perform what they promised was seriously doubted. The idea of crossing the continent from Missouri to California in nine days was looked upon as extravagantly ridiculous. As a consequence but few messages were entrusted to the care of the first Express.

As heartily enthusiastic as the celebration at Sacramento had been, California had not yet come to the end of its jubilation over the success of the Pony Express.

San Francisco was waiting to welcome the final courier in the greatest of all relay races.

4

Public affairs in San Francisco in the '60's were handled with an engaging gusto. Newspaper men, through their Reporters' Union, had a large part in arranging matters which had to do with parades and speeches—details which are taken care of in more or less perfunctory fashion by civic associations and political spokesmen in all large cities today.

From the newspaper chroniclings of early-day San Francisco life, it is learned that a preliminary meeting, to shape up a welcome to the Pony Express, was held at the Reporters' Union headquarters on April 13. It was known that the new courier service had been successful. The first of the messengers was well inside the border of California, and, in a few hours, rider and pony would be in San Francisco. California's metropolis, which had been leading in the fight for better mail service since the gold rush days, could hardly afford to be guilty of failure to pay tribute to this swift and picturesque organization which, at its first trial, had brought the Missouri and the Pacific closer together by days.

The details, as reported in the *Alta California*, indicate the complete success of the meeting. "The Pony Express was toasted and drank with enthusiasm," after which committees were appointed.

A number of other toasts were then drank, among which were "Major F. A. Bee," of Overland fame; "The

Memory of Henry Clay," this being the anniversary of his birth; "The citizens of St. Joseph, who are now celebrating the arrival there of the Pony Express" (by Mr. Kent); and "Mayor P. L. Solomon" (received with three cheers). The Mayor responded and gave a toast, "The mustang ponies of California; they have done more for civilization, with California boys on their backs, than their mailed ancestors did in conquering the Montezumas." "The Reporters' Union" having been given, Supervisor Biden, an ex-member of the press, responded very happily, when the meeting dispersed with many expressions of good feeling.

A further meeting was held at the chamber of Commerce at noon of the 14th. A sub-committee was appointed, according to the *Alta*, "to wait on the Monumental Engine Company and request them to fire a salute on the Plaza; and a committee was appointed to buy rockets."

A Grand Marshal and aids were appointed, and arrangements were made to light bonfires at various street-corners at 11 o'clock P.M., about the time when the boat from Sacramento was expected to arrive with the Pony Express courier.

A large crowd gathered in San Francisco's downtown district, an hour or two before the time announced for the arrival of the boat. The *Antelope*, one of the crack steamers in the river service, was heading down the river from Sacramento as fast as steam could drive it.

At 11 o'clock the bonfires were lighted, though the steamer had not arrived. But diversions had been planned to keep the crowd, now augmented by the nightly outpour of San Francisco's theatre-goers, from getting impatient.

The Monumental bell occasionally rang out its merry peal [says the reporter] and Five's boys, dressed in their uniforms, ran out their engine for the lark of the thing, racing at full speed around the block. The lateness of the hour at which the Monumentals were apprised of the wish for a salute prevented their getting necessary powder, but want of it was made up in fun and enthusiasm.

At 11:30 the *Antelope* arrived, amid a flare of rockets. The crowd cheered heartily as the "Pony" rider, on his gayly decorated mustang, took his place in the center of the procession, which, according to the *Alta*, marched in the following order:

California Band, playing "See, the Conquering Hero Comes"

Engine Company No. 2

Hook and Ladder Company No. 2

Engine Company No. 5

Engine Company No. 6

THE PONY EXPRESS

Citizens on foot and mounted

As Hamilton, on his pony, took his place in the procession, a woman darted from the crowd and, putting her bonnet on the mustang's head, tied the strings around the animal's neck. This individual demonstration was received with joy by the crowd, which no doubt appreciated the sacrifice in view of the prices charged for millinery at that day in San Francisco.

Among the onlookers was Jessie Benton Frémont, wife

of the "Pathfinder," General John C. Frémont, who had
first raised the American flag over California, and who
as an explorer had traversed the wasteland over which the
Pony Express had established this marvelous record of
speed. Mrs. Frémont tells in her "Reminiscences" how she
had taken a good position to view the celebration, when
her driver was ordered to "move on." After it was discovered that the occupant of the carriage was the wife of
the man who was known as the "Centaur of the Army" in
California, Mrs. Frémont was shown every attention.

The procession, cheered by non-marchers on the side-
walks, and its way lighted by bonfires at every street intersection, moved to the office of the Alta Telegraph Company, which the *Alta* reporter says, "was lighted up with
candles."

> A succession of hearty cheers were given for the Pony
> Express [he goes on]. Several speeches were called for,
> but, owing to the lateness of the hour—it was past one
> in the morning—none offered, and after three more and
> a "tiger" the procession dispersed. But until the "wee
> sma' hours" this morning the boys were "running" and
> in various boisterous ways manifesting their appreciation
> of the great event they had all been celebrating.

This first "official" trip of a pony and rider to San
Francisco was also the last. Thereafter the Pony Express
mail for San Francisco was sent by boat from Sacramento
in an ordinary mail pouch. San Francisco continued to receive the benefits of the Pony Express, even though the
living chain of riders ended at Sacramento. The newspapers of the coast city, their news service greatly augmented by the despatches which the "Pony" brought

through with such promptitude, were sympathetic toward the new institution. It was recognized that a hard fight for supremacy was on. San Francisco had long been hoping for the day when the Central Overland route would put the city in quicker communication with the "States." At the same time it acknowledged the remarkable achievements of the Butterfield line, in the face of the obstacles imposed by the longer route.

The starting of the Pony Express meant the opening of warfare through which San Francisco and all of central and northern California could not fail to benefit. It was to be a battle of giants—the wealthy freighters, Russell, Majors and Waddell, against the powerfully entrenched Butterfield. On the surface it was an even battle, but, when analyzed it was one-sided. The Pony Express organization, the Central Overland California and Pike's Peak Express Company, was virtually "on its own." Its remuneration from the government for transporting mail by stage was small compared with Butterfield's subsidy. The Butterfield contract with the Government had several years to run. Butterfield's opposition was politically weak. The spectacular and enthusiastic Russell had put faith in political promises which might or might not be fulfilled. The Pony Express itself was being run without a dollar of Government subsidy. Its only possible revenue was based on its necessarily high charges for letters and messages— charges which proved to be almost prohibitive.

Under such conditions it is not strange that a business man of John Butterfield's acumen was willing to sit back and let time decide the issue.

CHAPTER X

STATIONS IN THE SAGEBRUSH

1

LIVING conditions for the Pony Express riders were hard in Nebraska, harder in Wyoming and Utah, and hardest in Nevada. In California, the "and found" provision in a rider's agreement with the company was the only thing that kept him from starving to death. No "Pony" rider's wage would have gone far in the Golden State when the current quotations for beef stew and boiled potatoes, and corned beef and cabbage were $1.25 for each dish, with pie at 75 cents a wedge and other features of the menu in proportion.

The boys at the eastern end of the route, who lived in royal style at the Patee House, were the only riders who partook of anything that approached luxury. The outlying stations were dependent upon such supplies as could be hauled by slow-moving ox-trains.

Between St. Joseph and Marysville, Kansas, on the trail, there were settlements and numerous ranches. Beyond Marysville the ranches became more scattered. Some pioneer, who had taken up a homestead and had built himself a more or less comfortable habitation, jumped at the chance to make some extra money by boarding riders or attendants and caring for the livestock necessary at a relay or "home" station.

Board could be secured at these Kansas stations for $15 a month. It cost from $7 to $10 a month to feed one horse. Corn was $1 a bushel; coal was charged for at the rate of 25 cents a bushel. This was along the most thickly settled section of the trail. Out in the open country, from the western part of Nebraska, where the company was thrown on its own resources in the matter of providing lodging and food for its men, costs increased proportionately.

Without the resources of their overland freighting business at their command, Russell, Majors & Waddell would have been helpless in the face of these transportation costs. But they had established a freight schedule which was a marvel of regularity. Their oxen and mules were the best that could be procured. The bullwhackers in their employ were experienced men who took pride in getting their wagon trains through when trail conditions were at their worst.

Beyond the thin sprinkling of settlements that faded into the nothingness of the sagebrush a few hundred miles from the Missouri, the men who projected the Pony Express encountered their real difficulties in establishing stations. The distances between the regular stage stations had to be "filled in" for the relay riders. There must be at least two men at each relay station. A stable and corral must be built. Several horses must be kept in "top" condition. They could not be turned loose to rustle for themselves during the day or night, as not only thieving Indians but white men with a discerning eye for good horseflesh were always ready to run off Pony Express stock if given the slightest opportunity.

At the "home" stations a larger number of men and

horses must be kept. And there was blacksmithing to be done—a job that could not be entrusted to weaklings or the inexperienced. Some of the riders, like Frey and Keetley and "Pony Bob" Haslam, seemed to delight in choosing horses that were half outlaw. Shoeing a horse of that type was a good half day's job for two men.

Usually the work was done in a corral. The horse was roped and then thrown at the snubbing post. While the assistant sat on the horse's head, the blacksmith proceeded to the difficult and dangerous job of shoeing.

Most of the men assigned to this job had done blacksmithing for the Russell, Majors & Waddell freight outfit. This meant that they were accustomed to shoeing mules. Some of the best blacksmiths who went into the Army at the time of the Civil War were graduates of the hard school of the Central Overland route.

The men stationed at the points of relay were a rough, hard-fighting, straight-shooting lot. This goes far to explain why more of the stations were not attacked by Indians. Two such men would be sure to account for several of their foes, in case of an Indian raid. Later on, when the Indian wars were in full flame, after the Civil War, many of these guardians of Pony Express relay stations went back to the West and joined the Army on the frontier.

Darting between these relay stations, the Pony Express rider had little opportunity to form friendships among the men who were always on hand to speed him on his way. A distant figure in the sagebrush, a blast from a horn to announce his coming, and the rider was at the station. A fresh horse, prancing, excited and eager to go; the quick change of the mail from one saddle to the other;

a foot in the stirrup and the rider was gone, with hardly more than time to exchange a few words with the lean, sunburnt men who would be there, with ready hands and swift counsel, on his return trip. Brief advice from the station attendants:

"Look out for this black today—he's shore on the prod"; or, "The crick's up a foot—better hit the ford a little high"; or perhaps, "What's the latest from Pike and the rest of the states?"

The rider may toss out a newspaper in answer to the last question—a newspaper nearly a week younger than the one which the stage driver may throw off later in the day. But there has been no time for palaver, at this station or the next, or any one of the half dozen points of relay which must be touched before the rider reaches the end of his run.

Nor was acquaintanceship any more than casual among the riders themselves. I talked with several of them, in later years, and found that no one of them knew more than half a dozen other riders, and some of those only by hearsay. The reason was quite easy to figure out. Even at the "home" station there was little chance for human companionship, as far as the rider was concerned. He had a short "layover" which was chiefly devoted to the essential business of securing a little sleep. He was up and ready for another ride before the courier was due with the return mail. Unless a rider was hurt or sick, and was "laying over" at the "home" station, there was little chance for more than a friendly exchange of greetings.

Perhaps the people in charge of the "home" station were settlers, easing a harsh existence by "putting up" riders and horses. Or perhaps the station keeper was the most prosperous rancher in a sparsely populated neighborhood, his home, on account of its location, being the center of local activity. The old Cottonwood station, fourteen miles west and north of Marysville, Kansas, may be taken as an example. The station, still standing, was located on the Hollenberg ranch. The ranch house, a long, frame structure, was general store, post office and stage and Pony Express station. Six employees of the Overland Company were stationed there. One of the downstairs rooms was used for "store" purposes and the post office. The remainder of the downstairs portion of the house was taken up with dining room, kitchen, and bedrooms for the family. The Overland employees, including the Pony Express riders, had a common sleeping room in the "attic" which extended the entire length of the house.

Such quarters were luxurious to those occupied by the riders whose lonely beats were beyond the final evidences of settlement. Across Wyoming and the greater part of Utah and Nevada, the Pony Express couriers rode alone and became more accustomed to the barking of coyotes and howling of wolves than to the sound of the human voice.

The "home" stations in these solitudes had their quotas of stage and "Pony" employees—station keepers and stock tenders, augmented, perhaps, by an occasional long-haired trapper or prospector. There was a big dining-room, where travelers hastily gulped down such harsh fare as could be provided. At night this room resounded to the hearty snores of outdoor men, who were scattered about the floor, wrapped in blankets and "tarps." Many a time an exhausted rider of the "Pony" took his bed-roll outside and slept in the open.

It often happened that an Express rider, coming in late, would have to get his own meal. Most of the riders, having been brought up in the open could "juggle a frying pan" and knew the rudiments of Dutch oven cookery. It remained for "Pony Bob" Haslam, to establish lasting fame as a cook as well as a rider.

"Pony Bob" had boasted, in an idle moment, that he could make a pie. The bet was "covered," and there was nothing for the Express rider but to go ahead and make good his bluff.

In mixing the ingredients, "Pony Bob" in some way got hold of a can of sulphur which had been labeled something else. The sulphur pie created a sensation. The story was passed along the trail. It gave rise to a comparison which was heard for many years in the West:

"As yellow as a Pony Express rider's pie!"

2

The Oregon Trail, which the Pony Express followed to South Pass, had been made suddenly active, along its eastern stretches, through the discovery of gold in the Pike's Peak region.

The first announcement that gold had been discovered in the Rocky Mountains, in 1858, had started a rush which was checked before it was well under way. Word had come back along the trail that the discoveries had been small—that they had "petered out." All of which was true. "Color" had been found in Cherry Creek, where the future Denver was to stand, but there was nothing to warrant a stampede. Bewildered "Peakers" turned back—such as had sustenance enough to take them to the "States."—The others tried "homesteading" on the trail, right where they stopped.

Then came the news of further discoveries—real ones! The genuine prospectors who had been attracted by the first announcement did not sit down to bewail their misfortune, but started out to find the source of the golden grains that had been carried down to the lowlands by the mountain streams. Two of these prospectors, Gregory and Jackson, made discoveries almost simultaneously. Gregory's find was the basis of the Gregory Gulch "diggings"—placer deposits overlying rich and deep veins of ore. Jackson's discovery, only a few miles distant from Gregory's, proved to be the foundation of the Idaho Springs mining district.

It was not long before the new districts were overrun with miners. Those who were not fortunate in their locations pushed farther into the Rockies, and made one discovery after another. The new territory of Colorado was carved from the Territory of Kansas. The town of Denver, the "feeder" for the new mining districts, took on a swift and boisterous growth.

It took only a whisper of the word "Gold," to be magnified into a clarion summons along the great trail. The "Peakers" who had turned back in discouragement once more headed their lame and feeble oxen and mules to the West. Those who had driven homestakes in western Kansas and Nebraska deserted their claims. Reports of the richness of the gold discoveries became more frequent and insistent. Thousands of emigrants, with "Pike's Peak or Bust" on their wagons, swung into the trail from St. Joseph and other starting points. By the time the Pony

Express was put in operation, "Peakers" lined the road all the way to Julesburg, where they said farewell to the Oregon Trail and headed straight west for the golden mountains which were almost in sight.

Russell was one of the first to attempt to capitalize on the opportunities of this new gold field. After starting the Leavenworth and Pike's Peak Express, which was taken over by Majors and made the basis of the Central Overland, California & Pike's Peak stage line, Russell made investments in Idaho Springs mines and real estate. He believed the time would soon be at hand when transcontinental stages would be crossing the mountains close to Denver and Idaho Springs, over a route which had been surveyed through Berthoud Pass. This dream was not to be realized, on account of the steep grades over the mountains near Denver.

In the spring of 1860, when the Pony Express was established, the "Peakers" were in full swing toward the Colorado mining districts. The discoveries were not within one hundred miles of Pike's Peak, but the entire region was still popularly known to the enthusiastic emigrants as "the Pike's Peak country."

The trail to Denver forked from the Oregon Trail at Julesburg. The gold seekers who were bound for Colorado followed up the South Platte, while travel for the Oregon country, California and the silver mines of Washoe headed Northwest toward Fort Laramie.

This great stream of gold-seekers was a source of profit to settlers along the trail. The newspapers of Nebraska carried advertisements of outfitters and emigrant stations along the way. The following, from the *Huntsman's Echo*, of Wood River Center, one of the earliest newspapers printed in Nebraska, is an example of the appeal made to the emigrant:

Jesse Shoemaker's

RANCHE & EMIGRANT

Station

Shoemaker's Point

Ten Miles Above Lone Tree

Keeps Hay, Grain and Supplies.

First-rate Place to

CAMP.

Wood, water and grass abundant.

The editor of the *Huntsman's Echo* had an eye to any business possibilities that opened up along the trail—witness the following significant notice among the news items in his paper:

New Ranche—We learn that a ranche has been started at the junction of the Utah with the Pike's Peak road, about twelve miles above, but as the owner don't advertise or subscribe, nobody knows much about him.

Some of these places of "rest and refreshment for man and beast" along the way were run legitimately enough; others were refuges for the horse thieves and outlaws who prowled along the trail. Occasionally a traveler, who may have foolishly made a display of money, was "done in" and was never heard from again. Complaints about horse stealing were numerous. The fine stock at the Pony Express stations was guarded night and day. Without redoubled precautions under such circumstances, the "Pony" riders would soon have been afoot.

Horse thieves were shown no mercy. Near the "Pony" station at Cottonwood Springs, the junction of the north and south forks of the Platte, was an enterprising rancher known as "Frenchy," who had his own system of preying on the trail trade. Emigrants who camped at or near "Frenchy's" place would lose valuable horses. "Frenchy" would be all concern on hearing of the loss, but would suggest that perhaps the horses had strayed away. He knew the country well, and for a consideration—no inconsiderable price was named—"Frenchy" would absent himself from his business and try to hunt up the animals. If a deal was made, "Frenchy" would appear with the horses and receive his fee.

Unfortunately for the suave keeper of the ranch, he worked the same trick twice on the same travelers—once when they were going to the gold fields and again when they were returning. "Frenchy" was found, quite dead, hanging from the upraised pole of one of his own wagons.

The "Peakers," in their dingy-topped, creaking wagons, were but as a parade of phantoms to the Pony Express riders. But sometimes they proved all too real. A "Pony" rider on a night run in pitchy darkness might have a narrow escape from some wagon that had broken down and had been left in the trail until daylight made repair work easier.

Jay Kelley, one of the greatest riders in the service, was fired on in broad daylight as he came round a turn and bore down on an emigrant outfit.

"What did you do that for?" demanded the rider, embroidering his words as the occasion seemed to warrant.

From the wagon seat a frightened "Peaker" quavered the reply:

"I thought you was an Injun!"

3

All this travel and commerce on the Oregon Trail, from St. Joseph to Julesburg, meant that the Pony Express riders on that portion of the route were never actually without supplies. "Grub" might run low at a relay station but a small supply could always be secured at some emigrant "ranche."

Beyond Julesburg, the question of supply was not so simple. Through Wyoming there were from two to three relay stations between "home" stations. In Utah and Nevada the number increased, sometimes reaching as high as six. Supplies for relay stations were sent out from "home" stations, usually in a light wagon, drawn by mules. If the freighters had not come through on schedule, and supplies at the "home" station were low, or if the mules had strayed or been run off by thieves, the men at the relay stations suffered. Feed for the horses was brought from the "home" stations in the same way.

During the summer of 1860, the company spent a great deal of money putting the route in readiness for winter. The tents and makeshift shacks with which the relay attendants were compelled to put up during the opening weeks of the service, were replaced with better buildings. Wherever it was possible hay was raised for the ponies, thus cutting down the company's enormous outlay for feed. The station keepers and their helpers put in much of their time working on new quarters and putting up hay.

During the winter months, when there was little to do but wait for the arrival of the next "Pony," there were natural disagreements and a few attempted killings. Men, thrown together in such lonely surroundings, are quite apt to rasp each other's nerves. The Carson City *Territorial Enterprise* reported one such case when the Pony Express had been only a few months under way. In its issue of August 22, 1860 appears this item:

> One day last week, H. Trumbo, station keeper at Smith's Creek, got into a difficulty with Montgomery Maze, one of the Pony Express riders, during which Trumbo snapped a pistol at Maze several times. The next day the fracas was renewed, when Maze shot Trumbo with a rifle, the ball entering a little above the hip and inflicting a dangerous wound. Maze has since arrived at this place, bringing with him a certificate signed by various parties, exonerating him from blame in the affair and setting forth that Trumbo had provoked the attack.

Burton, in his description of his journey along the trail, pictures Dugway, a station beyond Camp Floyd in Utah, as "a hole, four feet deep, roofed over with split cedar trunks and with a rough adobe chimney. Water had to be brought in casks. We had to skirt an alkali slough to the next station."

At Deep Creek Valley, a "home" station on the Nevada-Utah line, Burton found supplies low, and the horses being fed wheat instead of oats. Commenting on this he says: "Wheat is believed to make the horses stumble by swelling of fellah and knee joint. The furious riding of the Mormons is the only preventive of its evil effects."

Commenting on the trials of the men at the stations,

this same observing traveler writes: "Diet is sometimes reduced to 'wolf mutton' or a little boiled wheat or rye; their drink is brackish water."

As scanty as their own supplies often were, station keepers at times found it necessary to supply Indians with food. Sometimes this was done as a matter of policy, to keep the Indians friendly, and again it was an act of common humanity. The Salt Lake City *Deseret News* in its issue of February 20, 1861, describes one of these incidents:

A person in the service of the Mail and Express company, situated on the route between this city and Carson, was in our office a few days since, and reported that the snow was very deep in places along the route; that the weather had been very cold, and that the Indians, particularly in the vicinity of Roberts Creek station [a "home" station between Ruby Valley and Reese River in Nevada] were in a destitute and starving condition. One Indian was recently found dead within a half mile of the station, who had perished of cold and starvation while on his way there for food. Another had fallen down nearby from exhaustion, badly frozen, who was seen, taken to the station and resuscitated before it was too late to save his life. Such a state of things among the red men is truly deplorable, but perhaps there is no way at present of ameliorating their condition.

While the Overland was thus playing Good Samaritan to starving Indians, the Government was maintaining reservations for the care of the red men. The condition in Nevada, which the *Deseret News* deplores, was merely the forerunner of worse conditions which were temporarily to close the mail route through that state and which later on were to result in bloodshed and property loss all along the line of the Central Overland.

This sharing of supplies with the Indians was not always a voluntary matter on the part of the station keepers of the Overland. The red man, having primitive ideas about the sacredness of privately owned property, would often steal whatever there was to be stolen. The fine horses, with which the station corrals were stocked, were not the only objects of his cupidity. It was the rule of the company to supply its men with blankets and clothing. To an Indian, such things were well-nigh irresistible. After an incident which occurred in Nevada, station keepers were warned not to allow any Indians to loiter about while such supplies were being received.

Bill Rogers, who had been wagon boss for the Russell, Majors & Waddell freighting outfit, was assigned to the job of stocking the "Pony" stations west of Salt Lake. At Ruby Valley, Rogers was unloading a supply of shirts and blankets from the front of his wagon, while several Pah-Utes, at first unobserved, were busy carrying away the choicest of his stock from over the tail-board.

When Rogers discovered what was going on, he took up his rifle and wounded one of the Indians. The fire was returned. Rogers' assistant joined in the battle, and wounded another Indian. Not until then did the Indians retire. This incident resulted in the burning of one or two stations and nearly precipitated a general war with the Indians.

Much of the responsibility for the efficient operation of the "Pony" depended upon the division agents. Bolivar Roberts at Carson, Howard Egan at Salt Lake, Joseph

A. Slade at Julesburg, and A. E. Lewis at St. Joseph—such men were on the trail most of the time, meeting and disposing of emergencies as they arose. It was "up to" the division superintendent to see that the livestock was kept in good condition; to apprehend horse thieves; to keep stations supplied when no supplies were in sight; to see that substitutes were available when riders were sick or injured, or had suddenly quit the service; and to build anew on the ruins of stations that had been destroyed by Indians. In addition they had to supervise the running of the stages and to look after the wants of transcontinental passengers, many of whom were unreasonable in their demands.

The division superintendents never announced their coming. They might descend from an incoming stage, or they might patrol the trail on horseback. Their word was law, and their law was harsh. Sometimes it had to be backed up with the gun.

All the way from Kearney to Carson each superintendent, on his allotted part of the "Pony" trail, was general, judge and jury.

CHAPTER XI

WILD BILL AT ROCK CREEK

1

WHEN a "shooting" happened at a Central Overland station, it did not take the news long to cover the trail between the Missouri River and California. It traveled with the ponies, two hundred miles a day or better, and it was not long until riders, stage drivers, station keepers and stock tenders were reducing the last morsels to shreds, while the ears of the casual traveler were stretched to hear more.

News of such an affair—a real killing—set the trail buzzing in July, 1861. One of the station men at Rock Creek, a young fellow named Hickok—Wild Bill he had been dubbed, though the front "handle" to his name was Jim—had cleaned out a gang that had attacked him, the number of fatalities varying according to the imagination of the one who had found an audience.

No doubt the tragedy at Rock Creek station would soon have become one of the forgotten episodes of the frontier, had it not been that its chief actor, Wild Bill, became a legendary figure, second only to Buffalo Bill in appeal to the popular imagination.

James Butler Hickok, 23 years old, a native of Illinois and quite unknown to fame, arrived at the Rock Creek station from Leavenworth in the spring of 1861 to assume his duties as stock tender. No doubt, on occasion, he acted as substitute rider, this being a rôle which many of the station attendants were called upon to fill.

No photographs of Wild Bill at this period are available, but he must have given promise of the superb bearing and ideal physical proportions which his interviewers never failed to mention in later years.

Rock Creek is a tributary of the Little Blue in Nebraska, a few miles north of the Kansas line. The Oregon Trail, extending parallel to the Little Blue, crossed Rock Creek about six miles east of the present town of Fairbury, Nebraska. Fifteen miles farther along the trail was Big Sandy station.

The Rock Creek crossing was the dread of emigrants on the trail. High water in the creek frequently made the crossing difficult. The creek banks were steep and slippery, and many an outfit "stalled" in the mud.

When Hickok arrived at the Rock Creek Pony Express station, conditions had been improved. The old station had been bought and the surrounding "one hundred and sixty" taken up as a homestead by David C. McCanles, a North Carolinian who, with his family, had joined the rush to the Colorado gold fields in 1859. Discouraged by the tales of the "Peakers" who had turned back at the first pessimistic reports, McCanles decided to stop on the trail, right where he was. He saw the business possibilities at the Rock Creek crossing. After coming into possession of the property, he built a bridge across the creek, charging a toll of from ten to fifty cents a wagon. He built a log cabin and lean-to on the west bank, opposite the old station. This he leased to the Central Overland company as a stage and Pony Express station.

David McCanles' brother, James, brought his family on from North Carolina and located a homestead in the bottom lands at the junction of Rock Creek and the Little Blue. Later on, James decided to move nearer the Missouri, and David took over his brother's homestead, and moved his family there.

These facts regarding the McCanles family are gleaned from an article by George W. Hansen in the *Nebraska History Magazine*, published by the Nebraska State Historical Society, which gives an entirely different version of the Rock Creek affair from the accounts previously published.

With young Hickok at Rock Creek were Horace Wellman, station keeper, Wellman's wife and J. W. ("Doc") Brink, stock tender. There was plenty to keep the station force busy. The company was running a daily stage service, and the Pony Express was operating twice a week. Changes of horse must be provided for the "Pony" riders, and refreshment for the stage travelers, both east- and west-bound. The tide of emigrant travel had set in again towards the Pike's Peak region. Wagons of the gold seekers were rumbling across the toll bridge. Frequently the emigrants stopped at the crossing and made camp. Mr. Hansen says:

They were not yet worn with travel, and were enjoying the excitement of their great adventure. The evenings were spent in games and dancing, and the woods and rock walls of the creek echoed with the sound of their song and laughter. Into all these sports David McCanles entered enthusiastically, often "calling off" and fiddling for the quadrille, or charming the camp with old-time tunes and

melodies on his silver-toned flute. Mormon emigrants
often camped here, and frequently remained at rest over
the Sabbath, holding their regular services of preaching,
Sunday School and prayer, the woods at night resound-
ing with their loud hozannas.

McCanles was an interested attendant at these services,
and delighted in debates and arguments with ministers of
different denominations on questions of dogma and creed.
. . . He was familiar with the scripture and the poems
of Shakespeare and Burns, and in public speaking or debate quoted freely from them all. In striking contrast
with this phase of his character was his fondness for hard
riding, horse racing, and all the rude sports of the frontier, calling for tests of strength and endurance. He
gloried in his strength and ability as a wrestler, and challenged the strongest men at local meets and in the evening
camps of overland travelers, and it is a well-established
tradition that he defeated all comers.

Bad blood seems to have developed between McCanles
and Hickok. Mr. Hansen says:

On account of some peculiarity of Hickok's nose and
prominent upper lip, not then covered by a mustache,
McCanles dubbed him "Duck Bill," and the name stuck
and irritated and exasperated him.

Factional differences, so common in the West at the
outbreak of the Civil War, are given in other accounts
as the real cause of the enmity between Hickok and Mc-
Canles. The McCanles brothers have been described as intent on the illegal gathering of horses for the Confederate
Army. This Mr. Hansen denies, saying that, because of his

Union sympathies, David McCanles had been selected as the Fourth of July orator at a patriotic meeting held at Big Sandy eight days before his death. James McCanles, the same writer points out, moved to Colorado in 1864 and became a banker and legislator in that state.

McCanles, besides being arbitrary and argumentative, seems to have been proud of his ability as a fighter. Whether these personal characteristics, or belief in the rumors of the McCanles' sympathy with the Southern cause, formed the basis of the ill-feeling, the fact remains that tragedy was impending at the Rock Creek Pony Express station.

2

Three men were slain at the Rock Creek station on July 12.

They were David McCanles, his nephew, James Woods, and a rancher named Gordon.

Hickok, Wellman and Brink were arrested on a charge of murder. So little known to fame was Wild Bill at the time that his name was written on the summons as "Duch Bill," a corruption of the "Duck Bill" nickname which McCanles had applied to him. Brink's name appeared on the same summons merely as "Dock."

Mrs. Wellman appears to have been the only eye-witness to testify. Monroe, the 12-year-old son of David McCanles, witnessed the tragedy, but was not permitted to testify, presumably on account of his youth.

The hearing was before a justice of the peace in Beatrice, Nebraska. The defendants were discharged, following the testimony of Mrs. Wellman and themselves, their plea of self-defense being sustained.

Money matters, growing out of the sale of the East Rock Creek property to the stage company for station purposes, seem to have been the direct cause of the quarrel which involved Hickok and cost the lives of David McCanles, Woods and Gordon. Mr. Hansen, in his account of the tragedy, says that McCanles looked to Wellman, as agent of the company, for payments, which were overdue.

Monroe McCanles in 1925—then William Monroe McCanles, attorney, of Kansas City, Mo.—made a sworn statement of his recollections of the tragedy at Rock Creek station. According to his statement, published by the Nebraska State Historical Society, Wellman had taken him to Brownville, on the Missouri, for supplies for the station and the McCanles ranch. Mr. Hansen says further that Wellman was to bring back an overdue payment on the property that had been sold to the stage company. In his statement, Monroe McCanles says:

> There was a little ranch upon the road, southeast of the station, owned by Jack Nye. . . . I ran up to Nye's and found father, Woods and Gordon there. Father seemed glad to see me and wanted to know if Wellman had treated me right while we were gone, and I told him that Wellman had treated me well. Then we all came back to the station.
>
> Father and I stopped at the house, and Woods and Gordon went down to the barn. Father went to the kitchen door and asked for Wellman. Mrs. Wellman came to the door and father asked her if Wellman was in the house and she said he was. Father said, "Tell him to come out," and she said, "What do you want with him?" Father said, "I want to settle with him." She said, "He'll

not come out." Father said, "Send him out or I'll come in and drag him out."

Here the narrator explains that while he and Wellman were at Brownville, McCanles and Mrs. Wellman had a quarrel over the affairs at the ranch and Mrs. Wellman had said that when Wellman came home he "would settle with father for his impudence." Continuing, the statement says:

> Now when father made the threat that he "would come in and drag him out," Jim (or Bill) Hickok stepped to the door and stood by Mrs. Wellman. Father looked him in the face and said, "Jim, haven't we been friends all the time?" Jim said, "Yes." Father said, "Are we friends now?" and Jim said, "Yes." Father said, "Will you hand me a drink of water?" and Jim turned around to the water bucket and brought a dipper of water and handed it to him. Father drank the water and handed the dipper back. As he handed the dipper back he saw something take place in the house that was threatening or dangerous. Anyway, he stepped quickly from the kitchen door to the front door, about ten feet north of the kitchen door, and said, "Now, Jim, if you have anything against me, come out and fight me fair." Just as he uttered these words the gun cracked and he fell flat on his back. He raised himself up to almost a sitting position and took one last look at me, then fell back dead.

Woods and Gordon, who came running up, were wounded by Hickok, the statement continues. They were "finished," according to the statement, one with a hoe and the other with a charge of buckshot. In neither case is the actual killing charged against Hickok. Further testimony

PRINCIPALS IN ROCK CREEK TRAGEDY

Upper photos, left to right, David C. McCanles and Wild Bill Hickok. Rock Creek stage and Pony Express station, McCanles shown on horseback. From daguerreotype presented by Mrs. Nat C. Stein to California State Library. McCanles Photograph, courtesy of Nebraska State Historical Society.

in favor of the McCanles side, as contained in Monroe's statement, is that Hickok fired the fatal shot at David McCanles from behind a curtain, and that the entire McCanles faction was unarmed.

This statement, made sixty-six years after the boy, Monroe McCanles, witnessed the affair at Rock Creek, is interesting, inasmuch as it is the only presentation from the McCanles side. Whether it would have changed the court decision, if it had been officially made, is problematical, inasmuch as there is no opportunity of weighing it against the testimony of the defendants and Mrs. Wellman. If their testimony became a matter of court record, it has not been brought to light.

Not a shot seems to have been fired by those on the McCanles side, though the statement that they were unarmed loses some of its importance when the life and times are considered. A frontiersman who went so far as to make threats was supposed to be prepared to back his words with gun-play if necessary. Guns were quite generally "packed," and if any party to a quarrel went without a weapon, his opponent was not supposed to be able to guess the fact.

If Hickok, as Monroe says, stood behind a curtain when he shot David McCanles with the latter's own rifle, which was in the cabin, he must have taken his position there very quickly. At one moment he is standing in the kitchen door, talking to McCanles. Then McCanles stepped quickly to the front door and up on the front step. Was this move indicative of his intention to carry out his threat to "drag out" Wellman or to attack Hickok, to whom the quarrel seems to have shifted?—questions which only the testimony of the defendants can answer.

On the surface, the affair at Rock Creek seems to have been a mere quarrel over money matters. What was underneath—whether there was deep-seated enmity caused by McCanles' alleged Secession sympathies, or belief in the stories of his outlawry, or a "showdown" brought about by his own belligerence—can only be matters of speculation.

Whatever the causes, three men were buried beside the trail. And, through a strange combination of circumstances, this tragedy at the Rock Creek Pony Express station set James Butler Hickok a long way on the path to national fame as "Wild Bill."

3

Before young Hickok started out on the career that was to make him one of the legendary figures of the West, what happened when he returned to Rock Creek station? How did he stand with his employers, who were not given to the hiring of known cutthroats and murderers? Did the stage and Pony Express people regard him as innocent or guilty?

These questions seem to have been answered, briefly but effectively, through a discovery made by Harry C. Peterson, now curator of the Sutter's Fort Historical Museum of Sacramento, formerly field research worker in California history for the California State Library and for years curator of the Museum of Fine Arts at Stanford University.

While gathering material of historical interest for the California State Library, Mr. Peterson was granted permission to search through some of the personal effects of the late Nat C. Stein. Mr. Stein, as General Superintendent of Wells, Fargo & Company, had supervision over thousands of miles of stage routes. He was on the road much of the time and was well known and highly respected throughout the West generally.

Among Mr. Stein's effects, Mr. Peterson found an old daguerreotype, so faded that he could not make it out at all. With the care of the born collector, Mr. Peterson proceeded to the work of restoring the picture. It responded to his skillful and patient treatment, and proved to be a picture of a stage station, with buildings and corrals in the background. In the right foreground was an overland stage and four horse team, taken, apparently, as the outfit was rolling into the station.

In the left foreground of the picture was a roughly dressed man on horseback, with a bottle in his hand.

Back of the picture was a note, in ink, reading as follows:

> View of the Rock Creek station on the plains, with the first coach from California by the new route. Also portrait of McCandless (*sic*) on horseback, a desperate character who, with two others, was shot dead at this station last August (1861) by our stock tender. It was done in self defense. Seven of these men attacked our stock tender, and he had to cope alone against them, but succeeded in killing three and putting the rest to flight. He was brought to trial, but soon honorably acquitted. Preserve this picture for me.
>
> N. S.

"I picked up the daguerreotype of the Rock Creek station either in 1921 or 1922 at Oakland," said Mr. Peterson to the author of this book. "It was very dim, and, taking it apart to cyanide and restore the image as far as possible, I found pasted to its back a message that thrilled me through and through. It was a message out of the past. It had not seen the light of day since it was penned over sixty years before, and that message settles for all time several very important points relating to the history of the Pony Express."

At the time of Mr. Peterson's discovery, the official documents relating to the arrest and hearing of Hickok and the other Pony Express employees at Rock Creek station had not been brought to light. Mr. Hansen, who found the documents in 1926, says that the "real" story of the affair—that is, the version by Monroe McCanles, which has been sketched here—had been told publicly on several occasions in Nebraska, but had been ignored by most writers. Most of the stories have been based on an account in an early-day magazine, which will be referred to later, picturing the affair as a desperate, hand-to-hand encounter between Wild Bill and ten outlaws.

The notation which Mr. Peterson discovered, places the date of the affair in August instead of July—a natural enough mistake. The statement to the effect that seven men attacked the stock tender, who killed three and drove off the others, indicates that the impression was strong that there were more than three men in the party faced by Hickok. The man on horseback in the foreground of the picture is holding a bottle, evidently of whiskey, in his left hand. The notation says that the portrait of the man on horseback is that of "McCanles, a desperate character." This would indicate that the writer had gathered an impression of McCanles not so flattering as that given by Mr. Hansen.

The declaration that the attack on the stock tender was

"unprovoked" and that the stock tender was "brought to trial but soon honorably discharged," would seem to reflect public sentiment at the time.

The writer of the note had no reason to favor one side or the other. Wells, Fargo & Company, which had then come into control of the Overland stage and Pony Express business, were notably strict with their employees. Hickok apparently was not known personally to the writer of the notation. He is alluded to merely as "our stock tender." If any minor employee had gone "on the rampage," shooting down three defenseless persons without cause, the company could not have afforded to keep such a man in its employ. It is more than likely that Mr. Stein, owing to the position of responsibility which he occupied, had "checked up" on the affair which had caused so much discussion along the line. That the case made an impression on him quite out of the ordinary is indicated by the notation, "Preserve this picture for me," and the impression seems to have been anything but unfavorable to James Butler Hickok.

The daguerreotype which was discovered in Mr. Stein's effects was presented by Mrs. Stein to the California State Library, and is now an item in that institution's large and valuable collection of material relating to overland transportation.

4

Hickok became a spy on the Federal side in the Civil War. Later he was a scout for Custer and other commanders in campaigns against the Indians on the frontier. Then he was marshal of Abilene, Kan., and other hard-to-manage towns in the cowboy era.

He became a popular hero—the dead shot who had killed many men, but always in upholding law and order. Innumerable books and magazine and newspaper articles were written about his career. Few authors neglected to mention the affair at Rock Creek, that station being located in Nebraska, Kansas, or whatever frontier territory appealed to the writer as most typically Western. These stories, as a rule, followed a pattern set by a writer in *Harper's Magazine* of February, 1867. The author, George Ward Nichols, was an officer in the Union Army. In his article he tells of meeting Hickok at Springfield, Mo., in 1865, after the close of the Civil War. His description of "the famous scout of the plains, William Hitchcock (*sic*) called 'Wild Bill' " is as follows:

Bill stood six feet and an inch in his bright yellow moccasins. A deerskin shirt, or frock it might be called, hung jauntily over his shoulders and revealed a chest whose breadth and depth were remarkable. These lungs had had growth in some twenty years of the free air of the Rocky Mountains. His small, round waist was girthed by a belt which held two Colt's navy revolvers. His legs sloped gradually from the compact thigh to the feet, which were small and turned inward as he walked. There was a singular grace and dignity of carriage about that figure which would have called your attention, meet it where you would. The head which crowned it was now covered by a large sombrero, underneath which there shone out a quiet, manly face; so gentle in its expression as he greets you as utterly to belie the history of its owner, yet it is not a face to be trifled with. The lips, thin and sensitive, the jaw not too square, the cheek bones slightly prominent, a mass of fine dark hair falls

below the neck to the shoulders. The eyes, now that you
are in friendly intercourse, are as gentle as a woman's.
In truth, the woman nature seems prominent throughout,
and you would not believe that you were looking into
eyes that have pointed the way to death to hundreds of
men. Yes, Wild Bill with his own hands has killed hundreds of men. Of that I have not a doubt. "He shoots to
kill," as they say on the border.

From others and from Bill himself, the author gets some
anecdotes of Wild Bill's career as a scout and spy. Bill
tells a story of swimming a river, under a hot fire from the
Confederate side. The author then goes on:

The scout's story of swimming the river ought, perhaps, to have satisfied my curiosity; but I was especially
desirous to hear him relate the history of a sanguinary
fight which he had with a party of ruffians in the early
part of the war, when, single-handed, he fought and killed
ten men. I had heard the story as it came from an officer
of the regular army, who, an hour after the affair, saw
Bill and the ten dead men—some killed with bullets, others
hacked and slashed to death with a knife.

As I write out the details of this terrible tale from
notes which I took as the words fell from the scout's lips,
I am conscious of its extreme improbability; but while I
listened to him I remembered the story in the Bible, where
we are told that Samson "with the jawbone of an ass slew
a thousand men," and, as I looked upon this magnificent
example of human strength and daring, he appeared to
me to realize the powers of a Samson and Hercules combined, and I should not have been inclined to put any
limits upon his achievements. Besides this, one who has
lived for four years in the presence of such grand hero-

ism and deeds of prowess as was seen during the war is
in what might be called a "receptive" mood. Be the story
true or not, in part or in whole, I believed every word
Wild Bill uttered, and I believe it today.

Hickok, according to the narrator, said he did not like
to talk about "that McKandlas affair," because it gave
him a "queer shiver," and sometimes he would dream about
it and wake up in a cold sweat. But the article proceeds
to quote him as follows:

> "You see, this McKandlas was the Captain of a gang
> of desperadoes, horse thieves, murderers, regular cut-
> throats, who was the terror of everybody on the border
> and who kept us in the mountains in hot water whenever
> they were around. I knew them all in the mountains where
> they pretended to be trapping, but they were hiding from
> the hangman. McKandlas was the biggest scoundrel and
> bully of them all, and was allers a-braggin' of what he
> could do. One day I beat him shootin' at a mark, and then
> threw him at the back-holt. And I didn't drop him as soft
> as you would a baby, you may be sure. Well, he got sav-
> age mad about it and swore he would have his revenge on
> me sometime."

The story then goes on to relate how Wild Bill, back
from a scouting expedition, dropped in at a cabin to see a
friend, a "Mrs. Waltman," and the "McKandlas gang"
surrounded the house. Bill had only one revolver, but took
down a Hawkins rifle from the wall and shot the leader of
the gang as he came in the door. Four more were killed by
Bill's revolver, the account says, as they "rushed" the
cabin.

"But that didn't stop the rest. Two of them fired their bird-guns at me. And then I felt a sting all over me. The room was full of smoke. Two got in close to me, their eyes glaring out of the clouds. One I knocked down with my fist. 'You are out of the way for a while,' I thought. The other three clutched me and crowded me onto the bed. I fought hard. I broke with my hand one man's arm. He had his fingers round my throat. Before I could get to my feet I was struck across the breast with the stock of a rifle, and I felt the blood rushing out of my nose and mouth. Then I got ugly, and I remember that I got hold of a knife, and then it was all cloudy like, and I was wild, and I struck savage blows, following the devils up from one side to the other of the room and into the corners, striking and slashing till I knew that every one was dead."

This account, for years had been accepted in many quarters as the real story of the affair at Rock Creek. In his introduction to Mr. Hansen's presentation of the case from the McCanles side, Addison E. Sheldon, secretary of the Nebraska State Historical Society, asks:

How did the extraordinary falsehoods with reference to the Rock Creek ranch fight gain such credence during the life of Wild Bill and since? Was he responsible for their origin, as stated in the *Harper's Magazine* story of 1867? Or did he simply acquiesce in them since they were to his advantage?

The chances are that Wild Bill, if he told the story in all its details as related in the magazine, was simply following a practice quite general in the West—"loading" an inquisitive tenderfoot. The story seems to have been somewhat of a strain upon the credulity of the man who set it down. That it has been repeated by other writers for so many years, in the face of contradictory evidence, is perhaps its most remarkable feature.

If the story was "embroidered" by Wild Bill for the delectation of an inquisitive stranger, he did not repeat the experiment in later years. He was not known as a braggart or falsifier. General Custer, in his book, *My Life on the Plains*, said of Hickok:

> He was free from bluster or bravado. He seldom spoke of himself unless requested to do so. . . . His influence among the frontiersmen was unbounded; his word was law; and many are the personal quarrels and disturbances which he has checked among his comrades by his simple announcement that "this has gone far enough," if need be followed by the ominous warning that when persisted in or renewed the quarreler "must settle it with me."

This attitude seems to have been consistently maintained by Wild Bill throughout his long career as scout and frontier marshal, which was ended when he was shot down by "Jack" McCall at Deadwood in 1876.

I have talked with many men who knew Wild Bill, including the late T. C. Henry, the first Mayor of Abilene. Mr. Henry appointed Hickok as Marshal to succeed the gallant Tom Smith, who had been killed. None of those men ever accused Wild Bill of being a boaster.

So far as the Rock Creek affair is concerned, it seems to have been well enough known at the time that three men, instead of ten, were killed. That much is proved by the notation found in Mr. Stein's effects, which says definitely that, in the attack on the stock tender, he "succeeded in killing three." But such things in those days, when there were few newspapers, were subject to astounding exaggeration. It is easy to see that these exaggerations, growing proportionately as the news was gossiped along the trail and beyond to the "States," may have reached the ears of Wild Bill's magazine interviewer in advance of his talk with Hickok. If Wild Bill's actual story failed to measure up to the trail legend, then current regarding the Rock Creek fight, the interviewer may have supplied the details from the "popular" version that had been passed along from the Western camp-fire and cabin recitals. Perhaps he preferred to liven up the story with the specific instances of slaughter that had been supplied by the officer who, "an hour after the affair had seen Bill and the ten dead men."

As it is, Wild Bill's first affair at arms, when he was an unknown tender of stock and substitute rider at the Rock Creek Pony Express station, still contains its element of mystery. This might have been cleared up had Fate decreed that Wild Bill should reach the age of reminiscence. But all chance of that was lost when James Butler Hickok made the fatal mistake of sitting down at his last card game in Deadwood with his back to the door.

CHAPTER XII

SLADE, OF JULESBURG

1

OLD Julesburg, on the South Platte, was a huddle of unpainted shacks. Paint and paint brushes had not begun to arrive on the frontier in the Pony Express days of 1860, and Julesburg looked ancient and haggard a few months after it was born. The Indians mercifully burned it to the ground a few years later, and a new town, some little distance from the contaminated site, took on more of the aspect of conventionality.

Julesburg marked a forking of the trail. The "Peakers" continued up the South Platte toward Denver and the gold camps. The Oregon trail travel and Overland mail followed up Lodgepole Creek north and west toward Fort Laramie. The Pony Express riders left their mail for Denver at Julesburg. A branch "Pony" line picked it up.

Old Julesburg never had a lid. If so, it had been blown off into the sagebrush right at the start, and nobody bothered to go out and recover it. By the time the "Peakers" reached Julesburg, they had taken on a second lease of enthusiasm. Things had been running pretty low, for the last three or four hundred miles, worn tires parting from shrunken felloes, grub boxes empty, and more ribs to be counted on the oxen and mules every day. But at Julesburg there were supplies to be had, and the hammers of blacksmiths kept time to the music of the honky-tonks. A few days more of travel and the emigrants would sight the tops of the Rocky Mountains,—faint triangles of white, peeping over the line of sage. What was to hinder a little "cutting loose" at Julesburg, the gateway to the newest El Dorado?

A socially-inclined stranger could not lean against the bars of Julesburg for long without hearing the names of its two most distinguished citizens, Jules and Slade. Perhaps, on coming into town, the stranger might even have glimpsed one of these civic leaders, Jules Reni himself, at his favorite diversion, making "whiskey bread." An old citizen of Julesburg explained this to me.

"When ol' Jules would get good an' tight," said my informant, "he would roll a bar'l of whiskey and a bar'l of flour into the street. Then he would dip whiskey into the flour an' make 'whiskey bread.' Many a time I've seen ol' Jules that way, with a bar'l of whiskey on one side an' a bar'l of flour on the other, playin' baker."

Jules had driven his homestakes on the site of the town. He was a French-Canadian, big and domineering, and said to have killed several men. His place, before there was any evidence of general settlement, was known as "Jules' Ranch," and later as "California Crossing." When it blossomed into a town it was called "Overland City," but there was nothing more natural, as a final thing, than to christen it Julesburg.

Jules, as first citizen of the town, was appointed division agent, with regulatory powers over the stage and Pony Express west to Rocky Ridge. Things did not go so well. Stage schedules were not maintained, chiefly owing to crippling losses of livestock. Somebody who would "clean up" the division was needed. Jules was deposed, and Joseph A. Slade took the job as division agent.

"*Captain* Slade, sir," was the new division agent's correction when somebody left off the title, of which he seemed inordinately proud. He had been in the Mexican War, but the title of Captain does not seem to have been acquired officially so far as records disclose. In conversation among themselves, when Slade was not within earshot, the men on the frontier called him "Jack." When he was around, they never forgot the "Captain."

I have talked with Overland officials, but none of them seemed to know just how or why Slade came to be appointed division agent. Yet he must have made a considerable record somewhere. Unknowns were not picked for executive jobs on the big trail.

Slade was from Carlyle, Illinois, and came of a highly respected family. The late Colonel C. G. Coutant, state historian of Wyoming, who made some inquiry into Slade's career, says the future scourge of the Overland was only thirteen when he killed his first man. A stone hurled by Slade is said to have killed a citizen who attempted to straighten out a difficulty between juveniles. The boy's father got him to Texas, where Slade grew to manhood and was married. He enlisted in the Mexican War, and, returning to Texas, engaged in freighting. He was next heard of on the Overland Trail, with a freight outfit from St. Joseph.

In Wyoming, according to Hugo Koch, a pioneer resident of that state, Slade killed Andrew Farrar, a man connected with the wagon train. The men had been drinking together, and Slade said that no man must dare him to shoot. Farrar had rashly replied:

"I dare you to shoot me."

Slade instantly fired, mortally wounding Farrar. Slade expressed contrition and dispatched a messenger from the Green River crossing, where the shooting had taken place, to Fort Bridger for a doctor. Farrar died, but Slade seems to have escaped punishment.

If there was more to Slade's record, it was not known when he supplanted Jules as division agent at Julesburg. Apparently it was not a record that greatly impressed Jules, who prepared for war.

The first clash between Slade and Jules came over some horses which the new division superintendent claimed were stage company property. The horses were being driven as Jules' own. When Slade possessed himself of the animals in the name of the stage company, Jules lost no time in seeking revenge. He lay in wait for the new boss and fired a charge of buckshot into Slade's body. Then Jules "went into retirement" in the mountains to await the news of Slade's death.

Apparently Jules had skimped a few slugs in loading the sawed-off shotgun which was to have ended Slade's career. One or two more buckshot and Jules' vengeance might have been complete. As it was, Slade had to go to St. Louis and have several buckshot removed from his body. Then he was back in Julesburg, intent on making a spectacular reprisal— something that would not only eliminate Jules but would make the name of Slade feared along the entire division.

Jules, when he heard of Slade's return, sent word that he would kill the new division agent on sight. Slade did not wait for Jules to act. First he went to Fort Laramie and explained the situation. The officers agreed that there could be no peace along the division unless it came through the removal of Jules by capture or death. Some have it that Jules was captured at Pacific Springs, by several of Slade's men. Calvin Downs, who "rode Pony" at the time, says Slade himself brought down Jules, after a chase, with a rifle bullet through the hips.

Jules was tied to a snubbing post in a corral. Then Slade practiced revolver shooting with his enemy as the target. Slade was a good shot, and Jules lived a long time before a bullet mercifully put an end to the torture.

Slade was not yet through. He cut off his enemy's ears. Bartenders, at the settlements along the trail, were startled for a long time after when Slade would reach into his vest pocket, and, throwing a withered ear on the bar, say:

"Give me change for that!"

2

Affairs along the division took a decided turn for the better after Slade's accession at Julesburg.

There was less stealing of livestock, for one thing— much less. A Pony Express rider was certain of finding a good horse ready at a relay station. Stage drivers were no longer compelled to get double duty out of their weary mules because stock had been run off.

Slade had given himself up at Fort Laramie, after the Jules episode, and had been released. The military officers and the stage company officials might have agreed that Slade's methods had been a trifle extreme, but the results were undeniable. Slade became the chief subject of discussion along the trail.

Slade himself never permitted the discussion to languish.

He was constantly on the trail, past Mud Springs, Fort Laramie, Red Buttes and other stations, all the way to South Pass and beyond, routing horse thieves out of their dens like so many wolves.

It was enough for Slade that any so-called rancher was merely under suspicion of using his ranch activities as a "blind" for horse stealing. Slade would burn his ranch buildings, and the suspect was lucky if he was merely driven out of the country instead of being shot.

The stage drivers and Pony Express riders out of Julesburg found plenty of new material to keep the Slade tradition going. Some of his exploits showed him to be possessed of a courage that was remarkable, even in a frontier country where personal hardihood was a common attribute. It took iron nerve to ride, as Slade rode on one occasion, to a ranch house occupied by four men who were suspected of complicity in a stage hold-up, and to kick open the door and begin firing. Two of the men were killed, a third was mortally wounded, and the fourth leaped out of a window and ran. Slade leaned through the broken window and brought him down, before he had run a hundred yards.

Other killings attributed to Slade were wantonly cruel. Occasionally he overstepped himself to such a degree that he became contrite and sought to make amends. It was said that a half-breed near Fort Bridger had incurred Slade's enmity, and that Slade had shot him and burned the man's house and driven his family into the brush. Then, to "square himself," he adopted his slain enemy's little son. It is certain that the Slades, when they finally removed from the scene of violent but effective reform on the Overland route, had an adopted son, partly of Indian blood, whom they called Jemmy.

There was little law between Fort Kearney and Salt Lake City. Denver was having its troubles holding its own against organized gangs of robbers and assassins. W. N. Byers, the courageous editor of *The Rocky Mountain News*, the first newspaper published in Denver, was trying to get the law-abiding element to work together. The gangsters nearly took his life on several occasions. At Fort Laramie the officers had all they could do in keeping the Indians more or less awed, and rendering some protection to the Government mail service and the Pony Express.

In this absence of any recognized form of law and order west of Kearney, the Overland company was virtually compelled to assume police powers over the larger part of its 2,000-mile route. Slade went further than any other official in exercising these police powers, but he had the most lawless element with which to cope. As in the case of any other mining excitement, the Pike's Peak rush had attracted many human vultures, whose activities were not confined to Denver and its adjacent camps. The trail was lined with them, and there was no crime they were not ready to commit.

So intent was Slade on clearing up the conditions along his division that he served notice on stage and Pony Express station keepers not to harbor any suspicious characters. Anything that looked like collusion with the horse-thieving element would mean not merely the loss of the station keeper's job, but death.

An instance, showing what a close watch Slade kept on the trail, is related by a former station keeper, whose post was near Fort Laramie.

Three youths known as the Davenport brothers, had been stranded from a "bull train" at Fort Laramie, at the beginning of the winter of 1860–61. They made camp a few miles below the fort, ostensibly as trappers. They were successful, as they sold mink, otter and muskrat furs to a French trader named Beauvais, five miles below the fort, and occasionally visited the post and traded at Judge Ward's store.

Two or three hundred horses, the property of military officers, the stage company and private citizens, were kept near the post, not under especially good guard. This entire herd was run off. At the same time the Davenports disappeared. The horses were not missed for several days, which gave the thieves a good start. A posse was organized to take the trail in pursuit. After a long chase the horse thieves were run down in Utah, close to the Nevada line. One of the Davenports was killed, but the others made their escape.

About the middle of February a footsore and hungry wayfarer applied for shelter at the stage and Pony Express station. The station keeper explained the strict rules Slade laid down regarding the harboring and feeding of anyone but company employees, but the weather was so cold and the case seemed so desperate that finally he gave in.

After he had eaten, the station keeper's guest crawled under a pile of gunnysacks in one corner of the room. About midnight the east-bound stage came in, with Slade aboard. While horses were being changed, Slade came in for his usual piece of pie. Much to the station keeper's relief, Slade departed, without having noticed anything of a suspicious nature. Next morning the wayfarer left, after having had his breakfast.

Two days later, to the station keeper's dismay, Slade

came back on the stage from the east. With him on the seat, shackled hand and foot and with a big iron bar between his ankles, was the young fellow who had hidden under the pile of gunnysacks. Not by a flicker of an eyelid did the passenger betray the fact that he knew the station keeper, who finally mustered up courage to ask Slade who it was that needed a hundred pounds of iron to keep him in his seat.

"That's one of the Davenports who got away," replied Slade. "The other was lynched in Nevada. This fellow was picked up near Scottsbluff and a Pony rider brought word to fetch him back to Fort Laramie."

The stage went on, with Slade and his prisoner, who never reached the fort. A delegation stopped the stage on the bridge over the Laramie River and the last of the Davenports was hanged from a cross-beam without having said a word that would implicate the station keeper who had sheltered him in defiance of Slade's wrath.

3

Slade's was a dual nature.

Under the influence of liquor all the courtliness, of which he made such a show, quickly vanished. He became a demon, committing atrocities which afterward seemed to cause him mental anguish. When drunk he failed to recognize his best friends, and, if they came in his path, they were no more to him than total strangers.

This Jekyll-and-Hyde strain in Slade is illustrated by the following anecdote which was related to me several years ago by the late Robert Spotswood of Denver. Mr. Spotswood was a valued official of the Overland. He had been driver, express messenger and superintendent and eventually became Slade's successor in charge of the Jules-burg division. He and David Street, paymaster and general executive head of the Overland, knew Slade intimately.

"Among all the men he knew, there is no doubt that Mr. Street stood highest in Slade's esteem," said Mr. Spotswood. "Yet he nearly lost his life at Slade's hands. Word came to Mr. Street that Slade was in Denver, on one of his sprees. Slade was in the process of wrecking a saloon in Denver—one of his favorite entertainments. He would shatter all the mirrors, drive everybody into the street and then shoot out the lights. Next day he invariably came and apologized, and paid the damages.

"When Mr. Street arrived, Slade had made a complete wreck of a saloon. Mr. Street tried to induce Slade to leave. Slade, apparently not recognizing him, shot him down, as it happened inflicting a wound that was not dangerous. Next day, when Slade was informed what he had done, he was nearly broken-hearted. He refused to go home until he heard that 'Dave' was on the way to recovery. No complaint was made against Slade by Mr. Street. Slade kept on in the employ of the company."

Thomas J. Ranahan, who was known along the trail as "Irish Tommy," a stage driver and "Pony" rider, told me that he had seen Slade on one of his sprees at Westport.

"A negro deckhand had done some slight thing that displeased Slade," said Mr. Ranahan. "Slade, who was drunk, 'took after' the offender. Slade's face was so terrifying that the deckhand jumped over the rail, into the river, and swam to safety."

The other Slade—the calm, gentlemanly director of divisional affairs—was met by Mark Twain at a station west of Julesburg, and is thus pictured in *Roughing It:*

He was so friendly and gentle-spoken that I warmed to him in spite of his awful history. It was hardly possible to realize that this pleasant person was the pitiless scourge of the outlaws, the raw-head-and-bloody-bones the nursing mothers of the mountains terrified their children with. And to this day I can remember nothing remarkable about Slade except that his face was rather broad across the cheek-bones, and that the cheek-bones were low and the lips peculiarly thin and straight. But that was enough to leave something of an effect upon me, for since then I seldom see a face possessing those characteristics without fancying that the owner of it is a dangerous man.

On the occasion of Sir Richard Burton's overland trip, an incident came up at Julesburg, tending to confirm Mark Twain's description of Slade as "the most gentlemanly, quiet and affable officer on the Overland service." In Burton's party was an army officer and his wife and baby daughter. Slade was so solicitous about the safety of the baby girl that he took the couple and their child in his own buckboard to Wind River summit, over the Rocky Ridge Road, "the most Indian infested and bandit frequented on the whole trail across the country," according to the officer's later statement. And for an outriding escort he provided "sixteen of the most villainous cutthroats on the plains." [1]

Slade's acts of violence were increasing to such a degree that they could no longer pass without official notice. He was overstepping even the wide bounds allowed by the stage company and the military authorities at Fort

[1] From *Sir Richard F. Burton at Salt Lake City,* privately printed for Richard Walden Hale, Boston, 1930.

Laramie. Slade was repeatedly warned, and promised
to do better. Then would come another wild outburst and
a saloon or store would be wrecked, and Slade's apologies
and his unfailing "squaring" of damages would not be
considered sufficient amends. The frontier was getting
tired of Slade's one-man riots—quite vocally so.

Finally it was decreed that Slade and the company
should part. In fact the separation was made necessary
by the action of the military commandant at Fort Halleck. The Overland route had been moved south of the
Oregon Trail through Wyoming. The new route, which
had been made necessary on account of Indian troubles
on the old trail, extended up the South Platte toward
Denver, past Fort Halleck and across the lower part of
Wyoming to Fort Bridger, instead of by way of Fort
Laramie and South Pass.

Slade had overstepped the limit when, with some com-
panions, he had "shot up" the sutler's store at Fort
Halleck. The commandant insisted on Slade's removal.
It was a demand that could not be ignored, and Mr.
Spotswood, who was selected as Slade's successor, was
also given the job of telling Slade that he was "through."

"When I left Denver to break the news to Slade," said
Mr. Spotswood, "friends cheered me with the information that I would never come back alive. They advised me
to take along a force sufficient for protection, otherwise
Slade would surely kill me.

"I knew that it all depended on the condition in which I
found Slade. If he were sober, I figured that I would have
no difficulty but I knew there was danger ahead if he
happened to be drunk. Anyway, I started out alone, feeling that was the best way to deal with the situation un-

der any circumstances. If Slade once started on a rampage, twenty men would be just the same as one to him.

"At that time Slade had moved division headquarters to Virginia Dale, in Colorado, just below the Wyoming line. It was a beautiful spot, which he had named for his wife. He had put up good buildings and corrals. A little stream wandered through the place. Slade was very proud of his new headquarters.

"Luckily, perhaps, Slade was sober when I arrived. He did not ask the nature of my visit, and I did not volunteer any information. Mrs. Slade prepared dinner. After the meal, I told Slade why I had come—that he had been discharged from the service and that I was to take his place. Both he and Mrs. Slade took the news calmly enough. Slade immediately went about making an inventory. He took me out and showed me the livestock that belonged to the company, and pointed out the animals that belonged to him. He was scrupulously exact about it all.

"In a few days Slade and his wife were gone from Virginia Dale. I next heard of him at Fort Bridger, but he was never again identified in any way with the Overland route."

4

A last look at this extraordinary man—probably the most outstanding figure among all the individuals identified with Overland transportation in the days of the stage and the Pony Express.

While Slade was at Fort Bridger, his attention was attracted by the news of gold discoveries at Virginia City, Montana. Millions were being scooped from the placer deposits of Alder Gulch. Men were flocking there, including some of the desperadoes whom Slade had driven from the Overland Trail.

At Fort Bridger, Slade had made the acquaintance of H. S. Gilbert, a prosperous trader. Acting on Slade's suggestion, Mr. Gilbert stocked a wagon train with supplies which could be sold at the new camp. Slade took the wagon train to Virginia City, and Mr. Gilbert followed later.

The new "diggings" were, in all probability, the wildest that the West ever saw. When Slade arrived, there were thirty thousand miners along Alder Gulch. One town fairly crowded into another for twelve miles along the gulch— Nevada, Adobetown, Grayback, Summit and others, with Virginia City as the metropolis. Dance halls, saloons, and gambling places kept Virginia City alive night and day. Organized road-agents were holding up and murdering miners who started for the "States" with gold dust. There was less law than along the Overland when Slade took charge at Julesburg. In fact there was no law at all. Henry Plummer, who had been elected sheriff, was head of the road-agent syndicate. Then the Vigilantes were organized and Plummer and about twenty of his accomplices were hanged, and Virginia City became a safer place in which to live.

Slade has been accused of having been an outlaw. It has been hinted that he "stood in" with the horse thieves and stage robbers along the Overland Trail. Mr. Spotswood and other officials have denied this. If there was truth in the statements that Slade was predisposed toward outlawry, Virginia City, when he arrived, would have been an ideal place for him. Plummer and his confederates would have welcomed such an ally as Slade, whose reputation as a "killer" had preceded him. But the

Vigilantes, who "checked up" on the outlaw element before they began their housecleaning, and who had a complete list of road agents, from Plummer down, never had an iota of evidence against Slade. In fact, Thomas J. Dimsdale, who wrote a review of the Montana law-and-order activities almost before the impromptu gibbets had ceased creaking, says Slade was a member of the Vigilantes.

If Slade had attended to the freighting business which he started, and looked after the ranch which he had located on the Madison River, across the Tobacco Root Mountains from Virginia City, he would have had no trouble and would have prospered. But drink had too strong a hold. He went on sprees and began to "shoot up" stores and saloons. His finances were running low, and he was unable to pay in more than promises for the damage he created. After the Vigilantes had put a Miners' Court in control, Slade gave offense by tearing up a warrant for his arrest, and threatening to shoot the judge.

Without giving him time to recover from his debauch and come forward with the usual apologies, a delegation of miners captured Slade and made preparations to hang him. He pleaded that his wife be sent for. His request was granted, but no sooner had the messenger been dispatched to the Slade ranch than the hanging proceeded. By the time Mrs. Slade reached the scene, after a wild ride on horseback across the mountains, Slade was dead. The miners were afraid to let him go, when once they had started proceedings against so famed a "killer."

In the crowd that saw Slade lynched was "Pony Bob" Haslam, who at that time was a Wells-Fargo guard between Salt Lake City and Virginia City. Calvin Downs and other riders on the Julesburg division had claimed that Slade had "held up" their pay. The story had spread along the trail. Haslam, speaking about it many years afterward, said he was the only rider who "saw Slade get his come-uppance for cheating the boys out of their pay." This is the only claim I have ever heard, reflecting on Slade's honesty, which seemed to be more than hearsay. On the contrary, I have had the assurance of Overland officials that no division was better run than Slade's, and that only the man's wild habits led to his discharge.

Mrs. Slade had her husband's body buried in the old Mormon cemetery at Salt Lake City, though Slade was not a Mormon. The cemetery records, which the writer recently looked up, are as follows:

> Bannack, Mont., I. A. Slade (*sic*) to be moved to Illinois in the fall; 20th July, 1864; cause, killed by vigilance committee at Bannack City. Buried in single.

The mistakes in this record are obvious, Slade's initials being wrong and Bannack being the place where Plummer was lynched.

The "temporary" burial was in the potter's field, with no identifying headstone. It proved to be Slade's permanent resting place. Dead at the hands of a vigilance committee, and surrounded by the pitiable derelicts of the frontier, whom he would not have permitted in the stage or Pony Express stations under his care—so ended the career of "Captain Joseph A. Slade, sir," the man who "from Fort Kearney west was feared a great deal more than the Almighty."

CHAPTER XIII

INDIANS

1

MORE than two-thirds of the Pony Express route
lay through hostile Indian country.

When plans for the fast mail service were announced,
the chief criticism was that it would be "suicide" for lone
riders to attempt to thread their way, unprotected, along
a trail that penetrated the hunting grounds of the most
warlike tribes. Emigrant trains, under the guidance of men
like Bridger, who could fairly sense "Injun trouble," and
backed by skilled riflemen, were never free from danger of attack. Occasionally the stage mail was lost or delayed, owing to Indian hostility. How was it going to be
possible for horsemen, traveling singly, to escape with
their scalps?

Almost at its very start from St. Joseph the "Pony"
trail plunged into Indian country. The Indians along the
Missouri were peaceable enough. They had come to a
realization, years before, that it was hopeless to oppose the
hordes of "long knives" whose domain stretched eastward
from the big river.

From Fort Kearney on, the Pony Express rider had to
keep a "stirrup eye" out for Indians. At first the riders
were armed with carbines, as well as two revolvers per man.
The carbines were soon discarded, as were the extra revol-

198

vers. The usual armament was one "navy" revolver. Occasionally a rider carried an extra, loaded cylinder for his revolver, in case of a fight with several opponents at close quarters. Even this extra weight was begrudged.

The "Pony" riders, most of whom had been brought up in "Injun" country, placed their chief reliance on the speed and endurance of their horses, and on the known shortcomings of their foes when it came to an actual brush. The average Indian was known to be a poor marksman. Not only did he "skimp" on powder, but it was his tendency to open fire at too great a distance to make his shots effective. Unless there was a general uprising, the Pony Express riders figured that they could get through without being "potted" on the trail.

As after events proved, only a few months following the discontinuance of the "Pony," it was fortunate that the warlike tribes whose hunting ground was in Wyoming were too busy fighting each other to combine their forces and institute a general war on the stations that dotted the Overland Trail. When that war finally broke, traffic was stopped and the losses of life and property were large.

The Oregon Trail, from Julesburg on, penetrated hunting grounds which were ranged by several powerful tribes. The Sioux sent their hunting parties down from the north and east, ranging far into central and southern Wyoming. The Crows, who were peacefully enough disposed toward the whites, but who never could resist the appropriation of horses, no matter whether the color of the rightful owners was white or red, came down from the Absaraka country to the north. The Shoshones, who held to the treaty with the whites, made by their wise chief, Washakie, came over from the central Wyoming region, where they ranged as far south as Fort Bridger, and the Arapahoes, from the same region, sent out hunting and horse-stealing parties of their own.

Occasionally the Sioux raided a ranch or wagon train, or threatened some isolated station. The Cheyennes and Kiowas, both warlike by nature, committed depredations which were mild compared to the damage done by the first-named tribe when it combined with the Sioux later on, but good hunting was the chief reason for all this concentration of Indians in Wyoming. There was no such buffalo ground anywhere else in the West, and it was not until the white men began killing off the bison that Indian strength was concentrated against a common enemy.

There were two military posts in Wyoming, along the Pony Express and stage route—Fort Laramie in the east and Fort Bridger in the southwestern part of the territory. A few soldiers were kept at Platte Bridge, later Fort Casper. A bridge had been built across the Platte at this point, which was a special object of Indian attack.

Fort Bridger was a comparatively small post, and, besides, was located in the Shoshone country, which was not hostile. It was garrisoned by not more than three companies of soldiers. For military protection the stage drivers and "Pony" riders must depend chiefly upon Fort Laramie. The records which were kept there, and at Fort Kearney, contain many references to detachments sent out to drive off Indians who threatened to hold up the mail.

This show of military vigilance sufficed to keep the trail free from any serious trouble. An occasional "Pony" rider was shot at or pursued, and one or two stations were attacked, the attendants driven off, the livestock stolen and the buildings burned, but the Express mail continued to go through with regularity.

These spasmodic attempts to stop the mail were the work of small marauding bands, from one tribe or another. Not until the spring of 1861 was there a real "Indian scare" along the Pony Express trail. The Sioux came out in force, likewise the Cheyennes, Shoshones and Arapahoes. Early in June there were war parties on both sides of the trail. The Sioux, Cheyennes and Arapahoes combined against the Shoshones, who were in camp on the Sweetwater. B. F. Lowe, a white man who was in the Shoshone camp, described the ensuing fight to Colonel Coutant, who thus pictures it:

> The Sioux, Cheyennes and Arapahoes advanced in solid column, with the rising sun reflected on their bright, burnished spears and shields. The Sioux dashed forward and cut off four hundred of the Shoshone horses and started back with them in an easterly direction. All was now excitement in the Shoshone village, and preparations were made instantly to follow the marauders. The war chief of the band was the eldest son of Chief Washakie, and he was the first to mount. He sat astride his noble war horse in front of his father's lodge, waiting for a few of his picked men.
>
> The old chief came out and his face wore signs of impatience. Casting his eyes on his young son, the chief said: "What are you waiting for?" The young man made no reply, but, brushing the flanks of his horse with his heels, the spirited animal bounded forward, carrying the war chief in pursuit of his fleeing enemy. He dashed along a distance of six miles, when he came up to eight Sioux Indians at the crossing of Willow Creek. These closed in

on him with their lances, but the Shoshone warrior, with a Colt's revolver in each hand, did not shrink from the unequal contest. With his right hand he brought down a Sioux and another with his left, but at this instant the remaining six crossed their spears in his body and he fell to the ground lifeless. His enemies had barely time to remove his scalp, when young Washakie's friends were upon them, and a running fight ensued, which lasted three hours.

The Shoshones recaptured their horses, besides securing a number of those belonging to the Sioux, who had retreated into a grove of quaking asp near Eagle Nest, on Little Beaver. The Shoshones assaulted their position, but were unable to drive the Sioux out of the timber and finally night put an end to the contest. After a brief consultation the Shoshones decided to return to their village, bury the dead and care for the wounded. The Sioux, taking advantage of the darkness, managed to escape, but they were on foot and had to travel many a weary mile to insure their safety. The Shoshones lost in this fight five killed and several wounded; the Sioux had forty men killed and lost a large amount of supplies. Chief Washakie never ceased to mourn the loss of this, his eldest son. He always felt that his own hasty words brought about the death of the young man.

Such affairs among the Indians served to emphasize the precarious position of those on the Oregon Trail. That the Pony Express continued to operate is one of those marvels past all explanation. As it was, only a few months after the last pony had sped on its final mission, such a blast of Indian fury descended upon the trail that the historic route up the Sweetwater had to be abandoned altogether and moved farther south, where additional military protection had been provided. Had the "Pony" relay stations been in existence then, it is probable that few men among the riders and attendants would have escaped with their lives.

2

The real war that held up the Pony Express and made it look as if the prophets of gloom were right, occurred in Nevada and Utah.

The Pah-Utes, a strong and warlike Shoshonean branch, numbering some 7,000 or 8,000 and led by Chief Winnemucca, had never been friendly to white settlement. They had opposed the first trappers to find their way among the far reaches of the Great Salt Lake Basin, and had taken toll of many emigrant trains in the '49 days, and had cut down several prospecting parties later.

At the time the Pony Express started, the Pah-Utes were in a particularly warlike mood. The winter had been unusually severe, and the medicine men charged this to the evil influence of the white invaders. The silver discoveries at Washoe had sent a swarm of prospectors from Carson City and Virginia City into distant hills in hope of uncovering another Comstock lode. These men, and the settlers who were establishing ranches and building mail stations, cut down the trees from which the Pah-Utes gathered the Indian nuts that provided a large share of their subsistence. The younger Indians, whose voice usually carried in such circumstances, were counseling war.

The Pony Express had made eight trips, and the mail had gone through without serious interruption until early in May. Then a "Pony" courier spurred his exhausted horse into Carson City, bearing the news that Williams station, about ten miles northwest of where Fort Church-hill was afterward built, had been destroyed. Five men at the station had been killed. The station keeper, J. O. Williams, escaped because at the time he was camping in the mountains.

Reports were received, telling of attacks on other stations and the destruction of ranches. The Pony Express suffered heavily. Every rider's life was in danger. A "Pony" courier, a Mexican, west-bound, rode into Dry Creek station, clinging to his saddle horn. He had been fatally wounded by Indians, and died in a few hours, but he had brought the mail through in its blood-stained *mochila*.

For two hundred and fifty miles the Pony Express route was in a state of siege. Stations were burned, and horses were driven off. Several station keepers and their attendants saved their lives by flight, engaging in battle with their pursuers as they fled.

The newspapers, deprived of a new and valued service, were not long in expressing concern. The *Sacramento Union*, on May 29, said:

> Up to the closing of the Alta Telegraph office last night, about half past ten o'clock, nothing was heard of the Pony Express, and we have fears that it has been interrupted by the Indian difficulties. Such a result will be much regretted by all the people of the state, who have just begun to appreciate the blessing of a ready transmission of intelligence from the East.

The newspapers of the East, which had established special correspondence, covering the latest news from Cali-

fornia and the mining districts of Nevada, were quick
to express regret over the threatened interruption of the
Pony Express service. The St. Louis *Globe-Democrat*
said:

Another Pony Express from California has arrived
with details of news from all parts of the Pacific Coast a
little over eleven days old. It is to be regretted that one
of the riders employed to carry this Express across the
Continent was killed by Indians on the plains between
Camp Floyd and Carson Valley, which detained the Express a day and a half and came near causing the loss of
it entirely. Now, as trifling as this occurrence may seem,
it calls loudly for action on the part of the Government.
Hundreds of troops are idling away their time in Utah,
who, if properly distributed at convenient distances along
the Pony Express route, would protect the riders and the
valuable property entrusted to their care.

The Pony Express is already assuming great importance to California, and large amounts of original drafts
are now forwarded by this conveyance. A considerable
amount was received in St. Louis by the last arrival, and
as the usefulness of this quick communication becomes
more and more apparent, these valuable trusts will increase. It is a matter, therefore, of the highest importance
that the bold and daring spirits who risk their necks in
carrying a sack of letters through the defiles of the
mountains, over unbroken prairies and through the rapid
rivers which divide us from the Pacific, should be protected. If these gallant fellows cannot perform their cir-
cuit unmolested, the Express will have to be abandoned,
and the whole country affected thereby. It is bad enough
that our Government compels the public to rely on private enterprise for this service, when a liberal encourage-

ment in the form of a mail contract should be extended. But to refuse protection afforded by the presence of troops already near the ground would be infamous.

The outbreak in Nevada had only begun to assume serious form. The preliminary attacks on ranches and Express stations were the result of a council of Indians at Pyramid Lake. While the older chiefs were pleading for peace, a party of young Indians left the council and launched the attacks which made war inevitable. On hearing this news, the older men ceased all resistance, and the tribe presented an unbroken, warlike front.

Hundreds of prospectors who were in the hills made their way to Carson City and Virginia City. From their ranks and from the residents of the two cities, a punitive force was organized, consisting of 105 men, Major Ormsby of Carson City being in command.

The expedition was looked upon as little more than a lark, and no trouble was anticipated in scattering the Indians.

"An Indian for breakfast and a pony to ride," was the slogan as the command started across the wastes toward Pyramid Lake. When within three or four miles of the council ground, a small body of Indians was sighted. Major Ormsby had his men dismount and tighten their saddle girths. Then about thirty of the command charged toward the Indians, who disappeared. Keeping on in a rather disorganized pursuit of the Indians, the volunteers were led into an ambush. At a given signal, a large body of Indians rose from concealment in the sagebrush and poured a heavy fire into the pursuing forces.

Major Ormsby sustained three wounds, and the volun-

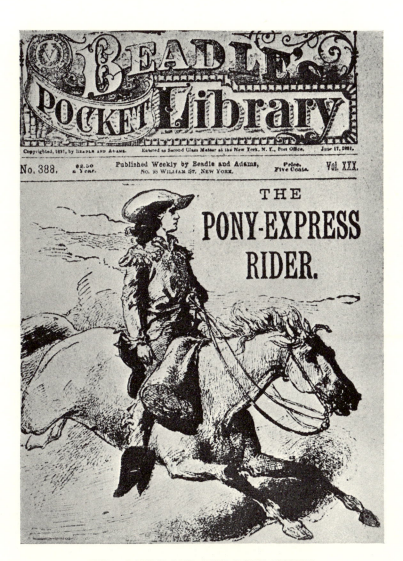

THE "PONY" AND THE DIME NOVEL

Cover of a "thriller" based on the Pony Express theme.

teers were without a leader. The retreat became a rout, the Indians following in close pursuit and in some instances lifting their foes out of the saddle before killing them. Major Ormsby was put on a horse, but pleaded to be left behind, saying that he was mortally wounded but perhaps he could arrange a truce with the Indians. The victorious Pah-Utes were in no mood for talking truce. They killed Major Ormsby and rolled his body into a ravine, as they had done with many other victims. Only about half the command reached the white settlements, the fatalities numbering forty-six.

News of this disaster at Pyramid Lake led to the forming of commands at towns and camps. The Governor of California sent arms and ammunition. Accompanied by a detachment of United States troops, this large force pursued the Indians into the mountains. Some fighting was done in snow two feet deep, but the losses on both sides were negligible and the Indians, being familiar with the country, managed to keep out of danger. The pursuing troops buried the remains of those who had been killed at Pyramid Lake; also they performed the same service for seven prospectors who had been killed by the Pah-Utes.

The expedition, which was chiefly valuable in impressing the Indians with the fact that the white settlers were fully aroused, did not remain long in the field. The Indians scattered and returned to their old haunts, contenting themselves with harassing the Pony Express line. Small, predatory bands of Pah-Utes wandered the trails which ran at right angles with the Express route. Whenever they saw a chance to waylay a rider or raid a station, they struck.

An appeal was made for seventy-five soldiers, to be distributed between Sand Springs, sixty miles beyond Carson City; Cold Springs, thirty-five miles farther east; Simpson's, forty miles farther; and Dry Creek, twenty-five miles beyond Simpson's. This appeal was denied, because most of the 2,500 troops that had been stationed at Camp Floyd when there were no Indian troubles, had been moved east. Later on, orders came from Washington to afford such protection to the trail as the commandant thought advisable, more for the United States mail and emigrant travel than for the Pony Express.

Undismayed by this apparently hopeless situation, Pony Express officials took matters in hand. In its issue of July 2 the *Union* reported:

We learn from one of a party of fifteen fitted out by W. W. Finney, agent of the Pony Express, to prospect the route from Carson City to Salt Lake and ascertain where the station keepers, riders, horses and Express were, that the party went half way to Salt Lake before they met the Express. They found the riders and station keepers scattered and about thirty horses gone, supposed to have been driven off by Indians. Two of the station keepers were killed, but none of the riders. . . . The express was coming under an escort of U. S. Troops at Sand Springs, where they met it. They also found about sixty emigrant wagons from Salt Lake, bound for California. The Pony Express party was in charge of Bolivar Roberts, who has for several years been engaged on the mail route and is well acquainted with the route as well as experienced in life on the plains. It is understood that the company will place five men at each station and will build stone houses and corrals where the materials can be had, and, when it cannot, will use adobe. Horses have been purchased to replace those stolen by the Indians.

The progress of this party is reported as follows in the *Deseret News*:

News from the West—Mr. Morrell, postmaster in this city, arrived on Wednesday night last from California. Mr. Morrell came from Carson to Roberts' Creek in company with Mr. Bolivar Roberts and a party of men, who brought through the mail and express which left California May 25. Mr. Roberts, being well acquainted with the country, by traveling some in the night time and taking every necessary precaution, succeeded in bringing the party through safely, contrary to the expectations of many at Carson City, who predicted that they would all be killed. At Roberts' Creek they, on the 16th, met Major Egan and his party with the mail, which left this city on the 6th. He was attended by Lieutenant Perkins and part of his command as escort, sent out to protect emigrants. The Indians were following in the rear of the troops and close to them, destroying the rebuilt stations, or whatever was left behind, before the soldiers were out of sight.

When these raids started, the riders who were on the trail did not know whether they would reach the next station alive, nor were they certain of the sight that would greet them if they did struggle through.

Thomas Flynn, the rider of the Pony Express from Genoa to the Sink of the Carson, not being met by the mail from the east, went on to Dry Creek. Here he found six terrified emigrants who had entered the station and found the keeper killed and scalped. The rider from the east had turned back in time to avoid an ambuscade near this point.

Hamilton, the California rider who was first out of Sacramento, took the stock from Smith's Creek, where the keeper had been killed, and camped the next night at Cold Springs. He was accompanied by C. H. Ruffin and others of the Pony Express. While on guard at night, Hamilton and Ruffin were fired on. The party lost no time in saddling up, and managed to escape, with the Pony Express stock they had gathered.

Major Egan had a narrow escape from death. According to the *Deseret News*, this veteran frontiersman, explorer and Pony Express rider had been not more than half an hour away from the station at Butte Valley, when Indians made an attack there. They drove off the station keeper and attendants, and burned the buildings.

Egan Canyon was the scene of one of the most thrilling events on the trail. Henry Wilson, the station keeper, and his stock tender, Albert Armstrong, were just sitting down to breakfast when arrows began whizzing into the cabin, a one-room affair which provided little protection. Wilson and Armstrong filled their hats with ammunition. They lay on the floor and shot through cracks until their ammunition was exhausted. They killed or wounded several Indians, but this merely enraged the remaining Pah-Utes and made them the more determined to get the scalps of the white men. Finally the besiegers burst in the door. Instead of killing Wilson and Armstrong at once, the Indians, after having bound their captives, proceeded to eat heartily of the supplies in the cabin. Then, having satisfied their hunger, they piled sagebrush around a stake and prepared to "finish off" their victims.

While they were in the midst of these preparations, the Indians were surprised by twenty soldiers, under Colonel Steptoe. In the fight that ensued eighteen Indians were killed. The surprise was so complete that the Indians retreated without having a chance to kill the station keeper and stock tender. They made up for this, however, in the course of their flight, by raiding the Shell Creek station that night, killing the station keeper and two assistants, and driving off all the livestock.

The Pony Express service was delayed only a month by the Pah-Ute war. Extra men were hired as guards, and stations were rebuilt. Adobe "forts" were constructed at the sink of the Carson and at Sand Springs, twenty miles east of the sink. For two months after the service was resumed, the raiders were fired at and harassed in every possible way by the Indians.

Major Egan came unexpectedly upon several Pah-Utes, who evidently were waiting for him at a lonely part of the trail. It was too late to turn back, even if the Pony Express rider had been so inclined. Egan drew his revolver, and rode full tilt at the Indians, firing as he went. The Indians scattered, and fired several shots which were ineffectual. Then they tried pursuit, but Egan quickly outdistanced them. One of the Indians told him afterward that the rider's bold action convinced the Pah-Utes that an escort must be following him.

"Pony Bob" Haslam ran into a bunch of thirty Pah-Utes, all armed with rifles. He was three or four miles from a station—and the way was blocked by the Indians. Haslam rode at full speed toward the Indians, revolver in hand. The leader, evidently impressed by his bearing, made a peace signal and cried: "You pretty good fellow

—you go ahead." Bob dashed through the crowd without a shot being fired.

The war, short as it was, was a heavy financial blow to the Pony Express management. It is estimated that the replacement of stations and livestock cost upwards of $75,000. The quick resumption of service aroused public admiration, but the Pah-Utes had cost the lives of some good men and had nearly wrecked the institution which they regarded as part of the white man's "bad medicine."

CHAPTER XIV

RIDERS ALL

1

GREAT exploits in horsemanship became almost commonplace in the Pony Express service. Records for speed and endurance were made, which, if established under different circumstances, would have aroused nation-wide interest. But most of such records were made as part of the day's work, with no time-keepers other than station men with an eye to the schedule, and with no glory to be won, other than the consciousness of a duty well performed.

The strain upon the riders increased proportionately after the service was made semi-weekly, instead of weekly, and relay stations were established from ten to twelve miles apart, instead of twenty-five miles. Perhaps the best evidence of the harsh demands made by the "Pony" upon its riders is to be found in the frequent changes of personnel. Among the eighty riders who started in the first interchange of mail between St. Joseph and Sacramento, few remained so much as a year. After the first twelve months of the service there were withdrawals due to two causes —enlistments on one side or the other in the Civil War, and the pushing of the transcontinental telegraph, which foreshadowed the doom of the courier service. In the main, withdrawals were for the reason that men could not stand the physical strain. It is probable that a complete roster of Overland Pony Express riders would total more than two hundred. Some of the men rode for a few weeks and others for a few days. Station keepers, stock tenders and even stage drivers were frequently required to substitute for saddlemen who were unable to go on. The riders who withstood the grind, month in and month out, were super-men of the saddle, whose extraordinary deeds have for the most part been lost, unfortunately, in the chaos of the frontier.

Riders were often called upon to "double" in the sad-dle—that is, to ride to the next "home" station, due to the non-arrival of the courier from the opposite direction. This meant from eight to twelve hours more in the saddle, and "taking the top off" at least six more of the fresh and speedy horses which were held in waiting at the relay sta-tions.

Twenty-five or thirty extra miles meant nothing to a Pony Express courier, though it would be a fair day's ride in itself to anyone not inured to saddle fatigue. It is related of Johnny Frey that, when he had trimmed a few minutes from his incoming schedule, he would rein his foaming horse in front of the old Troy House, the first hotel in the settlement of Troy, Kansas, and ask:

"Is breakfast ready?"

On being answered in the negative, the rider would reply:

"Well, put something on the fire, and I'll go on to St. Joe and will be back here to eat!"

St. Joseph was from fourteen to sixteen miles from

Troy, depending on the condition of the bottom lands along the Missouri and which one of several trails the "Pony" riders were taking to the Elwood ferry. Yet, in an incredibly short time, Frey would be back in Troy for the breakfast he had ordered!

"Johnny always sounded a special blast on his horn when he neared the Dave Hardy place near Cold Springs, where the widow Hargis lived with four grown daughters," said an old-timer who remembered the Pony Express days in that part of Kansas. "Johnny was always hitting a good clip, coming or going, when he reached Cold Springs, but he never failed to hold up for a second or two, so he could get the doughnuts or pie the girls brought out to him.

"At that time Miss Betty Hobbs, who was from New York State, was teaching the little school near Syracuse, the next station," went on my informant. "Clocks were scarce in those days, and you couldn't always tell whether they were running right or not. Well, no matter what the school clock said, Miss Betty always waited for the rider to go past on 'Pony day.' Those boys were so punctual, in and out of St. Joe, that you could set a clock by 'em."

Jack Keetley, a Marysville boy, was known as the "joyous jockey of the Pony Express." Keetley had the unusual experience of riding on more than one division—in fact he had ridden every mile of the trail from St. Joseph to Fort Laramie, though generally riding east of Marysville. Keetley, to settle a wager, once rode from Rock Creek to St. Joe and return, and then back to Seneca, a total distance of three hundred and forty miles. He was in the saddle thirty-one hours, without sleep or rest. Inasmuch as "Pony" riders frequently left the main trail in order to avoid bad road conditions, A. E. Lewis, then division superintendent at St. Joseph, went over Keetley's route with a "roadometer" which he possessed, to verify the distance that had been covered.

Alex Carlyle, who rode out of St. Joseph during the first two months of the "Pony," was a dashing, fearless rider, but had to retire on account of illness which developed into consumption and soon caused his death. Carlyle was once shot at, by an Indian in ambush. The Indian's aim was so good that the bullet knocked Carlyle's cap from his head. Thereafter Carlyle never would wear any kind of head covering, while riding.

Charley and Gus Cliff were riders who helped keep the "Pony" mail moving along the eastern division during the closing months of the service. They were appointed in the summer of 1861. Frey and several other riders had resigned to go into the army.

"Pony Express riding was not only hard work, but it was the lonesomest kind of a job," said Charley Cliff, recalling his days as a courier. "The only other rider I ever really knew was George Town, who took the mail from me at Seneca, when I had pounded out my eighty or eighty-five miles from St. Joe. My schedule called for eight hours on this run, but I could generally cut that time down considerably if I had to."

Jim Beatley was a notable figure along the route between St. Joseph and Rock Creek station. Beatley, like Frey, was noted for the wild horses he chose for his rides. In fact, any one of the Pony Express riders would have won popularity in the days of the Wild West show and the rodeo.

"It was common to find that you had drawn a bucking

horse when you started out of a station," said Gus Cliff. "That was one reason why we gave them the spurs right from the start and kept them going. A good many of the horses we had were half broke—some of the best of them, in fact. A few days on the trail cured most of them of bucking, but some never quit, especially right after they had been saddled."

Henry Avis, whose run was from Mud Springs, through Fort Laramie to Horseshoe Creek, made a remarkable ride through "hostile" country at a time when the Indians were threatening. In the spring of 1861 the Sioux were unusually defiant. Before he left Mud Springs, Avis heard that raiding parties had been sighted farther along the trail. At Horseshoe the rumors grew more definite. An incoming stage driver reported a war party, evidently out for trouble, in the vicinity of Deer Creek. He was going to have a party of soldiers sent out from Fort Laramie, as he was convinced there was trouble in store.

There was no incoming rider at Horseshoe to relieve Avis. Getting a fresh mount, Avis started on with the mail, despite predictions that he would lose his scalp.

Avis, before entering the Pony Express service, had been with Major Dripps, the fur trader and explorer, and knew the ways of Indians. He was convinced that his horse could outrun any Indian pony, but he knew that speed would be of no avail if he ran into an ambush.

The country through which Avis was traveling was rolling prairie. When he approached the crest of a hill, the Pony Express rider would dismount and lead his horse. In this way he was able to make a survey from each hilltop, without emerging into full view of any Indians who might be coming toward him. At one or two bad turns in the trail, where there were wooded creek bottoms favorable to an ambushing party, Avis "cut across" through the sagebrush.

In this way he succeeded in getting to the Deer Creek station with the mail, to find that the predictions of the stage driver had come true. The Indians had made a raid on the station, but had contented themselves with driving off all the livestock. The courier who was due to depart for the west decided to wait for the arrival of the soldiers, but Avis, with no remount available, returned to Mud Springs. He was sixteen hours in the saddle and on foot, covering the one hundred and ten miles to Deer Creek. For this exhibition of nerve, under trying circumstances, Avis received a monetary reward from the company.

"Seth Ward was the station keeper at Fort Laramie," said Avis. "When he heard that I was headed right for an Indian raid, he thought it was the last time I'd ever wake him up to sign a waybill."

"Pony Bob" Haslam established a remarkable record for courage and endurance while the Pah-Ute war was on in Nevada. Haslam's run was from Friday's station to Buckland's (afterward Fort Churchill) a distance of seventy-five miles. At the outbreak of the Indian war, Haslam found, on arriving at the relay station west of Buckland's, that the Pah-Utes had driven off all the stock. Pushing on to Buckland's, he found that there was no rider to relieve him. Going on through the sink of the Carson to Sand Springs, sixty-five miles, Haslam got a change of horses. He traveled to Smith's creek, a total of one hundred and ninety miles from his starting place, and there exchanged mail with Jay G. Kelley, who had come on from the east.

On his return trip, nine hours later, Haslam found that the Cold Springs station had been raided. The station had been burned and the station keeper killed. On reaching Sand Springs he advised the keeper to come with him to the sink of the Carson. If the keeper had not heeded Haslam's advice, no doubt he would have been killed when the Sand Springs station was raided the next day.

Indians had been seen at the sink of the Carson, but, after a short rest, Haslam went on, arriving at Buckland's with the mail only three and one-half hours behind schedule time. After he had completed his run to Friday's station, he had covered three hundred and eighty miles, being thirty-six hours in the saddle and traveling through a hostile country, with danger threatening him in every canyon and at every turn of the trail.

2

The Pony Express was launched at a time when news events of great importance were "breaking" regularly. Extra demands were made upon men and horses when anything of unusual interest was scheduled. No comparison can be made so far as the resulting records are concerned, for the reason that weather and trail conditions were always different.

The first "flash" announcing the election of President Lincoln was sent by telegraph from St. Louis to St. Joseph, on November 7, 1860. It was carried by special Pony Express to the telegraph station at Fort Churchill, Nev., in a few hours less than eight days, the San Francisco newspapers issuing extras on November 14. The courier who carried the news from Julesburg to the *Rocky*

Mountain News at Denver is said to have covered the last five miles at the rate of nineteen miles an hour.

President Buchanan's farewell message to Congress was sent by telegraph to Fort Kearney on December 6, 1860, and arrived at Fort Churchill on the evening of December 18, or twelve days *en route* by "Pony."

The greatest struggle against the odds imposed by bad weather conditions occurred when the Pony Express was called upon to carry through President Lincoln's inaugural message of March 4, 1861, in the quickest possible time.

Along the Pony Express line, division superintendents had been notified that the message must be put through, regardless of horseflesh. The superintendents had in turn notified station keepers to have the speediest horses in readiness. The riders themselves picked out the horses they were to be given at the relay stations, and the stock tenders had given these animals every care.

At the same time it was realized that the "Pony" was under its severest handicap. March is the worst time of year, as a rule, in the Rocky Mountains and the Sierras. On the plains it is generally a month of heavy snows.

The telegraph line had been completed to Fort Kearney on the east and Fort Churchill, Nevada, on the west, shortening the actual run of the Pony Express, so far as important messages were concerned, by approximately four hundred miles. But there were sixteen hundred miles to go, from one telegraph key to another, along the worst part of the route.

The Pacific Coast was all expectancy—witnessed by the following editorial in the San Francisco *Bulletin* of March 14:

The next Pony will bring us news of the inauguration of President Lincoln, and possibly his inaugural address. The arrival of that Express may be expected at any hour, as it is probable that the riders on the route will exert themselves to make fast time.

Exert themselves! No men ever strove harder, nor was more ever demanded of gallant horses. Men and animals floundered through snowdrifts in the mountains and faced cutting winds and heavy snowfalls on the plains. Years afterward I talked with W. A. (Bill) Cates, who rode with the Lincoln message through seventy-five miles of wind-swept, snow-covered hills in Wyoming.

"It was tough going," said Cates. "The message got a good start out of Kearney, but the closer it got to the mountains, the worse the conditions got. We had the best horses available—several of them were killed—and, considering what we had to fight, the record was the most wonderful ever made by the Pony Express."

When Salt Lake City received the message, it was March 12—seven days consumed by the plucky riders in struggling through from Fort Kearney. The *Deseret News* reported upon the arrival as follows in its issue of March 13:

> The Pony Express, with Eastern advices, up to the fifth of March, arrived here yesterday morning at ten o'clock, bringing the anxiously looked-for inaugural message of Mr. Lincoln, but no account of the ceremonies. The telegraph operator at Kearney leads us to expect full and more comprehensive details by next Pony.

Fort Churchill, on March 17, reported to the Sacramento and San Francisco papers the arrival of the Pony

Express at that station, at 8:30 o'clock that morning. The San Francisco *Bulletin* of March 18 printed the address in full.

So tense was the political situation at the time, and so eager were people to read what the new President had to say, that the newspapers made no comment on the struggle of men and horses to get the message across the desert and mountains in the quickest possible time. One can only read between the lines of the *Bulletin's* explanatory "bank" under its stock heading, "By Magnetic Telegraph":

"Per telegraph to St. Louis; thence by telegraph to Fort Kearney; thence by Pony Express to Sacramento; thence by telegraph to San Francisco."

In this is packed a lot of romance of early-day journalism. Twelve days to get news through from Fort Kearney to Sacramento, with couriers fighting blizzards and snowdrifts on the way! Twelve day of urging staggering horses along trails suddenly made white and unfamiliar. Twelve days of changing an icy *mochila*, with its all-important message, from one saddle to another! Editors, compositors and pressmen waiting in Pacific Coast newspaper offices —waiting for the "big news" which might be delayed by any one of a hundred happenings—a pony's misstep in the dark, a rider shot from ambush by Indians, a snowslide in the mountains, or a prairie trail lost by a half-frozen courier.

Many writers have mistakenly said that the Lincoln inaugural message went through *from St. Joseph to Sacramento* in seven days and seventeen hours. The newspaper records of the day, showing that the message was telegraphed from St. Louis to Fort Kearney, and that it took twelve days to reach Fort Churchill, Nevada, are in themselves sufficient refutation of this misstatement.

The winter schedule of the "Pony" varied from eleven days to seventeen days between Kearney and Churchill. It is to be assumed, from the bad weather conditions along the route early in March, 1861, that, had not extraordinary efforts been made, the seventeen-day limit would have been reached. The fact that the couriers who carried the Lincoln inaugural message cut *five days* from the time which they would have taken ordinarily, speaks eloquently enough of the struggle which men and horses waged against the elements.

CHAPTER XV

YOUTH IN THE SADDLE

1

THE West of Pony Express days differed materially from the West through which the Forty-Niners hurried.

The gold seekers were animated by one desire—to get to the mines and scoop out treasure ahead of the competitors who were back there in the trail dust. The West of 1860 was more inclined toward adventure for adventure's sake. There were other excitements besides gold hunting. Not all eyes were turned toward Pike's Peak, as they had been toward California. Homestakes, as well as mine location stakes, were being driven. People had discovered that "the Great American Desert" had its oases. Ranching, freighting, staging—a dozen vocations were making their appeal. If any employment developed that paid more dividends in adventure than in cash, there were plenty of young fellows to be enlisted. Youth was turning to the frontier, not with any dreams of sudden wealth, but to escape from the humdrum of life in the "States."

These young adventurers of the trail supplied the Pony Express with some of its best riders. Among the half a dozen Overland "Pony" riders whom I have chanced to know, every one, at some place in his story, has brought out the fact that he had drifted west in a search for excitement. It was the same spirit that sent thousands of others to the West, later on, to seek jobs as cowboys.

Typical of this class of adventure-seeking youths from east of the Missouri was William Campbell, who at the time this book was written, was living at Stockton, California, and who kindly consented to talk about his experiences as a Pony Express rider.

The Santa Fé trail was the lure that first attracted Campbell to the West. At eighteen, in company with his older brother, he left his home in Illinois and headed for Westport, then the great receiving point and outlet for the Santa Fé trade. Russell, Majors & Waddell, with army contracts to fulfill, were sending their big freight outfits along the trail connecting with military posts. It was not long before both the Campbell boys were "signed up" as bullwhackers and were headed for the real West.

"Our work was to carry provisions and military supplies to the forts located north and east," said Mr. Campbell. "Alexander Majors was the local manager, while Mr. Russell stayed in Washington to get contracts. Our wages consisted of twenty-five dollars a month, with plentiful rations of bacon and beans—good fodder for hungry young fellows, especially when supplemented with fresh game killed on the way.

"Before we started out, Mr. Majors made us promise that we would not abuse the cattle or swear at them. My job was driving a team of four yoke of oxen, hitched to a wagon carrying four tons of freight. I had never driven more than one yoke of oxen. To make matters worse, we had to break our cattle to the work—a slow process. After the cattle were broken in, our normal speed was fifteen miles a day with the loaded wagon. There were twenty-six wagons in the train, one of them carrying the supplies for the men. The crew consisted of twenty-five drivers, or bullwhackers, a wagon boss and four extra hands.

"We were headed for Fort Union, New Mexico, with a three months' trip in prospect. In about three weeks we struck the buffalo country and buffalo meat became a regular feature of our diet. Along the Arkansas River it seemed as if the buffaloes must have numbered millions. Traveling along the Cimarron cut-off, and crossing a sixty-mile desert without water until the Cimarron was reached, we pushed on to Fort Union, near Santa Fé.

"We did freighting for two seasons. Once, when headed back toward Fort Leavenworth with our wagons empty and our number reduced to eighteen men, we ran into an Indian scare. The Comanches were on the warpath, and Indians seemed to be everywhere. We were forced to retreat to the Cimarron, which we reached after a day and a night on the trail. Here we joined a party of topographical engineers, under an escort of fifty soldiers. They were headed back toward Fort Leavenworth. We were glad to have this military protection.

"Once, on a return trip, we nearly had our cattle stampeded in a buffalo 'surround.' We were in the Pawnee country. The Pawnees were friendly. They were out on their annual buffalo hunt, a long way from their reservation on the Loup Fork, west of Omaha. The hunt had carried them into the country of the hostile Comanches. There were frequent battles between the tribes, but, as their firearms consisted of very poor rifles, there was little bloodshed. The first warning we had of the 'surround' was when several old buffalo bulls came over the Arkansas sandhills. Then came a herd of about five hundred buffaloes, pursued by at least one hundred and fifty Pawnees. The Indians were sinking arrows into the animals which they had selected for slaughter. A warrior would follow a choice buffalo cow, shooting arrow after arrow into her until finally the animal dropped.

"The general course of the hunt was directly toward us. We had hardly time to group our wagons in bunches of three, and to station each driver holding his lead oxen by the horns to prevent a stampede, when the buffaloes were upon us. You can imagine the mêlée that ensued, the buffaloes charging between the teams, hotly pursued by the Pawnees, and the frantic oxen trying to get away. Fortunately it was all over quickly, and the buffaloes and Indians were past us. In a little while the plain near us was strewn with the bodies of dead buffaloes. Not a rifle had been fired, the hunters doing all their killing with bows and arrows. In a little while we were bartering with the Indians for choice buffalo meat, in exchange for crackers, sugar and other provisions."

In the early spring of 1860, when Russell, Majors & Waddell had determined upon establishing the Pony Express, young Campbell was sent north to the Oregon Trail, to freight supplies to stations and to haul lumber and other materials for the buildings that were being erected to complete the relay chain. Campbell tried to get in the service as a rider when the Pony Express was started, but was unsuccessful.

"It was not until December, 1860, that I had an opportunity to ride," he said. "The boys were dropping out pretty fast. Some of them could not stand the strain of the constant riding. It was not so bad in summer, but when winter came on, the job was too much for them. The men who bought the horses knew their business. Sometimes we used to say that the company had bought up every mean, bucking, kicking horse that could be found, but they were good stock and could outrun anything along the trail.

"My relay was along the Platte, between Fort Kearney and Cottonwood Springs, or Fort McPherson, one hundred miles west of Kearney, with changes at Plum Creek, Pat Mullaly's, Midway and Gilman Ranch. I was over the average height, and I weighed one hundred and forty pounds. In fact, with my six feet, I was one of the tallest men in the service, but they weren't so particular that winter, if they could find men who could get the mail through. My first ride was in a heavy snow storm, and it pretty nearly used me up. After that, I began to get used to the pounding in the saddle, though it was strenuous work at any time.

"The hardest ride I ever had was when I had to spend twenty-four hours in the saddle, carrying the mail one hundred and twenty miles to Fairfield, twenty miles beyond my regular station at Fort Kearney. The snow was from two to three feet deep along the Platte, with the temperature down to zero. It was impossible to make more than five miles an hour. Often I had to get off and lead my horse. I met no one on the trail, as even the stages had stopped running. The only way I could tell where the trail lay was to keep an eye on the tall weeds, which showed above the snowdrifts on either side.

"There was no rider to go on with the mail when I reached Fort Kearney. The station men refused to go out in such a storm, so I started for the next station, twenty miles distant. I reached there at four o'clock in the afternoon, just twenty-four hours from the time I had started. I had used up four horses in making this ride. I was so exhausted that I slept until ten o'clock the next morning. I refused to ride back to Fort Kearney, preferring to wait for the stage which finally came through, traveling at the rate of two or three miles an hour. Even with four good mules, this stage took between three and four days to cover the run which I had made in twenty-four hours. Later on, in better weather conditions, I made the same run in twelve hours.

"The telegraph had been extended to Fort Kearney, and often I had to wait for big news that was coming in, or that was expected. A lot of important things were happening, and of course there was great interest in the latest news all along the trail. The telegraph operator at the fort was a good fellow, and always had a supply of cookies on hand. He would say: 'Sit down here, Billy, and eat some cookies and wait a little while longer. There's more news scheduled to come in over the wire.' Well, I had my own schedule to maintain, but I had things figured out pretty well and knew just where I could save time on the run; so I would wait till the very last minute.

"The greatest danger I faced on the trail was buffaloes. They were along the trail in western Nebraska by thousands. If a rider ever ran into a herd, he was gone. Wolves were numerous—big fellows. One winter night I saw some fifteen or twenty of them around a crippled horse which they had killed. They followed me for fifteen miles to the next station. The next day I went back and doctored up the carcass of that horse with strychnine. Twelve dead wolves were lying around the bait, the next time I went back. I got some Indians to prepare the hides, and had twelve beautiful pelts, two of them white, which I had no trouble in selling at a good price.

"Often it was hard work keeping on the trail in the dark. One black night, I remember, I was completely lost. I calculated that the Platte was half a mile away on my right. Finally I made my way to the river, and threw in one end of a rope which I carried and in that way found out the direction in which the current was flowing. I managed to make my way back to the trail and get going. One night I was riding a horse named Ragged Jim, a fine animal. The horse stepped in a buffalo wallow in the dark, and I went over his head, dragging the mail with me. I couldn't locate the horse in the dark, so I set off on foot for the next station, which was fifteen miles away. I remembered that the stage had just gone past, and I started to run, taking a chance on catching it. Fortunately for me, the driver was not trying to make any time in the dark. I kept shouting as I ran, and finally the driver heard me and pulled up, carrying me to the station where I got another horse and went on.

"Nebraska was pretty rough in those days. Often I would hear the invitation: 'Step up here, Pony Boy, and have a drink.' I never had any trouble when I refused. The only comment would be: 'Well, you're a funny feller to be runnin' around out here in this country.' Just the same, I was glad for my Presbyterian bringing up.

"There was an occasional ranch along the trail. One rancher had a bulldog which would always run out at the passing stages and riders. One night I thought I would scare this animal. I fired my pistol in his general direction, but my aim was a little too good, for I killed him. The station tenders told me the next day that the rancher had threatened to shoot the next Pony Express rider who passed. The regular trail led between his house and a barn on the ranch, but there was a branch road outside. Thereafter I took the branch.

"The telegraph company continued to extend the line westward. It was our duty to stop at the last station along the trail to receive the latest news. On the return trip we stopped long enough to give the operator the most important Western news to be telegraphed ahead. Of course we continued to carry the mail regularly, as it was sent from St. Joseph or Sacramento. Sometimes we carried as high as two hundred and fifty letters.

"Richard Cleve was the rider who rode 'opposite' to me on my run. At Big Sandy, Jack Keetley was one of the riders who took the mail and carried it on East. I saw Slade on one of his sprees at Cottonwood Springs where he shot out the lights and had the place terrorized. Wild Bill Hickok I met a few years later at Wichita.

"The Indians were peaceable enough, at least on my run, while the Pony Express was going. In fact several Sioux were employed as stock tenders at some of the stations. The men at the stations never failed to have a horse ready when a rider arrived. I generally blew the horn which I always carried, but there was little need for that, as a rule. On a clear, frosty night, the men could catch the sound of horse's hoofs when a rider was a long way off.

"One of the hardest rides I ever had made was when I carried President Lincoln's inaugural address from the telegraph station at Fort Kearney. Another was when the news came that Fort Sumter had been fired on. Such things broke the routine, and made every Pony Express rider feel that he was helping to make history."

2

Another adventure-seeking youth from the "States" who found plenty of thrills along the big trail was W. A. (Bill) Cates, who carried on west from Cottonwood Springs.

Cates entered the service at the start and remained until the end. Then he continued as a rider, carrying messages between Leavenworth and Fort Riley.

"If you ask me about my biggest thrill as a rider," said Cates years afterward in Denver, "I got it on the Leavenworth-Riley run, after the Overland 'Pony' was discontinued. The Indians were pretty quiet on my run while the overland service was going. A good many of them couldn't 'savvy' the idea of a lone rider pelting across the country at such a speed, with no particular object in view. Then, when they got over the idea that we were just crazy, they began to get bothersome. The Kiowas went on the rampage, and one day about three hundred of them, in full war regalia, took after me. I knew what those war bonnets meant, and I didn't stop for any parley. I had a good horse, but some of those Indians were as well mounted as I was. In fact they were gaining a little on me when I got within a few miles of the fort. It was customary for the commandant, about the time I was due at the fort, to send some soldiers out to meet me, just in case I happened to be having any trouble. I was in a sweat this day, wondering if I was to be met, as usual. It was going to be rough on me, in case the commandant figured that maybe he'd skip a day in taking this little precaution. Maybe

I wasn't thankful when I saw an escort coming out to meet me. The Indians saw the soldiers at the same time. They were out for raids and not for battle, so they turned around and went the other way, and I took my scalp on to the fort."

Cates was from Illinois and had headed west along the trail at the time of the Pike's Peak excitement. When he had a chance to sign as a "Pony" rider, he forgot all about gold.

"That was the way with most of the young fellows in the service," said Cates. "They were looking for something exciting, and the 'Pony' was just what they wanted."

3

"Irish Tommy" was a name well known along the trail. It was the nickname of Thomas J. Ranahan, a blue-eyed, courageous little stage driver, "Pony" rider and scout whom I knew in after years.

Ranahan was just as capable in the saddle as he was on the stage-driver's seat, and a good deal of his time was spent as a substitute rider.

"My stage run was over South Pass," said Ranahan. "It was a hard run in winter, on account of the storms. Many a time 'Pony' riders would come in totally exhausted. In that case there was nothing to do but go on with the mail for him, and turn the ribbons over to someone else till I could pick up the stage at the next station. One night I got into Green River Crossing and heard rumors of trouble at the station. It was just about the time the war broke, and feeling was running high on both sides. The station keeper was for the South and had become 'riled' at a stage driver known as 'Rowdy Pete' who had come in wearing a Union Flag. The station keeper had told Pete not to come in again wearing that flag. Pete was due from the west; so I waited to see what happened. When he arrived Pete's coach was all decorated with flags, even to the wheels. The crowd was mostly for Pete, and the station keeper didn't have a word to say."

4

From Fort Bridger to Salt Lake City and through Utah, Pony Express riders were nearly all Mormon boys. Some of them, young as they were, had been with Lot Smith when Johnston's supply train had been cut off and burned. They were splendid, fearless riders, and cheerfully faced many hardships that arose in a rough and sparsely populated country.

One of the Mormon boys riding out of Fort Bridger was Thomas Owen King, his next "home" station being Echo Canyon. King had helped in the work of building stations between Salt Lake City and Fort Bridger, and, when the Pony Express was started, he was among the first riders.

On the first trip of the "Pony" in April, 1860, King started out and rode twenty miles in fairly good weather. Then he changed horses, but five miles farther on he encountered a heavy storm. The trail was very narrow and the footing was bad. King's horse stumbled and the rider and *mochila* were thrown off. Before King could grasp it, the mail had been blown over a cliff. He quickly recovered it, and, by the time King reached the next station, he was on schedule.

"My longest ride," said King, "was from Salt Lake City to Ham's Fork, one hundred and forty-five miles, which I covered in thirteen hours. I don't know how far I could have ridden in those days, with just time to eat a little. I don't remember that I ever felt tired. Many a time I went to sleep in the saddle, and the pony would keep up his pace. Other riders would sleep, also. I remember once I came into Bear River after a night ride of eighty miles from Salt Lake, and reported to the station keeper that I had not passed Henry Worley, who was riding in the opposite direction. Worley had reported the same thing about me at the other station. We had both been so sound asleep in our saddles that we did not know when we passed each other. The ponies, when they learned what was expected of them, would keep up the pace from one end of a run to the other."

Accidents on the trail were few, when one considers the pace that was maintained, even on the darkest nights. As young " 'Ras" Egan, son of Major Egan, was on his way from Camp Floyd with the mail from the west, on a cold and stormy night toward the end of November, 1860, his horse stepped in a hole in the trail and fell, breaking its neck. Stripping the *mochila* from the saddle, young Egan trotted five miles to Camp Floyd with the mail.

Danger was not in the reckoning, so long as youth was getting its thrills out of the Pony Express.

CHAPTER XVI

THROUGH OTHER EYES

1

ANYTHING so romantically spectacular as the Pony Express could not fail to attract public attention. Correspondents of Eastern newspapers sent back glowing accounts of the working of the service. Editorials were printed, commending the enterprise of the men who, quickly and effectively, had brought East and West so much closer together, and who had disproved the contention that the Rocky Mountains, in their northern reaches, formed an impassable barrier to transportation in winter.

Amazement was expressed at the magnitude of the business conducted by Messrs. Russell, Majors & Waddell. That any single firm could, out of its own resources, overcome the frontier obstacles to communication was something well-nigh incomprehensible.

Horace Greeley, bent on telling the readers of the New York *Tribune* the truth about the Pike's Peak gold discoveries, made an overland trip, with Denver as his main objective, in June, 1859. At that time Jones & Russell, backed by Majors, were operating the Leavenworth & Pike's Peak Express to Denver. Their eastern head-

quarters were at Leavenworth, with the Russell, Majors &
Waddell freighting outfit. A few months later the business
of the company was greatly expanded when the coaches
were moved to the Central Overland route and the Pony
Express was added. Even so, the sight at Leavenworth
seems to have made a profound impression on Mr. Greeley,
who wrote:

> Russell, Majors & Waddell's transportation establish-
> ment, between the fort and the city, is the great feature
> of Leavenworth. Such acres of wagons; such pyramids of
> extra axle-trees; such herds of oxen; such regiments of
> drivers and other employees! No one who does not see
> can realize how vast a business this is; nor how numer-
> ous are its outlays as well as its revenue. I presume this
> great firm has at this hour two millions of dollars in-
> vested in stock, mainly oxen, mules and wagons. They
> last year employed six thousand teamsters and worked
> forty-five thousand oxen.

The Pacific Coast, rejoicing in shortened schedules of
coach transportation and its first "fast mail," accorded
warm support to Russell, Majors & Waddell. The newspapers, fearful of losing a valuable news service, gave
every support to the Central Overland, especially in its
operation of the "Pony." As early as the fall of 1860,
rumors began to be circulated to the effect that the Pony
Express was to be discontinued—that the anticipated
Government support was not to be forthcoming, and that
the support accorded by the public was not sufficient to
meet operating expenses. In answer to these rumors, the
Sacramento *Union* said editorially in its issue of October
18:

If there is one thing upon which men of this State are agreed, it is the absolute necessity of continuing the Pony Express. We cannot but think that the Post Office Department is fully aware of the great outlay of money and labor to which the Pony Express Company has been subjected in establishing this speedy means of communication between the Atlantic and Pacific States, of the indomitable spirit and energy which have been manifested in keeping up this connection in the face of the greatest difficulties, and the immense benefit which has been secured by this agency to the people of the East as well as on the Pacific Coast.

When the first Pony Express arrived in California it was made the subject of congratulatory resolutions, adopted by the General Assembly; when the "Pony" was discontinued, the General Assembly went further and adopted resolutions of regret, at the same time calling for the state to come to the rescue and continue the service. Only for the fact that the telegraph had then been established, no doubt California would have come to the rescue of the "little animal" which had won such a large measure of public favor.

Europe soon took cognizance of the notable "speeding up" of communication with the Pacific Coast. The era of European investment in western America was just dawning. Business houses on the Pacific Coast, with European connections, found the "Pony" invaluable. European investors in the mines of California and Washoe received speedy reports from their representatives, besides the general news which was received in New York by Pony Express and telegraph. In many cases the Pony Express was used in exchanges of diplomatic correspondence which had to do with affairs in the Far East in which not only Washington but European capitals had an interest.

Attracted by the picturesque phases of the subject, the London *Illustrated News* sent a representative to St. Joseph to cover the details. The correspondent prefaced a very complete descriptive article as follows:

> Some of our readers may possibly be puzzled, when reading American news, to find most important intelligence from California, Oregon, British Columbia and the Pacific side of North America contained in a short paragraph headed "By Pony Express"; and the question naturally arises, what is meant by a Pony Express? where does it come from? where does it go? and why is it a Pony Express and not a horse, or a stagecoach, or a railway express? For the purpose of giving some information on this point, our correspondent has taken the trouble to visit the locale of the Pony Express, to see it arrive and depart at its Eastern terminus, and also to get a view of it en route on the plains.

French and German publications printed articles and pictures descriptive of the "Pony"; and a poster, in colors, entitled "Le Poney Post," showing a Pony Express rider pursued by Indians, had a large sale in France.

In this country it was not long before dime-novel readers were regaled with the exciting adventures of a handsome hero, who more than carried out the promise of a striking, if not faithful, frontispiece, and who slew his quota of redskins.

The dashing saddlemen, out on the frontier, had, without knowing it themselves, become figures of international interest.

2

Samuel L. Clemens and Richard Burton were the most distinguished of the writers who traveled over the long trail when the Pony Express was in operation. Both succeeded in catching rare details of the trail life.

In his journey to Nevada, which he describes in *Roughing It*, Mark Twain gives the following picture of a meeting with a Pony Express rider:

> In a little while all interest was taken up in stretching our necks and watching for the "pony-rider"—the fleet messenger who sped across the continent from St. Joe to Sacramento, carrying letters nineteen hundred miles in eight days! Think of that for perishable horse and human flesh and blood to do! The pony-rider was usually a little bit of a man, brimful of spirit and endurance. No matter what the time of day or night his watch came on, and no matter whether it was winter or summer, raining, snowing, hailing, or sleeting, or whether his "beat" was a level, straight road or a crazy trail over mountain crags and precipices, or whether it led through peaceful regions or regions that swarmed with hostile Indians, he must be always ready to leap into the saddle and be off like the wind! There was no idling time for a pony-rider on duty. He rode fifty miles without stopping, by daylight, moonlight or starlight, or through the blackness of darkness— just as it happened. He rode a splendid horse that was born for a racer and fed and lodged like a gentleman; kept him at his utmost speed for ten miles, and then, as he came crashing up to the station where stood two men, holding a fast, impatient steed, the transfer of rider and mail-bag was made in the twinkling of an eye, and away flew the eager pair and were out of sight before the spectator could get hardly the ghost of a look. Both rider and

horse went "flying light." The rider's dress was thin and fitted close; he wore a "roundabout" and a skull cap, and tucked his pantaloons into his boot-tops like a race rider. He carried no arms—he carried nothing that was not absolutely necessary, for even the postage on his literary freight was worth *five dollars a letter*. He got little frivolous correspondence to carry—his bag had business letters, in it mostly. His horse was stripped of all unnecessary weight, too. He wore a little wafer of a racing saddle, and no visible blanket. He wore light shoes, or none at all. The little flat mail pockets, strapped under the rider's thighs, would each hold about the bulk of a child's primer. They held many and many an important business chapter and newspaper letter, but these were written on paper as light and airy and thin as gold leaf, nearly, and thus bulk and weight were economized. The stage-coach traveled about a hundred to a hundred and twenty-five miles a day (twenty-four hours), the pony-rider about two hundred and fifty. There were about eighty pony-riders in the saddle all the time, night and day, stretching in a long procession from Missouri to California, forty flying eastward and forty toward the west, and among them making four hundred gallant horses earn a stirring livelihood and see a good deal of scenery every single day in the year.

We had a consuming desire, from the beginning, to see a pony-rider, but somehow or other all that passed us and all that met us managed to streak by in the night, so we heard only a whiz and a hail, and the swift phantom of the desert was gone before we could get our heads out of the windows. But now we were expecting one along every moment, and would see him in broad daylight. Presently the driver exclaims:

"HERE HE COMES!"

Every neck is stretched further and every eye strained wider. Away across the endless dead level of the prairie a black speck appears against the sky, and it is plain that it moves. Well, I should think so! In a second or two it becomes a horse and rider, rising and falling, rising and falling—sweeping toward us nearer and nearer—growing more and more distinct, more and more sharply defined—nearer and nearer still, and the flutter of the hoofs comes faintly to the ear—another instant and a whoop and hurrah from our upper deck, a wave of the rider's hand, but no reply, and man and horse burst past our excited faces and go swinging away like the belated fragment of a storm.

So sudden is it all, and so like a flash of unreal fancy, that but for the flake of white foam left quivering and perishing on a mail-sack after the vision had flashed by and disappeared, we might have doubted whether we had seen any actual horse and man at all, maybe.

Richard F. Burton, then a Captain, intent on gathering first-hand impressions of Mormon life, started from St. Joseph for Salt Lake City on August 7, 1860. With a fine disregard for the dollar-a-pound charge for all luggage over the twenty-five pound limit, Burton packed his portmanteau as he would, even including chimney-pot hat, frock coat and silk umbrella. "As you value your nationality," he said in his account of these Western travels, "let no false shame cause you to forget your hat box and umbrella."

At Guittard's, one of the first "home" stations out from St. Joe, Burton saw a Pony Express rider arrive, and makes a brief mention of the fact in his notes. This part of Kansas interested Burton chiefly because of its physical aspects, and not because of the life at the stations. He describes the first miles of the trail from St. Joe as "deep, tangled wood, elms, hickory, basswood, black walnut, poplar, hackberry, box elder and willow, bound and festooned by wild moss and creepers, and an undergrowth of white alder and red sumac."

Farther on, in the Indian country, Burton is said by certain of his fellow passengers to have provoked a row at a stage station, all through a hasty sketch of an aboriginal native. Burton says he made the sketch of an Arapahoe at Platte Bridge, to see if Indians registered the same dislike of portraiture which he had noted among African tribes. Further, he says that the Indian, on being shown the sketch, merely grunted and walked away. The outside testimony is to the effect that the incident happened at Julesburg, and that the offended Indian and his companions attacked the station and were only stood off by Slade, the express messenger (or "Pony" rider), the stock tender and quite a supporting cast of stage passengers and hangers-on. If Burton set down any information, further than that contained in his book, his niece, Miss Sisted, who edited his note-books, seems not to have given it out.

Between South Pass and the rim of the Utah Basin, Burton's stage met a "Pony" rider who seemed to have more time on his hands than the intent courier described by Mark Twain. Burton pictures the meeting as follows:

Advancing over a soil alternately sandy and rocky— an iron flat that could not boast of a spear of grass— we sighted a number of coyotes, fittest inhabitants of such a waste, and a long, distant line of dust, like the smoke of a locomotive, raised by a herd of mules which was being driven to the corral. We were presently met by the Pony Express rider; he reined in to exchange views which, *de part et d'autre,* were simply nil.

On past Salt Lake City, among the various Indian groups of Utah and Nevada, Burton reveled in the opportunities for acquiring knowledge of the various dialects. He says:

> I preferred to correct my Shoshonee vocabulary under the inspection of Mose Wright, a Pony Express rider from a neighboring station. None of your "one horse" interpreters, he had learned the difficult dialect in his youth, and had acquired all the intonation of an Indian. Educated beyond the reach of civilization, he was in these days an oddity. He was convicted of having mistaken a billiard cue for a whip handle, and was accused of having mounted the post supporting an electric telegraph wire in order to hear what it was saying.

At Ruby Valley station, Burton found Colonel Rogers ("Uncle Billy") in charge—a former marshal in California and now assistant Indian agent and in charge of a model farm. At Diamond Springs, where the party went on past the station, he tells of camp being made where "the wind blew sternly through the livelong night," and pictures the camp as surrounded by "heaps of hills, white as bridal cakes." At Sheawit, or Willow Creek, renamed Roberts Spring Valley for Bolivar Roberts of the "Pony," Burton met his friend Mr. Mose Wright, "who again kindly assisted me in correcting my vocabulary."

At Dry Creek station Burton made note of one of the tragedies of the Pah-Ute war. "I inspected the grave for two," he wrote,

Loscier and Applegate, who were killed on May 21 by Indians. The former fell at the first fire; the latter, shot in the groin and unable to go, secured a revolver under pretense of defense, bade good-bye to his companions and put a bullet in his head. The others escaped.

Burton, at Simpson's Park, which station was destroyed by the Pah-Utes, found replacements going on. In true soldierly fashion he noted that the new station "was commanded by a neighboring height and the haystacks were exposed to fire."

In a deep canyon, Burton had a spot pointed out where a Pony Express rider named Miller had been badly wounded and had lost his horse. A young rider named "Jim" explained to the traveler that there was a system to getting past an Indian ambuscade—always keep an eye out to see if anyone were taking aim, and if so, throw oneself almost out of the saddle, clinging to the horse's neck, or make an unexpected rush to disconcert the Indian.

A very simple and illuminating explanation, which goes a long way toward explaining how the Pony Express mail came through "Injun country" so regularly, but perhaps not a plan which a tenderfoot would care to attempt.

3

What were a Pony Express rider's sensations on a long and grueling ride?

Joaquin Miller has, perhaps, come nearest to answering that question. Miller, who had his fling at gold mining and nearly every outdoor employment in California, tried Pony Express riding. In an article in the San Francisco *Call*, May 12, 1892, he said:

Ike Mossman of Oakland started an express from Walla Walla to Orofino, two hundred miles, and, as usual, all alone. When I came along a month or two later, he took me as partner. This was partly because I knew so many old Californians, and partly because he was threatened with competition by Wells-Fargo. We formed our partnership at Orofino, and he wanted to get back to Walla Walla in the next twenty-four hours. In fact he not only wanted to get there in that time but had to, or find the dreaded rival in the field.

This two hundred miles, strange as it may seem, was Mossman's habit, and he did it twice each week. . . . "Oh, yes, I can ride it with you. If you have horses down the road, I can ride them, and will be at your side as you enter Walla Walla." I remember Mossman gave me an inquiring look, but had I not helped drive cattle from Portland to Yreka? And had I not helped drive mustangs from Texas to Shasta? Why, of course I could ride— ride anywhere and ride anything!

And we set out at sunrise. The next sunrise must see us two hundred miles away. Pleasant the first forty miles, woods, cool waters, wildflowers that brushed our feet at the trailside as we shot forward. Then up a long, tortuous mountain-side; then down, down, down. It began to get rough. A horse likes the change of levels, and it rests a man, too, but neither "ups nor downs" should be too continuous. However, a horse will make a longer distance, and do it in better condition, over a hilly road than on a road that is entirely level. The reason is that he rests his uphill muscles while going downhill, and the reverse.

At Lewiston, the first hundred miles, I dismounted slowly. But fresh, well-fed horses always refresh the rider. We had a long pull of it from the bank of Snake River. Then the plains. No sign of habitation—only our Indians waiting by the roadside every ten, twenty or thirty miles, as water allowed, with fresh horses.

I became tired, then sleepy—oh, so sleepy! I pinched myself, sang old California songs, gave the Modoc war-whoop, told whopping big lies to keep myself awake, but almost tumbled from my horse dozens of times that long, long night. We made it in a little less than twenty-four hours. Mossman instructed me what to do till he returned, and, leaving me at the hotel, set his face back across the same long road. . . .

I shall never forget little Bill A——, with his bright, black eyes flashing from under a great, heavy brow like a chieftain's. He would not even get off his horse to die. "Stick to me, will you, till we get in?" I had caught up to him, passed him, and was going to leave him there, reeling in his saddle, holding onto the mane; nothing left of him at all but his blazing black eyes. He was riding for the hated rival express line, and the best rider they had—gentle and daring, even unto death.

I got to the door of his office, before going to my own, and all the town looking on and wondering. And when they lifted him from the saddle he was dead, his thin little fingers twisted in the mane and clutching it as if they had been the claws of a bird.

This was the courage that animated every rider who carried the fast mail of the "Pony" days. There are few records of riders "quitting" under the innumerable dangers of the desert trail.

It was this die-in-the-saddle spirit which focused the eyes of the world on the Pony Express.

CHAPTER XVII

ROUGH GOING FOR THE "PONY"

1

IF the story of the Pony Express could be confined to the uplands of the West it would, perhaps, be more gratifying to the reader who prefers to follow the exploits of sunburned, heroic men, rather than the doubtful expedients of politicians and lobbyists.

Unfortunately, as pointed out, the success of mail enterprises along Western routes depended largely upon political favor at Washington. The Pony Express was launched merely as a gesture. It was to prove that a certain route was more feasible than another route. That much being proved, it was reasonable to suppose that a mail contract, of appropriate richness, would be awarded to the individual or the corporation which had produced the evidence.

In the case of the Pony Express, the firm of Russell, Majors & Waddell was the sponsor, with Senator Gwin, of California, because of his supposed influence with Congress and in the White House, acting as godfather. At the proper time the godfather, like an amateur magician, would draw a properly rich bauble from his hat, and all would be well.

In order to further the financial affairs of the company

which had gone in for everything in the transportation line ranging from ox-teams to stages and the swift "Pony," William H. Russell, then known as "the Napoleon of the West," was stationed in the East. His route lay between the office of the Secretary of War in Washington and the financial district of New York. His partner, Alexander Majors, remained for the most part in the West, dealing out Bibles to his bullwhackers and "Pony" riders.

On December 24, 1860, the newspapers of the country published hints of a startling robbery at Washington— the disappearance of some $3,000,000 worth of Indian bonds, part of the Indian Tribal Fund. The loss was reported by Jacob Thompson, then Secretary of the Interior in the Cabinet of President Buchanan. The bonds had been in charge of a clerk in the Department of the Interior, one Godard Bailey, who had disappeared.

On the same day William H. Russell, projector of the Pony Express, was arrested in New York, at the offices of the Central Overland, California & Pike's Peak Express Company in Fulton Street. It was charged that Russell had accepted the bonds from Bailey and hypothecated them, leaving in their stead "acceptances" from John B. Floyd, Secretary of War, which had been issued in advance of services to be performed by Russell, Majors & Waddell in transporting supplies to Western Army posts.

The New York *Herald* gave this summary of the case at the outset:

Mr. Russell, not finding himself able to negotiate these acceptances, and being greatly embarrassed financially, and ascertaining from Godard Bailey, with whom he was intimately acquainted, that the latter had control over $3,000,000 of Indian trust funds invested in lands of different states, arranged with Bailey to let him have about half a million dollars, these bonds to be hypothecated in New York, and as surety for which he gave Bailey the acceptances of the War Department, which Bailey placed in the safe where the bonds were kept. Recently these bonds have greatly depreciated, and the bankers in New York who made advances on them therefore called for additional security. Bailey, in order to save the bonds, delivered over $300,000 worth of them additional—in all $870,000. On the 18th inst. he wrote a letter to the Secretary of the Interior, frankly imparting these facts and demanding an investigation.

Russell and Bailey were put in jail, pending bail arrangements. Russell's bail was put at $200,000. Almost immediately he had more than $2,000,000 in securities pledged by friends in Missouri, Kansas, Virginia, Baltimore and New York. Bailey was released on $3,000 bail.

A special committee from the House of Representatives was appointed to make inquiry into the case, which was creating a tremendous stir and was being "played" in big headlines all over the country. Floyd's explanation, in which the burden was laid on Russell, was given as follows in the *Herald:*

Floyd had allowed Russell to draw upon his department for $100,000. This had been repeated six or seven times, Floyd's friends saying that each time he thought Russell was merely renewing and not accumulating the drafts. A friend approached Bailey (who was said to be married to a niece of Floyd) and told him that his uncle would be ruined and that Bailey could save him by allowing him to use the state stocks held in trust for the Indians as against the acceptances given to Russell.

This charitable view that Floyd had been imposed upon was not sustained in the report made by the House Committee, a few weeks later. Floyd, who had cast his lot with the Confederacy, was by this time in Virginia. The *Herald* printed the voluminous report of the committee in full, leading it with a "scare" head:

THE GIGANTIC ROBBERY OF THE INDIAN TRUST BONDS AT WASHINGTON

————

Report of the Special Committee of Five to the House of Representatives

————

John B. Floyd, Late Secretary of War, Captain of the Forty Thieves

————

Godard Bailey a Mere Catspaw of the ex-Secretary and His Chums

————

The Government Involved in Losses and Liabilities Hard Upon Six Millions of Dollars

————

The report declared that Floyd had issued "acceptances" to others besides Russell; that the practice had been brought to the attention of the President, who had forbidden its continuance, and that the acceptances issued to Russell, Majors & Waddell amounted to from $2,000,-000 to $3,000,000 more than had been earned. It characterized Bailey as "a bankrupt in fortune and a political adventurer." The Secretary of the Interior was scored for "carelessness" in not taking better care of the bonds, and Russell was severely criticized for evasiveness on the witness stand.

As a matter of fact, Russell was on the stand only a short time. He was asked a few questions, pertaining to his business affairs with the War Department and his answers were stigmatized as "vague, rambling and unsatisfactory, and he shows such utter ignorance of the details of his business, or unwillingness to make an exhibit of his affairs that your committee have considered it much safer to base their conclusions on the records furnished by the War Department."

Russell, soon after he had taken the stand, was asked: "Did you ever directly or indirectly give to any person any present for services rendered to you, connected with your business with the War Department?" Russell then asked to be excused to consult legal counsel and appeared later with a written statement which the committee characterized as "no answer to the question that had been asked as introductory to more important ones, but an elaborate effort made by Mr. Russell, with technical adroitness and legal acumen, to avail himself of the Act of Congress (with regard to voluntary testimony) and to interpose it as a shield between him and his deeds."

What was Russell's version of the affair which a Philadelphia journalist described as an "unfortunate breach of official trust"? Dr. Victor M. Berthold, in an article on William H. Russell, as the originator and developer of the Pony Express, says, in *The Collectors' Club Philatelist,* that Russell's statement which he presented to the committee apparently has never been made public. Dr. Berthold states:

> Despite a most careful research in the *Congressional Globe* and a request addressed to the Library of Congress for information as to whether or not there exists in their records "Russell's version" we have been unable to discover such document, and this despite our knowledge that on January 18, 1861, when cited before the committee, Russell presented a statement of the transaction.

Bailey, Russell and Floyd were indicted by the Grand Jury in Washington on January 30, 1861—three cases against Bailey for larceny in abstracting the bonds intrusted to his custody; one joint indictment against Bailey and Russell for abstracting the bonds; three indictments against Russell for receiving the stolen bonds; and one joint indictment against Bailey, Floyd and Russell for conspiracy to defraud the United States Government.

A dispatch from Washington the next day pointed out the fact that Bailey, who abstracted the bonds, had not been examined by the Committee of Investigation. The dispatch said further:

> The Act of 1857, which is supposed to relieve witnesses of Congressional Committees from prosecution, will doubtless be pleaded for the benefit of some of the parties to this mammoth robbery. Lawyers already maintain that the indictment against Messrs. Russell, Floyd and Bailey for a conspiracy to defraud the Government is for

a crime not known in the criminal statutes. They will probably all escape punishment.

Floyd being beyond reach and Bailey, for some unknown reason, not being called upon to testify, the investigations of the committee seem to have centered upon Russell. The historian, H. H. Bancroft, intimates that Russell was made the victim of a plot. In his *Chronicles of the Builders,* Bancroft, says:

> In January, 1861 . . . Russell, president of the company, fell into difficulty—if, indeed, it were not a trap set for him by friends of the southern route. The company was largely in debt, owing about $1,800,000; and, although a large company, and with considerable assets, was embarrassed to a degree which made borrowing necessary to a greater amount than was convenient. The Government was also in debt to the company on its contracts, Congress having failed to pass an appropriation bill. While Russell was in Washington, endeavoring to secure some relief, he was induced to take $870,000 in bonds of the Interior Department, as a loan, and giving as security acceptances on the War Department furnished him by Secretary Floyd, a part of which was not yet due. The bonds, as it turned out, were stolen by Godard Bailey, a family connection of Floyd's, and law clerk in the Interior Department. . . . In the temporary confusion which followed the discovery of the fraud, Russell lost his opportunity, as perhaps it was meant that he should, and Congress in February authorized the Postmaster General to advertise for bids for a daily mail over the central route.

The House committee of investigation in its report spoke of the "tortuous windings of vast and complicated

interests and extensive though concealed ramifications."
Whether this refers in any way to the rivalry over mail
subsidies, at which Bancroft hints, can only be guessed,
as the great fraud case which so stirred the nation seems
never to have come to trial.

Jacob Thompson, who, as Secretary of the Interior, was
merely criticized by the investigating committee for carelessness in looking after the bonds entrusted to his care,
resigned in January, 1861, (the month of the bond fraud
discovery) according to Orville J. Victor, author of *The
History of the Southern Rebellion*. The same author says
of Thompson:

> He was appointed aid to General Beauregard. From
> 1862 to 1864 Thompson was Governor of Mississippi.
> After the assassination of Lincoln, Thompson was ac-
> cused of complicity and a price was put on his head. He
> then escaped to Europe. When he returned he was
> brought to trial and a civil suit was brought in 1876 for
> the money taken by Bailey while Thompson was Secre-
> tary of the Interior.

With regard to the case against Russell, Mr. Henry C.
Needham, in his introduction to Dr. Berthold's mono-
graph, to which reference has been made, says:

> It was probably quashed, for the record shows that
> apparently Russell made the amount good. To realize the
> sum necessary it is more than likely that Russell liqui-
> dated many of his business assets and borrowed quite
> heavily from Holladay and the Wells-Fargo people.

The charges brought against Russell do not seem to
have injured his standing among his friends and associates in the West. To them he was still the "Napoleon"

who had imagination and daring. He was still the brilliant genius of business who had given Denver its luxuriously equipped stage line from the Pike's Peak region to the "States." He was still the master mind who had not only proved that the Central Overland could be kept open all the year round, but who had confounded the gloomy critics by organizing and establishing on that route the swift and efficient Pony Express.

A few months after all the publicity he had received as a result of his financiering in Washington and New York, Russell visited Colorado. The *Rocky Mountain News*, speaking of his intended visit, said: "The people of Pike's Peak will extend him a warmer welcome than to any other man who has visited us."

A complimentary ball was given in Russell's honor at Golden, Colorado, and Governor Gilpin, the first Governor of the new territory, and other officials were there to pay tribute to the man whose swift ponies had beaten a trail for the telegraph and railroad across the continent.

Public opinion, at least, seemed to have returned a verdict of "not guilty" in behalf of William H. Russell.

2

It is a remarkable fact that while the New York newspapers were "playing up" the scandal that shook the Pony Express management, news by "Pony" was coming in regularly. Next to the "scare" heading which told of the latest developments in the fraud case at Washington, the reader found the "stock" heading which topped the regular grist of news from the West "by Pony Express and telegraphed from Fort Kearney."

In some mysterious way, even with debts pressing and

its chief promoter under indictment, the Pony Express kept clicking off the miles with as great regularity as weather conditions would allow. The operator at Fort Kearney never missed getting his semi-weekly sheaf of news from the Pacific Coast to be telegraphed ahead of the rider, who swung on toward St. Joe with the letters in his charge.

For months it had been the current rumor that the "Pony" was in financial difficulties. The freighting business of Russell, Majors & Waddell had fallen off with the approach of war. Soldiers were withdrawn from Western posts, the Indians being happily quiescent. Skeleton garrisons were left, to be increased somewhat later on, by detachments of Confederate prisoners, on parole. These "galvanized Yankees," as they were called, were only too glad to be relieved of prison routine and fare. In return for a minimum of duty, which they performed cheerfully and well, they were better fed than if they had been in some Eastern prison, but there were not enough of them to make the freighting of supplies worth while. The big commands were gone from the posts, with horses and mules. The old days of fat contracts for hauling Army supplies in the West, if not gone forever, were at least in a serious decline.

The stage business, too, had suffered, and the mail contract alone kept it from showing a heavy loss. Friends of the "Pony" were beginning to look anxiously about for financial support, as evidenced by this editorial in the Sacramento *Union*, as early as August 21, 1860:

Discontinuance of the Pony Express—There is a strong probability that the Pony Express will be discontinued. Our correspondent in St. Louis says it is pretty well settled that Russell & Co. will get no mail contract, and, as the Pony Express is now a total loss, almost, to them, there is no inducement to continue it. Our correspondent adds that the people may thank Postmaster General Holt and our plotting Senator, Gwin, for it. The former is about one hundred years behind the age and should go home and cultivate a tobacco plantation. The latter should be expelled from California just as soon as the votes of the people, through the Legislature, can be brought to bear upon his Senatorial aspirations.

Russell, the official spokesman for the "Pony," was quick to counteract these early rumors about the suspension of the Express. In November, 1860, he announced that election news would be carried free to newspapers on the Pacific Coast. This brought a protest from newspapers that were paying for their press service, and the idea was abandoned.

Through the *Alta California* Russell announced that the directors had decided to continue the Pony Express until January 1, 1861, and then, if Congress refused aid, to abandon the enterprise. No aid was forthcoming, but the "Pony" continued running. After the news had "broken" regarding the financial scandal at Washington, there were numerous expressions of public concern over the prospect of losing the "Pony." The California Legislature, on February 4, passed a resolution "that our Senators in Congress be instructed, and our Representatives requested, to use their earnest endeavors to obtain an appropriation from the General Government in aid of the Pony Express Company."

Obligations, apparently, were pressed as a result of the

exposé at Washington. The *Deseret News* of February 27 reported that

> all the stock belonging to the Mail and Express Company in this Territory had been attached in the suit of Livingston, Bell & Co., in consequence of which mail and express would be stopped, and no further communication might be expected from the East very soon, which, in these exciting times would certainly be a great inconvenience, not to say calamity.

The fears of the *News* editor were allayed by the explanation of the plaintiffs that, while they had attached the animals, it was not intended to interfere with the mail, nor to prevent the "Pony" from making its regular trips.

The people of the Pacific Coast and the intermediate West were genuinely alarmed over the transportation and mail situation on the Central Overland route. All eyes were turned to Congress to see what relief, if any, would be forthcoming.

CHAPTER XVIII

BEHIND THE SCENES

1

IN all the proceedings of Congress during the year preceding the Civil War, and for several months after the outbreak of hostilities, one finds the Pony Express mentioned only a few times, and then, generally, quite unofficially.

The members of Congress, when they opened their newspapers, looked for the latest news from the Pacific Coast under the familiar "By Pony Express" heading. But officially the Pony Express did not exist, in the minds of the nation's lawmakers. Here was an institution that had bridged the appalling gap of "the Great American Desert" and had proved that the impossible was possible, and yet it was ignored.

This attitude was not exceptional. An "example" was not being made of the Pony Express. It was merely a continuation of the treatment which had been accorded to the private express companies in the East and in California when they had proved that they could outdo the Government in the efficient delivery of mail. Anything that cut into the revenue of postmasters injured the prestige of the party in power. When Henry Wells offered to take over the entire mail service of the United States, including delivery, at the rate of five cents a letter (then about one-fourth of the price being charged by the Government) he was met with the reply:

"Do you realize, sir, that it would throw sixteen thousand postmasters out of office?"

In the case of the Pony Express, some aid might have been expected from Washington in the early months of the service, had there been a more determined effort in its behalf.

Senator Latham introduced a bill which called for remuneration on the basis of service performed, but this measure failed. Senator Gwin, for all the claims made for him as the "father" of the project, had little to say about it officially. The senior Senator from California became absorbed in a larger proposition—a trio of routes to the Pacific Coast.

> I hope nobody will take spasms [said Senator Gwin on the floor of the Senate] when I say that I am in favor of all the routes and always have been, and always intend to stand up for them. I look upon this policy of extending routes across the continent and establishing connections with various sections of the Union as one of the most important policies adopted by the Government. I will go so far as to say, notwithstanding that I expect to be looked upon almost as a monster, that I am in favor of a route from St. Paul to Puget Sound.

In accordance with this declaration, Senator Gwin in May, 1860, introduced a bill calling for a triple overland mail system, to do away with steamer mails. He proposed a semi-weekly mail between St. Joseph and Placerville; a similar mail from St. Paul to Puget Sound, with a connection from New Orleans to be added to the southern route, and a daily mail service between San Francisco and Puget Sound. This all-inclusive bill, coming at a time when most Senators were declaring that one overland route was enough, was lost.

Besides this lack of any effective support in Congress, there was another reason why the Pony Express received no recognition at Washington during its first months of operation. It was inevitable that a transcontinental telegraph would soon be completed. In fact a survey had already been made, over the very route traversed by the "Pony." From the start it was recognized that the "fast mail" service in the West could be only temporary.

Rumors of the straits of the "Pony" were numerous. As early as August 9, 1860, the St. Louis correspondent of the San Francisco *Bulletin* said:

> The Pony Express, I suppose, will now jog along for a considerable time, as Russell, Majors & Co., the proprietors, received on the 18th a warrant on the United States Treasury for $67,000, the money being, says the paragraph announcing it, "in consideration of past mail service." Whether the payment is made on account of the Pony enterprise itself, or the mail contract between St. Joseph and Placerville (which they bought out from Hockaday & Co., and Chorpenning) does not appear. Russell & Co. are said to have other large claims against the Government for trains of merchandise destroyed on the plains by Indians during the Utah rebellion, in consequence of the failure of the Government to furnish the necessary escort authorized by the contract.

Russell, evidently in answer to this article, had the following letter published in the *Bulletin:*

The only fear of the Pony Express being discontinued is through the action of the Postoffice Department. The company now runs the mail from St. Joseph to Salt Lake, thence to Placerville. It is now in prospect to continue it only from Julesburg, on the South Platte, four hundred miles west of St. Joseph, to Salt Lake. If this is done we cannot maintain the Pony Express. A continuance of our present contract till Congress makes some provision, would at least keep it till they decide to give the mail to us or to some other party. If once the Express is broken up, I doubt much if any other parties can be found who would invest so much money on an uncertainty. We have, however, attained our principal object, that of practically demonstrating that the route is feasible and practical, and with a good mail contract, and in that way only, the Express can be maintained.

No contract was awarded in November, however. It was recognized that mail service to the Pacific Coast must be improved, but how this was to be brought about was a problem which took several months of consideration. The idea of a daily coach service seemed to be uppermost, but, as late as February 23, 1861, the Committee on Post-offices and Post Roads considered, instead of such a ser-vice, "if we had not better recommend to the Senate that they take a tri-weekly service and a Pony Express three times a week, the Pony Express to run alternately with the coaches."

While these debates were going on, the "Pony" con-tinued to run between St. Joseph and Sacramento, heavy losses being footed by its promoters in the hope that they would be the successful bidders when the contract was finally made.

2

The transportation of printed matter to and from the Pacific Coast was one of the chief items of the Government's problem. The charges for letter mail were high, and the bulk of such mail was comparatively small. It could be easily handled on the coaches and added little to the burden of the four-horse teams. But stage drivers were often in despair when they were called upon to transport hundreds of pounds of newspapers, books, pamphlets and the "franked" and bulky publications sent out by legislators at Washington.

The Pony Express riders had the advantage when it came to getting their mail through numerous streams which were innocent of bridges. The "Pony" letters were light, and were enclosed in oilskin wrappings. In addition, the *cantinas* which held them were waterproof, or nearly so. If a stream was too deep to be forded without submerging the *cantinas*, a rider could strip the *mochila* from the saddle and hold it over his head.

There was no such happy solution for those in charge of the stage-coach mail. Congress, in 1825, had authorized "every printer of newspapers to send one paper to each and every other printer of newspapers within the United States, free of postage." This meant a great addition to mail carried in bulk. Frequently the publication mail was so heavy that it was arranged in the bottom of a coach, and the passengers had to dispose themselves among the mail sacks as best they could. This mail rarely came in without damage in time of high water, as shown by the following items of complaint in the *Deseret News:*

The mail from St. Joseph arrived at Hank's station,

twelve miles out of the city on Friday evening last, but, owing to the breaking of the carriage or some other cause, it was not brought in until Monday at 5½ p. m. There was more than the usual amount of mail matter, most of which was as wet as water could make it, though not badly damaged, excepting the books, which will have to be rebound.—June 13, 1860.

The Eastern mail arrived at 10.30 on Monday morning, bringing twenty-one sacks, all inside the coach. The conductor, Mr. Charles McCarty, states that the mail matter has always been carried in his charge, and that if any newspapers or other documents in this or any other previous mail carried by him have got wet, it has been occasioned by the water in the numerous creeks along the route being so deep as to strike through the bottom of the coach.—June 27, 1860.

The mail from the States arrived on Monday, but our portion of it was too wet to be opened, and we have hung it up to dry. Report says that the coach was upset in one of the mountain streams this side of the Weber.—February 27, 1861.

The great amount of matter in bulk, which had to be handled in a limited number of coaches, led to the practice of "caching," or hiding, mail along the roadside. A driver would start out with several hundred pounds of printed matter, duly disposed about his coach, but would find his team "playing out" under the combined weight of mail-sacks and passengers. In such a case the mail was sacrificed. Sometimes it was hidden in some convenient cave along the way; at others it was simply thrown off by the roadside. The *Deseret News* of May 2, 1860, thus reports an arrival of "cached" mail:

The "way mail," that is to say an ox-wagon load, as reported, of mail bags that have been left by the wayside, some of them nearly or quite six months, arrived Wednesday night the 25th, and from that time till Monday afternoon we were daily in receipt of a variety of old papers and other documents, which were delivered as fast as the clerks in the postoffice could distribute the heterogeneous mass, comprising dates from November, 1859, to April 4, 1860.

In a later issue the *News* editor calls upon those to whom documents in this "way mail" are addressed to call for them without delay. Incidentally he remarks that "the caching of public documents is not a matter of so much consequence as the leaving by the way of the mail more liable to be wasted and destroyed, as most of the valuable seeds have been that were forwarded from Washington during the past winter."

Such "caching" of mail was forbidden, but the driver of a "Pitching Betsy," as the old Concord was called, was not inclined to let instructions stand in his way when his mules were flagging on the road. Alex Toponce, in his *Life and Adventures*, tells of having two Army officers as passengers, with several hundred pounds of reports. The printed matter, in sacks, was piled on the seat in front of the officers. On a steep hill the driver's assistant cut the string that held the mail sacks, and the heavy documents fell on the Army officers. The reports were piled in the back seat, and the Army officers seated themselves opposite. This time, going downhill, the string was cut and the Army officers were again buried under the falling documents. One of the officers suggested "dumping" the troublesome mail. Says the author:

George was horrified at the suggestion. "General," he said, "that is Government mail. There is a heavy penalty on losing any of them Patent Office reports."

"Rot!" the General says. "Get rid of them some way, only don't you dare let me see you. My aide and I will walk on up the trail, and when you catch up with us I don't want to see any more of those big sacks."

The cost of transporting such mail was enormous, even with drivers practicing "caching" at every opportunity, as they did on both the central and southern stage lines.

3

There was occasional renewal of the talk of establishing a Pony Express service on the Butterfield line, but this died out as war became more imminent.

The Butterfield route was not proving the success which the Postmaster General had prophesied for it in his glowing prospectus. The service was continued regularly, but patronage was not what had been expected. The competition of the Central Overland had cut in heavily. Senator Yulee of Missouri estimated that the expense to the Government in maintaining service over the Butterfield route was between $60 and $70 for every letter to or from the Pacific Coast.

It took war to end the dissension over the respective merits of the Butterfield and central routes. As early as February, 1861, when it was realized that civil strife was inevitable, the Butterfield company received orders to move its coaches and livestock to the central route. The Central Overland, California and Pike's Peak Company, and its subsidiary, the Central Overland Pony Express Company, virtually passed out of existence, being merged

with the Butterfield-Wells-Fargo interests under the title
of the Overland Mail Company. Under the Postal Appropriation Bill, which became effective March 2, the Butterfield and Wells-Fargo interests received a contract,
with an annual subsidy of $1,000,000, to carry the mails on
the central route. The contract specified a coach service
each way, six days a week, and ordered the continuation of
the Pony Express service, beginning July 1. Thus, for the
first time, the Pony Express became "official," receiving,
as it did, the benefits of a Government subsidy.

Benjamin Holladay, who, at the start of the Pony Express, saved the institution by advancing money for buying feed for the stock at the western end of the line, and
who evidently was one of the company's creditors during
the later days of financial difficulty, was to operate the
stages and "Pony" east of Salt Lake City. The Butterfield-Wells-Fargo interests controlled the business west of
Salt Lake.

Russell and his associates were eliminated from active
management before the new Government contract went
into effect on July 1. So much is indicated by the following
notice appearing on May 16 in the Sacramento *Union:*

> *Pony Express Notice*—Orders having been received
> from W. H. Russell, President Pony Express Company,
> I hereby transfer the office and everything pertaining
> thereto to Messrs. Wells, Fargo & Co. All letters to be
> forwarded by Pony Express must be delivered at their
> office on Second Street, between J and K, Sacramento.
> J. W. Coleman, Agent Pony Express Co.

The men who had founded the Pony Express and had
thereby proved the feasibility of the central route, no

longer figured in overland transportation. John Butterfield had won his long fight for overland supremacy, and
had a few more sheets of figures to add to the sheaf of
loose papers in his beaver hat.

CHAPTER XIX

CARRYING ON

1

THE Pony Express route was soon buzzing with stories about Ben Holladay, the new "boss" of the line from Salt Lake east. Another "Napoleon" had succeeded Russell, promising to carry everything before him —a dominating figure, calculated to turn the lethargic into models of human energy.

Even the ever-present topic of Slade was sidetracked at intervals while station gossip turned to the most masterful personality that ever dazzled the overland trail. Slade had been kept on by Holladay as a man whose methods were not to be questioned as long as he secured results—and so was every other man in the service who could ride roughshod to success in whatever he undertook.

Ben Holladay had ridden that way—had overcome and trampled down one handicap after another. Born in Bourbon County, Kentucky, he had turned to the frontier gateway in western Missouri and Kansas. At Leavenworth, among the freighters and stage-drivers and outfitters of emigrant trains, he found an atmosphere that suited him. His compelling personality soon made itself known and he was looked upon as a likely young fellow who would make his way in the world. He became a friend of General Rufus Ingalls and other prominent men.

The war with Mexico had given Holladay a start. He

had bought mules for the War Department and had sufficient funds to equip himself as a freighter in the California trade. The future which he saw for himself in California was in transportation, not in mining. He engaged in staging and made money. When the silver field of Nevada really developed, Ben Holladay was one of the chief owners of the rich Ophir mine.

Holladay had only fairly embarked on his career when he became head of the overland stage business east of Salt Lake. The next few years were to be crowded with achievements, ending in financial failure that was close to tragedy, but amid all his successes and in the midst of many personally-owned enterprises, he liked best to think of himself as "boss" of the greatest stage line in the world.

Business on the Overland "bucked up" as soon as Holladay took hold. He put on more coaches and more livestock and more employees, to maintain the daily schedule demanded by the new contract. He had made for himself a coach that was royal in its appointments—a coach fitted with sleeping accommodations like a Pullman. The candles by which Holladay read at night were fitted into silver candlesticks. The drivers who held the "ribbons" on Ben Holladay's coach swaggered and bragged about it long afterward.

Holladay had an office in New York and another in San Francisco, and he liked to visit each unexpectedly. He traveled at top speed—no other way would suit him. He would wait until the last minute, and then the driver must make up time on the way.

The "Pony" gave Holladay much pride, and he watched its arrivals regularly and checked them with the schedule.

If he thought the service was lagging, some division agent was sure to hear from headquarters.

Alex Toponce, in his book of reminiscences, tells a story which illustrates how closely Holladay watched affairs on the Overland. Toponce was "riding Pony" for about two months, out of Fort Kearney. He says:

> They furnished us with a fine lot of horses to ride. Many of them were Oregon horses, with some mustang blood, and there was one famous strain called "Copper Bottom," mostly dark grays.
>
> Just west of Kearney was a long, sandy hill to climb, and going out one morning I overtook a lot of soldiers in Government ambulances. They were walking their teams up this hill. I had to turn out of the road to pass them, and my horse changed from a gallop to a walk while going up the hill.
>
> Suddenly a man put his head out of the window of a stage and called to me, "Hey, young man."
>
> I rode over and said, "Yes, sir."
>
> It was Ben Holladay, the boss of the mail line. "Young man," he said, "the company furnishes the horses. You furnish the spurs."
>
> I took the hint and went up the hill on a lope. Soon after that I quit the fast mail business.

Holladay had taken a leaf from Barnum's rule-book of success, with regard to the value of advertising. He put on a "show" trip by stage from Sacramento to St. Joseph, just to see how close he could come to the record made by the "Pony." Everything else along the stage route was sidetracked, to make way for the big man in the luxuriously appointed coach. Holladay made the trip in twelve

BENJAMIN F. HOLLADAY

The picturesque genius of stage transportation, who controlled the eastern division of the Pony Express during the later months of the service.

Photograph by courtesy of Purd B. Wright, Kansas City, Mo.

days, or seven days under the schedule time. The trip cost him considerable money, but this expense was made up many times in publicity received, as the Eastern newspapers gave much space to the story of Holladay's ride.

One stagecoach line after another, connecting with the Overland, was acquired by Holladay. Soon he was running a daily line of coaches to and from Atchison, Omaha and Nebraska City, connecting at Denver with daily stagecoach lines for the Central City, Gregory, and Clear Creek mining districts; also with tri-weekly coaches for Taos, Santa Fé and other points in New Mexico. From Salt Lake he ran a tri-weekly line of coaches to and from Virginia City, Mont., Helena, Boise, Walla Walla and Portland.

Holladay did not scruple to use his great power when occasion seemed to demand. He became angered at a Denver newspaper, which launched an attack on him for alleged overcharge for express on exchange, the local bankers having protested that the rates were excessive. Holladay changed his stage route and left Denver sixty miles away.

In New York and San Francisco, Holladay entertained lavishly. He built a veritable palace, which he called Ophir Hall, north of New York City, in Westchester County. Ophir Hall is still one of the "show places" of Westchester. [1]

---

[1] Holladay had steamers operating on the Pacific from San Francisco to Oregon, Panama, Japan and China. In 1866 he sold out his interest in the Overland line to Wells, Fargo & Co. for $3,000,000. This money he invested in a railroad which he was building from Puget Sound to California. The panic of 1873 wrecked the enterprise, which was about all that remained to Holladay of his one-time vast holdings. He died soon afterward, a comparatively poor man.

Holladay went in for expensive jewelry. One of his fads was fancy vests, of which he owned many—each one having fancy buttons inlaid with jewels.

The story of Ben Holladay's holdup became almost as famous in the West as Horace Greeley's ride with the stage-driver, Hank Monk. Holladay's coach was held up by "road agents," one of whom stood at the window and saw that the Overland "boss" kept his hands in the air. Holladay complained that he was getting tired, but was gruffly told to "keep 'em up." Then he said his nose itched.

"I'll scratch it for you," said the obliging "road agent," who thereupon thrust the muzzle of his shotgun a little farther forward and scratched Holladay's nose so vigorously with the weapon that, as the "boss" told reporters afterward, he "took off some of the skin." Holladay considered that he came well out of the affair, despite his bruised nose and the loss of considerable money and jewelry, as he saved a particularly valuable emerald which the robbers overlooked.

The holdings of Holladay on the Overland route have been variously estimated, but a summary contained in a Government document relating to claims because of the depredations of Indians may be accepted an authentic. In this document Holladay says that on the Overland route he "carried more than fifty tons of mail per quarter; employed one hundred and ten coaches, 1,750 horses and mules, and 450 men; that he erected buildings, houses, stations, stables, corrals and shelters and provided food, forage and wood."

Holladay's chief losses on the Overland came in 1864, when, under military orders, he had to move the entire stage route between Julesburg and Fort Bridger many miles south. Even then, Indian attacks were frequent and disastrous along the new route. Like Chorpenning, Holladay battled for his claims many years. They would come back from committees and the Court of Claims "recommended paid" but there is no record that there was even a partial payment made on more than $500,000 said to have been due.

2

The forts along the Pony Express route were often the scenes of tragic incidents. This was especially true of the forts in the present-day state of Wyoming—Laramie and Bridger.

The first-named fort was named for Jacques La Ramée, a trapper who settled at the mouth of the Laramie (or La Ramée) River, and who was killed by Indians. The second was founded by the celebrated trapper and scout, James Bridger. These forts were the first places to which appeals were made in case of Indian attacks, holdups, or other incidents of life along the great trail.

A Pony Express rider, who galloped up to the station at Fort Laramie in the summer of 1861, knew, by something which swung against the sky, that one more frontier crime had been expiated.

The details of this crime and its sequel were finished to me by Robert Spotswood, who at the time of the tragedy was on a tour of inspection over the division.

Owing to the difficulty of supplying meat to its outlying stations, the stage and "Pony" line had followed the expedient of hiring professional hunters. These men, mostly old trappers, and all of them skilled with the rifle, brought in fresh game to the stations, which not only varied the menu in behalf of the stage passengers, but afforded a welcome change of diet for the stage drivers, "Pony" riders and their assistants.

One of these hunters, supplying meat for the stations around Fort Laramie, was Bob Jennings, who had come over from the vicinity of Fort Bridger to fill the place of a hunter who had quit. Little was known of Jennings, but he soon built up an unenviable reputation along the line. He was six feet two inches in height, with an enormous head, topped with a thick shock of sandy hair.

Jennings' sullen disposition made him disliked, but he was a skilled hunter and kept his stations well supplied with meat, so the division superintendent did not feel called upon to discharge him. One of the relay stations was in charge of a man named "Hod" Russell, a slim, inoffensive fellow who was inordinately fond of poker. In one of the games in which Jennings participated, the hunter lost in the neighborhood of one hundred dollars, Russell being the winner. Jennings was not going to pay, but Russell's friends made him settle. He left, threatening vengeance and declaring that Russell had cheated.

A day or two after the episode of the card game, Spotswood, who was making his inspection trip in a light buckboard, came upon Russell playing cards, not at his own station, but the next one along the line. Russell said he was going back on the next stage, which was due right after the arrival of the "Pony" rider.

The Pony Express courier came in and the change of horses was effected, Russell helping. Then the stage came, and Russell and Spotswood both helped change the mules. Spotswood had just stepped to the head of the near leader, to adjust some piece of harness, when he heard the report of a rifle and a bullet whizzed past his head.

"Looking around," said Spotswood, "I saw a white puff of smoke from some bushes fifty yards away. Then I heard a cry, and saw that Russell, who had climbed up to the seat next the driver, had fallen forward, dead. Everyone surmised that Jennings had done the shooting. Several started at once for the bushes, but I stopped them, telling them that Jennings was a dead shot and had the advantage of concealment and could kill half a dozen of them before they could reach him. We took the body of Russell on in the coach, and buried him near his station. Then I reported the murder to the commandant at the fort, who immediately organized a searching expedition for Jennings.

"The soldiers hunted for several days, to no avail, and the commandant said it looked as if Jennings had succeeded in 'making his getaway.' I was convinced that the hunter was still in the neighborhood, however, and called in one of the greatest frontiersmen the West ever knew —'Buffalo Bill' Comstock. He was the first man to earn that title in the West, the name being given to him because of the great numbers of buffaloes he had killed while hunting in behalf of various Army posts on the plains. He had some Indian blood in him, I believe, and had lived much with the Brulé Sioux. He was rugged, able and sincere, and had gone through marvelous experiences in his life on the plains. The commandant at the fort said he would coöperate with the stage company in giving a reward to Comstock if he brought in Jennings, dead or alive.

"When we called Comstock into consultation, he said quietly:

" 'I'll get him alive.'

"Comstock got three companions, and all disguised themselves as Indians. No one could have guessed they were not Sioux. They spent a few days hunting, fishing and looking about. Then they discovered that Jennings had hidden in a secluded spot on a little creek. He had built himself a brush wickiup and was living on game and fish.

"The next morning after their discovery, Comstock and his companions strolled into Jennings' camp. The hunter raised his rifle, and seemed about to fire, but the supposed Indians made peace signs and he allowed them to approach. Then all sat down and had a talk in Sioux. Jennings' suspicions vanished, and he invited his visitors to breakfast. He laid aside his rifle and his revolver and cartridge belt while he broiled an antelope steak.

"This was the opportunity which Comstock and his companions had awaited. They flung themselves on Jennings, and soon had him bound and helpless, though he put up a hard fight. Then, putting Jennings astride one of his own horses, and binding his feet underneath, they took him to the nearest station on the trail, where they were lucky enough to catch a west-bound stage. The passengers aboard marveled at the ways of the West when they saw Jennings bound to the rear boot of the stage with heavy chains. Not satisfied with that, Jennings' captors buckled him with stout straps. Then they rode behind the stage as an escort until the fort was reached and Jennings was delivered to the commandant."

The hanging that followed was entirely unofficial, but it was surprisingly quick. Stage employees and others along the trail, who had gathered on hearing that Russell's slayer had been captured, assisted in the execution, which had its unique features.

Jennings, without even being blindfolded, was led to an immense pole, like a well sweep, which was used for hoisting fresh meat in the air, to keep it away from flies and wild animals.

It was his body, swinging from the end of the pole, which attracted the attention of the next Pony Express courier to arrive, in the early morning hours.

CHAPTER XX

WIRES AHEAD

1

A SHORT time before the first Pony Express riders flashed across the western half of the country, a man on mule-back traversed the trail on a self-imposed mission which eventually was to end the era of saddle and spurs in transcontinental communication.

He was Edward Creighton, a young contractor who had been successful in constructing lines of telegraph in the East, and who was convinced that he could replace horseflesh with wire in bridging the gap between the Missouri River and the Pacific Coast. On his preliminary trip of inspection he traveled the whole route of the Hockaday & Liggett and Chorpenning stage lines. He jogged along, out of Kearney, up the Platte, past the crossing of the South Platte to Fort Laramie and over South Pass to Fort Bridger and Salt Lake City. From the Mormon capital he went on through the unpeopled stretches of the Great Salt Lake Basin to Carson City, Placerville and Sacramento. All the time he was making notes concerning the best places for telegraph stations and the possibilities of securing poles in the vast stretches of desert where not a tree was in sight for miles.

By the time Creighton arrived in California he was

fortified with answers to the objections which had always been supposed to be unanswerable when the subject of a transcontinental telegraph was brought up. The chief objections were that poles could not be secured and planted, and, even if they were, the Indians would never allow a wire to be strung across their hunting grounds.

The Pony Express in itself was a good answer to the argument concerning the danger from Indians. Aside from the brief interruption caused by the Pah-Ute war, the telegraph line of flesh and blood had continued to operate. Creighton shrewdly saw that Indian superstition constituted a big point in his favor. If the Indians looked upon the Pony Express couriers as "bad medicine," it was likely that a telegraph line would impress them even more strongly as something to be shunned.

"To facilitate communication between the Atlantic and Pacific states by electric telegraph," Congress had passed an act on June 16, 1860, guaranteeing an annual subsidy of $40,000 for ten years to any company which succeeded in bringing about the desired result. In January, 1861, the Pacific Telegraph Company was incorporated in Nebraska. F. A. Bee and Benjamin F. Ficklin, who had been prominent in the encouragement of the Pony Express, were among the incorporators. In California the Overland Telegraph Company was incorporated. These eventually were merged with the Western Union system.

The company reaching Salt Lake City first was to receive a very considerable bonus in the way of tariff preferentials. James Gamble was in charge of the construction for the western company; Creighton had supervision over construction from Omaha to Salt Lake City. To facilitate construction, both forces were divided. Creighton worked west from Omaha and Stebbins east from Salt Lake City, while Gamble's two forces worked toward each other between Salt Lake and Carson City.

The work was pushed at an average rate of about five miles a day, though in one stretch of desert in the Southwest, Gamble completed sixteen miles in a day in order to reach a point where water could be obtained. But for the pioneer work of the stage company and the Pony Express company in establishing stations along the way, such a rapid rate of progress could not have been maintained. The fact that there were "Pony" relay stations between the stage stations, not more than ten miles apart, meant that help could be secured by the construction crews any time it was needed.

Creighton, working from the east, had four hundred men, all heavily armed and with the necessary provisions, including one hundred head of cattle for beef. Five hundred head of oxen and mules and more than one hundred wagons were used for the transportation of materials and provisions.

With the idea of impressing the Indians with the mysterious power of the "wire express," Creighton, then at Fort Bridger, asked Washakie, chief of the Shoshones, if he would like to talk with a Sioux chieftain at Horseshoe station, a few miles west of Fort Laramie. The Shoshone chieftain asked a question, which the Sioux answered. Then followed several questions and answers, back and forth, between the two chieftains. Greatly mystified, but hardly convinced that some trick had not been played upon them, the chiefs agreed to meet at a place midway between the stations and compare notes. This was done, with the result that the Indian tribes soon learned, through their chieftains, that the wire was really the instrument of Manitou.

In even more forceful ways were the Indians impressed by the crews engaged in stringing the wire. A number of Pah-Utes had been employed by Gamble, in Nevada. At one time, when the crews was working about two hundred miles east of the Sierra Nevada, a thunderstorm broke over the valley, and the wire became charged with electricity. The white workmen wore heavy buckskin gloves, which afforded insulation. Some Indians who were called upon to help in tightening a wire, took hold with their bare hands. The wire was just sufficiently charged with electricity to knock them down. This word was passed around among the Indians, and thereafter when any Pah-Ute had occasion to travel under a telegraph wire he went at full gallop with his head bent low in fear.

Outer stations were established as fast as connections were made. One of these stations was raided by Indians who evidently had not heard of the mysterious powers of the white man's wire, or who were skeptical. Thinking it to be whiskey, the Indians carried off a carboy of nitric acid. The first one to take a drink was "laid out," and the telegraphers in that neighborhood were looked upon as supermen, who could drink a particularly powerful brand of firewater!

2

The planting of telegraph poles began early in July, 1861—truly a time of momentous events along the Overland trail. The Pony Express at that time was carrying to the Pacific Coast the day-by-day news from the battle fronts. It had carried the news of the firing on Sumter, the seizure of Harper's Ferry and the great navy yard near Norfolk, and President Lincoln's call for volunteers. Soon it would bear the news, throughout the West, of the Federal disaster at Bull Run.

The West was beginning to feel that its isolation was disappearing. The new contract on the overland route called for daily stage service; the faithful and efficient "Pony" was testing the endurance of men and horses to bring the news; and work had been started on the telegraph. The *Deseret News* of Salt Lake City summed up the local situation in the following comprehensive paragraph, on July 10:

> *Anticipated Events*—The arrival of the Pony Express from the East is expected in the course of the forenoon today. In the afternoon the first daily Overland Mail coach from St. Joseph may arrive, and before the setting of the sun the first telegraph pole on the Western line hence to California will unquestionably be erected on East Temple Street, not far from our office.

As fast as outer stations were established, the important news of the day was sent to them by wire and transferred to the Pony Express. This meant that, so far as telegraphic communication was concerned, the Pony Express was playing a constantly lessening part. The newspapers, in introductory lines which were significantly descriptive, told of the progress of the telegraph across the country. Thus, the San Francisco *Bulletin* on August 6, printed over its dispatches: "By telegraph to Fort Kearney from St. Louis, thence by Pony Express to Roberts Creek Station, thence by telegraph to San Francisco." By August 13 the Pony Express rider was leaving his dispatches for the *Bulletin* and other Pacific Coast papers at Dry Creek station, thirty-six miles east of Reese River station and one hundred and sixty-eight miles east of Fort Churchill. By August 26 the outer telegraph station was at Grub's Wells.

Similarly, at the eastern end, outer stations were established, as rapidly as progress was made, at points not exceeding fifty miles apart. Occasionally there was an unavoidable lapse in the news, witnessed by the following explanation, published in the San Francisco *Bulletin* of August 17:

> Outer Station, Pacific Telegraph, fifty miles west of Kearney, August 9. Owing to moving the outer station from Kearney to this place on Tuesday and Wednesday, and line being down yesterday and today, I have not been able to get a word of news for this Pony.

Creighton, on September 6, reported his part of the line completed west from Fort Laramie to within four hundred miles of Salt Lake City. About the first of October, Gamble reported his line complete with the exception of a gap of fifty or sixty miles between Ruby Valley and Schell Creek, midway between Carson City and Salt Lake. For that section of the line, Gamble and his men were obliged to go into the mountains themselves to get poles, and narrowly escaped being snowed in. Gamble had had trouble in having his first contract in Utah fulfilled. The contractors were Mormons, and one of Gamble's assistants, James Street, shrewdly went to Brigham Young about the matter. Young called in the contractors, found that they were at fault, and denounced them from the pulpit, saying

that their contracts should be fulfilled, even if they lost
every cent they had. The contractors went back to their
work, and there was no further trouble on that score.

While construction work was in progress, the Pony
Express riders rendered invaluable assistance by report-
ing breaks in the wire, where some of the younger Indians,
who were not inclined to look upon the telegraph as a
mysterious agency, had shown contempt for the white man
by destroying his work. At Ruby Valley, where the "Pony"
riders had always had to keep on their guard against
possible ambush, it was learned that the Pah-Utes were
planning a descent on the telegraph construction camp.
A Pony Express rider carried the news to Camp Floyd
and a sufficient military guard was hastily dispatched
to the scene.

Creighton's crew from the east finished their connections to Salt Lake City on October 18, and on that day
Brigham Young sent the first telegram from the Mormon
capital to Washington. Two days later, Gamble's men
from the west had completed the line between Salt Lake
City and the Pacific Coast. A few days were spent in making necessary connections at Salt Lake City, and October
24, the first congratulatory messages from Washington
were sent to San Francisco.

The "brass-pounders," at their clicking keys, had closed
the last gap on the Pony Express trail.

3

The carrying of news dispatches was, from the start,
the chief function of the Pony Express. If it had not been
for its importance as a bearer of press dispatches during
the troubled days at the outbreak of the Civil War, it is

more than likely that the "Pony" would have been discontinued when it passed from the control of Russell, Majors & Waddell.

The contract with the Government, made in March, 1861, when the Butterfield line was transferred from the southern to the central route, specified that the Pony Express was to be continued "until the completion of the transcontinental telegraph." Official Washington saw bad psychology in cutting off the fast mail service in such a crisis and leaving the people of the Pacific Coast a prey to rumors while the slow-moving stages were coming in. Therefore the new contractors were required to keep the Pony Express going until telegraph service was installed. It was the Government's first recognition of the value of the Pony Express, but it came at the eleventh hour.

The truth was that while he had "traveled light," as far as rider and saddle were concerned, the gallant "Pony" had been loaded down with a hopeless burden of debt. It cost between $25,000 and $30,000 a month to operate the Pony Express, according to reasonable estimate. Eighteen months of actual service, even at the lower figure, would amount to more than $400,000, of which expense Russell, Majors & Waddell bore the larger share, besides having to foot the losses caused by the Pah-Ute war.

The returns did not begin to balance the heavy outlay. From the beginning the company was handicapped in not having sufficient offices where Pony Express mail could be received. The California newspapers printed editorial appeals for better support for the new institution. In response they received communications from readers in the interior of the state, complaining that, much as they would like to patronize the "Pony," there was no way by which they could get letters to the main offices at Sacramento and San Francisco.

When the service was started the rate was set at $5.00 a half ounce. In May, 1861, when the Wells-Fargo interests took charge, the rate was reduced to $2 a half ounce, effective until July 1. On that date, under the terms of contract with the Government, the rate was reduced to $1.00 a half ounce. This resulted in an increased volume of mail business, but not enough to make the service profitable at such a low rate. The fact that Wells, Fargo & Company had a large number of offices where "Pony" stamps and envelopes could be bought, also served to increase the volume of business. [1]

[1] During its months of operation by the Central Overland California and Pike's Peak Express Company, Pony Express mail was canceled by handstamps. The first adhesive stamps, issued by Wells, Fargo & Company, were of $2.00 and $4.00 denominations. When the $1.00 rate went into effect on July 1, 1861, the same company was ready to supply the public with Pony Express stamps of $1.00, $2.00 and $3.00 denominations. These adhesive stamps bore the picture of a pony and rider. Some of the handstamps at first in use bore the outline of a pony, without a rider. Other handstamp cancellations do not show the running horse, but most of them contain the name "Pony Express" in some form. The first of these cancellations used at St. Joseph carried the name of the Central Overland California and Pike's Peak Express Company. Later a circle was added, enclosing the oval and containing the name "Pony Express." Wells, Fargo & Company issued a specially prepared envelope, with a printed frank on the left end of the cover, which paid the $1.00 per half-ounce rate for Pony service. Pony Express stamps and cancellations are quite rare, and many are collectors' items. Dr. Victor M. Berthold has gone very thoroughly into the subject in a monograph entitled *Handstamped Franks Used as Cancellations on Pony Express Letters 1860 and 1861, and the Pony Express Stamps and Their Use,* reprinted from the *Collectors' Club Philatelist.* H. C. Needham, also an authority on Pony Express stamps and cancellations, has written an introduction to the work by Dr. Berthold from which this information has been secured.

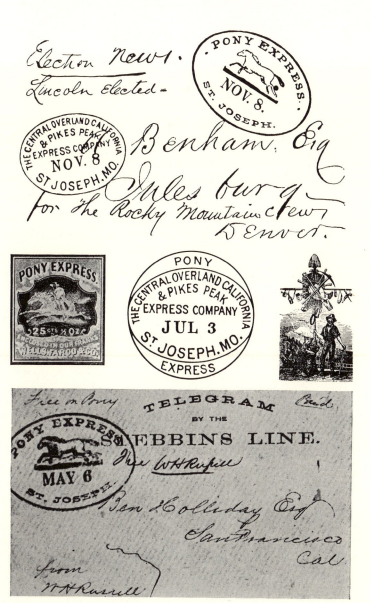

Pony Express envelopes (upper and lower). Wells, Fargo & Co. adhesive stamp; handstamp first used in cancellations, and envelope corner of California private mail carrier, showing "miner's coat of arms."

Courtesy Alfred F. Lichtenstein, New York.

All told, it is questionable if Pony Express receipts totaled $100,000. Russell, Majors & Waddell, having had to equip the line, build stations, and shoulder the operating expenses for at least a year unaided, sustained the heavy part of the ultimate loss. Their successors lost proportionately, during the final months of operation.

Not even the most liberal of mail contracts would have made up for such an outlay. As an object lesson the Pony Express succeeded, but as a business enterprise it belonged in the realm of chimeras.

Russell and his partners had put on the first Wild West show, and the public had cheered the performance but had neglected to pay at the gate.

CHAPTER XXI

SADDLES OFF

1

THE last Pony Express rider swung out of Atchison, Kansas, in late October, 1861.

St. Joe for several weeks had ceased to rejoice in its title as the jumping-off place for the West. There was no more booming of the cannon which told the ferry captain to be ready to shove off for the Kansas shore with the "Pony" mail. Ben Holladay had moved the stage and Pony Express headquarters to Atchison. His superlative Concord coach was there, in the midst of a host of weather-scarred "Pitching Betsies." The Patee House, where riders were fêted, and where Russell and Majors used to play host to distinguished travelers, was just a hotel, and St. Joe had become just another town.

Along the familiar trail, covered by the last rider, a great change had taken place. Emigrants still struggled westward. Stage-coaches—daily now!—still rumbled through the sagebrush, like strange animals invading the haunts of the buffalo. But at many of the stations there was an ominous clicking going on, day and night.

All along Slade's division—at Julesburg, Mud Springs, Fort Laramie, Horseshoe, Deer Creek, Three Crossings and Rocky Ridge, there were telegraph operators. They were scattered on the trail—at Bridger and beyond Salt

Lake, at Egan's Canyon and Ruby, and at the sink of the Carson. From San Francisco to the Missouri there was not a hundred-mile stretch without its telegraph station and its man in charge.

Routine orders had suddenly whisked away a lot of romance from the trail and substituted the dullness of which civilization has always had plenty and to spare.

Orders had come through to sell the horses or to add them to the livestock at the stage stations—the gallant ponies which had outrun the swift mustangs of pursuing Indians. It had been ordered that relay stations were to be dismantled or turned over to the telegraph company. Station keepers, stock tenders and horseshoers were ordered to find new jobs, and with them went the "Pony" riders—the men who had made possible a mail service without equal in Christendom.

New jobs! Well, no doubt they were to be had, but what could offer any excitement equal to the mad scramble of men and horses at the relay stations? What could there be, to make up for the rhythmic swing of the racer's long stride?

New jobs! There were plenty in the young and growing West, but the Pony Express rider who hung up his saddle for the last time felt in his heart that there could be no other job in the world quite worth while.

2

The disbanding of the Pony Express came at the time of the greatest expansion of the stagecoach business in the West.

Wells, Fargo & Company and Ben Holladay were acquiring rival companies and starting new lines wherever opportunity offered. New mining districts were being opened in Colorado, Idaho and Montana. The mines in Nevada were booming. Growing towns in the Northwest were demanding stage and local Pony Express service. The San Francisco newspapers carried advertisements for "Wells, Fargo & Co.'s Pony Express to Washoe; through in 24 hours." Crowded off the main highway, the "Pony" was still active on the by-ways.

Some of the overland riders were not long out of the saddle. Among them was "Pony Bob" Haslam, who was sent by Wells, Fargo & Company to ride an express route of one hundred miles between Queens River and Owyhee River in Idaho. The Modoc war broke out, and Haslam quit his run after he had counted ninety dead Chinese within ten miles along the trail, all slain by Indians. The rider who succeeded him was killed on his first trip.

Haslam's next job, as express messenger on the stage line between Salt Lake City and the bandit-ridden Virginia City district in Montana, was hardly less dangerous. Not until the Vigilantes had made a "clean sweep" of Plummer and his road agents was any express messenger safe in pulling out of Virginia City in charge of gold dust. After the wholesale lynchings, which wound up with the execution of Slade, "Pony Bob" concluded that he had had enough of the excitements of life in Montana. He served as deputy United States Marshal at Salt Lake City, and for a while was Wells-Fargo messenger between the Mormon capital and Denver.

Haslam was called back to Nevada to do some riding for Wells, Fargo & Company, between Reno and Virginia City, in 1868. The Pacific Union Express Company was running in sharp competition. A Pony Express run had

been put on between the two cities, and Haslam was summoned to make the first ride in opposition to Frank
Henderson, the rider for the rival concern. The race had
been widely advertised, and considerable money was
wagered on the outcome. Each rider was to have five
changes of horses in twenty miles.

Both received their packages before the mail train
stopped at Reno. The Pacific Express rider got about
ten rods' start, Haslam having delayed to see that his mail
packages were firmly adjusted. Bob soon overhauled his
rival and kept ahead of him during the rest of the distance.

In later years "Pony Bob" lived in Chicago, where
he was connected with one of the big hotel companies. His
business card was unique, bearing a sketch of himself
when, as a youth of twenty, he made his famous ride on
the "Pony" trail through the hostile Pah-Ute country in
Nevada. Many persons, after conversing with a quiet, affable stranger, who seemed to be taking life easy in the
lobby of the Congress Hotel, were amazed to find, on ex-
changing cards, that they had been talking to "Pony
Bob," of Pony Express fame. Haslam died in Chicago in
1912, at the age of 72.

Among the several riders in the Overland Pony Express
service who enlisted on the Federal side at the outbreak of
the war—all employees having been required to take the
oath of allegiance to the Union—was Johnny Frey, the
daredevil of the St. Joe end of the route. Frey entered the
cavalry service, with every prospect of making a brilliant
record, but was killed at Baxter Springs, not far from
his home at Wathena, Kansas, in one of the early en-
gagements of the war. Johnny was of German and Eng-

lish descent and came of a well-to-do family. His father was one of the first to introduce blooded horses and cattle in Kansas, and Johnny, at the time he entered the Pony Express service, was carrying on this business, as much for pleasure as for profit. He had a small herd of fine cattle, and several Kentucky-bred horses. He rode these horses in local races and nearly always carried off first honors. He was famous as a rider in the Kansas-Missouri region near St. Joe before he became a "Pony" courier.

The West still had some thrills in store for Thomas J. Ranahan ("Irish Tommy") when the Pony Express service was ended. After a few years of stage-driving, Ranahan turned the reins over to someone else and joined Colonel George A. Forsyth's scouts. Forsyth, setting out to punish the Sioux and Cheyennes who had been conducting raids in Kansas and Colorado at the close of the Civil War, headed about fifty unenlisted men, mostly trappers and hunters who were used to Indian campaigning.

On the trail of a war party on the Arickaree branch of the Republican River, near the Colorado-Kansas line, Forsyth was suddenly attacked at dawn by fifteen hundred Cheyennes and Brulé Sioux under the Cheyenne chief, Roman Nose. The result would have been annihilation had it not been that every man in Forsyth's command was a seasoned fighter and "savvied" Indian methods. Withdrawing to a tiny island in the stream which was hardly more than knee-deep in any place, the scouts killed their mules and converted the animals into breastworks, behind which they made a desperate fight. The Indians, confident of wiping out the little command of fifty men, charged again and again. Colonel Forsyth was wounded, and Lieutenant Fred Beecher, a nephew of Henry Ward Beecher, was killed with several others. One of the sharpshooters among the scouts finally managed to kill Chief Roman Nose, after which the Indians ceased their frontal attacks and settled down to a siege.

With nothing but mule meat on which to live, and with several of their number wounded, it looked as if the scouts were doomed. At the end of three days, four scouts managed to slip through the Indian line by twos, under cover of darkness. After terrible privations, and narrowly escaping being discovered by Indians, the messengers reached Fort Wallace. Rescuers did not arrive until the seventh day of the siege, by which time the surviving scouts had nearly succumbed to starvation.

Even this experience did not cure Ranahan's desire for adventure. He continued scouting for several years under General Carr and other leaders in the Indian campaigns which followed. The author of this book met Ranahan on the Beecher Island battle site, where a memorial, commemorating this now famous engagement, was being dedicated. Ranahan even then preferred to talk about his stage-driving and Pony Express days rather than his experiences in Indian campaigning. In his later years "Irish Tommy" lived at Weiser, Idaho, where he was engaged in business.

Jay G. Kelley, who faced many dangers and frequently "doubled" his run through the Nevada section of the trail where the Pah-Utes were particularly menacing, became a mining engineer in Colorado. Sam and Jim Gilson found wealth in the Utah mines, the former being the developer of Gilsonite, a mineral with an asphalt base, used in road making. It was originally known as Uintahite, but was renamed in honor of Gilson, who developed a practical use for it.

For many years W. A. (Bill) Cates was a familiar figure in Denver, where he had settled down in business. Few were aware, from anything Cates had to say on the subject, that he had been a Pony Express rider. After much urging he consented to appear as a "Pony" courier in a procession which was part of a festival being staged by Denver. There was no Pony Express saddle to be had, and Cates refused to ride a "stock" saddle. So he hunted up the best saddle-maker in Denver and had him make a replica of the type of saddle, *mochila* and all, which had been designed for the Pony Express riders.

Robert J. Spotswood, who succeeded Slade as Superintendent of the "toughest division on the Overland," became a resident of Denver. No man along the entire route was more respected or better liked than Bob Spotswood, who could drive a four-horse team or ride a pony with the best and who had had an active part in every branch of the Overland service. This all-round experience stood Spotswood in good stead, some years after the discontinuance of the Pony Express, when he ran stage lines of his own between Denver and the mining district of Central City and between Denver and Cheyenne. Spotswood died in Denver about 1900.

In his book, *Seventy Years on the Frontier*, Alexander Majors gives a place to William F. Cody ("Buffalo Bill") among the Pony Express riders. In his introduction to this book, Cody says:

Family reverses, after the killing of my father in the Kansas war, caused me to start out, though a mere boy, to seek aid in the support of my mother and sisters, and it was to Mr. Alexander Majors that I applied for a situation. He looked me over carefully, in his kindly way, and, after questioning me closely, gave me the place of messenger boy, that is, one to ride with dispatches between the overland freighters—wagon trains going westward into the almost unknown wild dump of prairie and mountain.

Cody was fourteen years old at the time the Pony Express was started. If the company broke its rule of not hiring men under twenty, it was the only time that a difference of six years was passed over. Unfortunately, perhaps, for history if not for public enjoyment, some of Cody's numerous biographers have ascribed riding feats to this "mere boy," as Cody described himself, which quite outshine the performances of Jim Moore, Bob Haslam, Jay Kelley, Jack Keetley, and others who made endurance rides which were exceptional. It is only fair enough to a deservedly popular character to assume that Cody was too busy as a showman in later years to curb every enthusiastic pen that was taken up in his praise.

The Egans, father and son, prominent among the Mormon riders who so impressed Burton, settled down in Utah after the days of the "Pony" were over. The son, Richard Erastus (" 'Ras") Egan, was known as a particularly daring rider, and once "doubled" on his run from Salt Lake to Rush Valley, making a continuous trip of one hundred and fifty miles in a blinding snowstorm. At another time he rode a double route, one hundred and sixty-five miles, and then made the return trip without resting—three hundred and thirty miles in all. On this route young Egan came on a stage which had been held up by Indians. The driver and passengers had been killed, and the Indians had taken the stage horses. One of the mounted Indians started in pursuit of Egan. Having the better horse, the Pony Express rider kept his pursuer just out of gunshot. Then Egan suddenly turned and rode directly at the Indian, yelling and waving his revolver and putting the pursuer to flight.

Nick Wilson was another Utah rider who had many encounters with Indians. He was shot in the forehead with an arrow from the bow of a Goshute Indian, and bore the scar during the remainder of his life. William Streeper of Salt Lake City was a famous rider, and others who helped put the mail through Utah and Nevada were Billy Fisher, John Fisher and "Wash" Perkins.

Theodore Rand, who rode out of Kansas, became a railroad man at Atchison. Don Rising, who was credited with some of the fastest endurance rides made on the eastern division, went back to his boyhood home at Wetmore, Kansas, where he spent his remaining years.

3

William Campbell, whose experiences as a Pony Express rider are related elsewhere in this volume, was one of the Russell, Majors & Waddell "graduates" of freighting days who made good after the completion of the telegraph had ended his career in the saddle. His after-adventures show the opportunities which the West then held for the young and ambitious.

After his last ride out of Fort Kearney with the Pony Express mail, Campbell turned to freighting. He and his brother bought ox-teams and hauled lumber to build houses in the new town of Denver. Then they were engaged to haul freight to Virginia City, Montana. On arrival there, with a load of paints and oils, they sold their five ox-teams, of five yoke each, for $5,000 in gold dust.

The next problem was to ride horseback 1,500 miles to Nebraska City, through a country infested with road agents and Indians. Joining with other travelers until they had made a party of eight or ten, the youths arrived at Nebraska City after a ride of fifty days on short rations. Their gold was shipped through to the Philadelphia mint and brought greenbacks at the rate of $1.40 for every dollar in "dust," a margin of $2,000 to their credit.

Most of this money was invested in mules, which the Government was selling at the end of the war. Fifty young animals were corraled near Nebraska City. An armed guard was maintained over them, to prevent theft by Indians. Campbell's brother, who was a harness-maker by trade, worked all winter making sets of harness for the mules. In the spring the brothers took a large freight contract, hauling merchandise to Salt Lake City. They made three trips in one season, and then sold their complete outfit at a good price. For the next season's work, more mules and wagons were bought. At the end of another successful season, the brothers took a contract for grading along the line of the Union Pacific Railroad, which was then being built. This work proved the most profitable of any in which they had engaged. At the end of eleven years of such experiences, the boys—now men of affairs —returned to Nebraska City and settled near there, each on three hundred and twenty acres of prairie land. Both married girls they had been "courting" for several years. William was elected State Senator. In later years he settled in the San Joaquin Valley of California, where he took an active part in financing and constructing some three hundred and sixty miles of irrigation canals.

When the author of this book talked with the former Pony Express rider, late in the summer of 1931, William Campbell, though in his ninetieth year, was erect and sturdy, and keen in his enjoyment of life. The girl he married in Nebraska was at his side, and he spoke proudly of her and her influence on his life, and of their family of seven sons and daughters. He exhibited the little leather-bound Bible which had been given him when he became an employee of Alexander Majors.

"I was glad to get that Bible," he said simply; "and have always prized it, though collectors have made me offers for it."

Of the few score picked riders of Pony Express days, not many, like William Campbell, lived to see the airplane beacons flashing along the trail which they rode in darkness. Many of them were gone when the "horseless carriage" first pushed its way across the continent.

Nine out of ten of the riders, after they had quit the saddle, went into occupations utterly prosaic. Nor is that a subject for wonderment. The West could offer no other cup of adventure which would not seem flat and unprofitable after the one they had just quaffed!

CHAPTER XXII

CONCLUSION

1

THE Pony Express came officially to an end on October 26, 1861, two days after the completion of the transcontinental telegraph.

On the next day the San Francisco *Alta California* published this brief editorial:

> *Suspension of the Pony Express*—Wells, Fargo & Company, having received a dispatch from the East, directing the stopping of the Pony Express, that active animal may be considered as withdrawn from the Overland course. *Peace to his manes!*

As a matter of fact it was nearly a month later, on November 20, to be exact, when the *Bulletin* announced that the last Pony Express, on the steamer *Eclipse*, had left Sacramento that morning for San Francisco with a total of seventy-eight letters addressed to individuals and firms in San Francisco. Why this final mail was so late in coming through does not seem to have called for any reportorial inquiry. There were no crowds to greet the last rider, as in the case of the first courier who arrived in San Francisco, which is no indication that the Pacific Coast was not sincerely mourning the passing of the "Pony."

As a matter of fact, the substitution of the telegraph

for the Pony Express did not prove, at first, to be the godsend which had been anticipated. The tolls were high. To send a message from San Francisco to St. Louis cost $5 for ten words, with 45 cents for each additional word; to Chicago, $5.60 and 50 cents; to New York and Washington $6, and 75 cents; to Boston, $7, and 60 cents. In the ten words were included the place, month and day, leaving only seven words for the message. Whatever press rate was established seems to have been too high to suit the newspapers, which may have had something to do with flavoring this editorial, regarding the passing of the Pony Express, published in the *Pacific* and quite generally reprinted:

A fast and faithful friend has the Pony been to our far-off state. Summer and winter, storm and shine, day and night, he has traveled like a weaver's shuttle back and forth till now his work is done. Good-bye, Pony! No proud and star-caparisoned charger in the war field has ever done so great, so true and so good a work as thine. No pampered and world-famed racer of the turf will ever win from you the proud fame of the fleet courser of the continent. You came to us often with tidings that made your feet beautiful on the tops of the mountains; tidings of the world's great life, of nations rising for liberty and winning the day of battles, and nations' defeats and reverses. We have looked for you as those who wait for the morning, and how seldom did you fail us! When days were months and hours weeks, how you thrilled us out of our pain and suspense, to know the best or know the worst! You have served us well!

A season of disastrous floods in the Carson Valley followed the installation of the telegraph. Poles were uprooted and wires were down. So bad were conditions that rumors were heard to the effect that the entire overland service would be abandoned, as the stage line had suffered with the telegraph. The California Legislature petitioned Congress to have the overland mail service maintained, and pointed out that the stage stations were necessary, as the telegraph could not be kept in order without the aid rendered by the mail company. The petition asked faster stage service, "and, in addition to this service, that the Pony Express be restored."

Neither editorial sentiment nor the petitions of legislators could restore the "Pony." The next step in progress was to be the transcontinental railroad, but, strange to say, there were business leaders on the Pacific Coast who did not realize that fact. Holladay and other stage company officials could not be made to see, until the last, that the stage, as well as the Pony Express, was doomed. The drivers of the Concord coaches had only a little way to go until they, like the Pony Express rider, were to say good-bye to the trail.

2

The Pony Express was in actual operation seventy-nine weeks, deducting four weeks' suspension due to the Pah-Ute war.

During the first month of operation the trips between St. Joseph and Sacramento were weekly. After that they were semi-weekly each way, constituting a total of 308 one-way trips.

The route of the Pony Express was approximately 2,000 miles in length. The riders covered a total of 616,-

000 miles, or more than twenty-four times around the world.

At one hundred letters a trip, a reasonably high estimate, the total mail was something over 30,000 letters.

Estimating the expense of operation at $25,000 a month, the total cost of the Pony Express must have been about $475,000.

The returns per letter ranged from $5 to $1, as the charges were lowered. Three dollars would have been a high average return, which meant that total mail receipts may have been in the neighborhood of $90,000, plus any charges made to newspapers for their "special" service.

Figuring on a basis of letter mail only, outside of any newspaper charges, it cost about $16 a letter to serve the patrons of the "Pony." As balanced against a $3 return per letter, this left a deficit of $13, a per-letter loss not as high as that sustained on the Butterfield coach route through the Southwest—the main difference being that in the latter case the Government footed the loss, while in the case of the "Pony" during most of its time of operation, the deficit was borne by individuals.

Some writers have estimated the total loss of the Pony Express at approximately $200,000, which apparently is much too low. Alexander Majors, in his book of reminiscences, says the loss was "several hundred thousand dollars."

The bulk of Pony Express business was in "through" mail, there being comparatively little for Salt Lake City, Denver and other "way" points. The lists of "Pony" letters received on the Pacific Coast, as printed in the San Francisco and Sacramento newspapers, indicate that returns could have gone only a small part of the way toward balancing the costs.

The failure of expected political support, and the unfortunate publicity attendant upon the "great bond scandal" at Washington, which came just prior to the awarding of the Overland mail contract, ended the long struggle of the "Pony" against financial odds.

3

Along the two-thousand mile front of the Overland trail, one transportation general after another had fought and lost.

The big trail "broke" nearly every man who tried to master it. Woodward lost his life and Chorpenning a fortune trying to make the route pay—first in the days of pack mules and later by wagon and coach.

Woodson, Kimball—both were losers when they sought to conquer that part of the trail which lay between Salt Lake and Independence, and McGraw was glad to turn over his contract to another. Hockaday & Liggett sold out their mail contract for what they could get—Hockaday on the verge of nervous collapse due to the strain of fighting Indians and storms.

Russell, the man of many daring schemes, was the next to succumb, and with him went the once prosperous firm of Russell, Majors & Waddell, whose freight wagons had lurched over every important trail in the West. Ben Holladay, the forceful and picturesque, seemed to be on the verge of success until the Indians appropriated his expensive horses and mules and laid his stations in ashes from one end of Wyoming to the other. It was a blow that staggered even so doughty a fighter, and Holladay soon quit the trail for quieter prospects.

New men seemed always ready to step into the breach. Figured on paper, the attractions of the Overland proved irresistible to one investor after another. Stage fares were high, and could be made higher; there were mail subsidies to be had, and there was treasure to be carried, at high rates, from the branches of the trail that penetrated the mining districts. The West was certain to grow rapidly, and local transportation must increase proportionately.

Audacity was more common than caution in business enterprise beyond the Missouri in those days, and men were not inclined to look on the other side of the picture—the high cost of stage operation through uninhabited districts; the damage and delays caused by storms, and the constant threat of Indian depredations. Moreover, there were the losses due to organized bands of horse thieves—men who would risk the hemp to secure horseflesh. In spite of the large rewards offered for their capture, and undeterred by lynchings, these gangs operated for years along the Overland, usually contriving to have the Indians blamed for their misdeeds—witness the following item from the San Francisco *Bulletin:*

It is strongly surmised that the horses and mules recently stolen from the station at Bear River have all gone westward, to the California market. The company offers $1,000 reward for their delivery. They are sufficiently branded XP (Express) so that there can be little deception practiced upon purchasers. At the time they were stolen, the Indians were blamed, and also for the disappearance of the herdsman, who was at first set down as killed by the redskins; but the indications point westward—and no murder.

The losses due to these organized thieves, who sometimes contrived to get one of their number employed as an Overland stock tender, amounted to many thousands of dollars. In the matter of Indian depredations, the claims of Chorpenning, Holladay and others who had government contracts amounted to more than $1,000,000.

Heavy as these losses were, it was the high cost of day-to-day operation that sapped one treasury after another. One Indian "scare," even though it never developed into reality, could cut off thousands of dollars in passenger receipts. One bad storm might hold up an entire division and stop the mail service long enough to endanger a government contract. A mining camp might turn in a profit for a year or two and then it would be "played out." There would be a rush to some other district, and the stage company would be left with a "dead end" from which coaches and livestock must be removed.

Capricious, even to the point of treachery, the Overland continued to lure men to financial ruin.

If the Pony Express had succeeded, it would have been against all the precedent of the trail.

4

Yet the Pony Express was a success in ways other than financial.

Every newspaper reader who saw the headline, "By Pony Express," found a dull world brightened. The idea of a chain of horsemen braving the dangers of the West, night and day, was something to quicken the imagination.

Like Balzac, who on reading one of Cooper's stories, exclaimed, "Oh, to be a red Indian!" the fireside sitter on the Atlantic shore let himself soar in imagination across the prairies and over the mountains with the daring saddlemen of the "Pony."

Nothing ever attracted more attention to the West. The rawest tenderfoot who turned westward knew there was a Pony Express and would have been disappointed if he had not seen a rider. Later on, in the Wild West show era, no performance would have been complete without its Pony Express race, with the riders making swift changes of saddles. Even today, when a big rodeo is staged in the West, the relay race, born of the Pony Express, is a feature that brings the crowd to its feet, shouting with enthusiasm.

The *mochilas* of the Pony Express riders carried the "air mail" of 1860–61. The "Pony" was as far ahead of the stagecoach in those days as the airplane is ahead of the railroad train today.

It was the Pony Express that gave the newspapers of the country a long-desired opportunity to "speed up" their news service to and from the Pacific Coast. Most important of all, the "Pony" disproved the theory that the Rocky Mountains formed an impassable barrier in winter. It did much to minimize the terrors of "the Great American Desert," and to hasten the development of the West.

The Pony Express was the greatest school of horsemanship ever developed. Riding under the most difficult and dangerous conditions, the men of the "Pony" established records for endurance in the saddle which will remain unequaled for all time. Selected from the most promising applicants at a time when the saddle played a part in every-day life, these men went joyously about a task which tested human stamina to the very limit. Their so-called "Ponies" were anything but such in reality—powerful animals, clean of limb, deep of lung, and "outlaw" in disposition. Only resilient youth, born to the saddle, could have ridden such animals at top speed, day after day.

The youngsters who took so gayly to such an unheard-of task must have amazed even the dreamer, Russell, whom the world has to thank for a "failure" so glorious that it will be remembered forever. The riders of the Pony Express made that institution greater in reality than it could have been in the fondest imaginings of the romanticist who planned it.

The clattering hoofs of the "Pony," and the sound of the rider's horn, aroused echoes which never can be stilled.

BIBLIOGRAPHY

ALTER, J. CECIL. *Utah, the Storied Domain; a Documentary History.* The American Historical Society, Chicago; 1932.

—— *James Bridger, Frontiersman, Scout and Guide.* Shepard Book Co., Salt Lake City; 1925.

ATHERTON, GERTRUDE. *California, an Intimate History.* Boni & Liveright, New York; 1927.

BANCROFT, HUBERT HOWE. *Chronicles of the Builders of the Commonwealth.* The History Co., San Francisco; 1891.

—— *History of California.* The History Co., San Francisco; 1891.

BANNING, WILLIAM AND GEORGE H. *Six Horses.* The Century Co., New York; 1930.

BARNARD, HELEN M. *The Chorpenning Claim.* Bancroft Library, Berkeley, Calif.

BERTHOLD, DR. VICTOR M. *William H. Russell, Originator and Developer of the Pony Express.* The Collectors' Club Philatelist, Fredericksburg, Md.; Vol. VIII, Nos. I and II; 1929.

BRADLEY, GLENN D. *The Story of the Pony Express.* A. C. McClurg & Co., Chicago; 1913.

BURTON, SIR RICHARD F. *The City of the Saints.* Longman, Green, Longman & Roberts, London; 1927.

BUTTERFIELD, JULIA LORRILARD. *A Biographical Memorial of General Daniel Butterfield.* Grafton Press, New York; 1904.

CHORPENNING, GEORGE. *Case of G. Chorpenning vs. the United States of America*. Petition to the Forty-second Congress, Washington; 1870.

CLARK, C. M. *A Trip to Pike's Peak*. S. P. Rounds, Chicago; 1861.

CONNELLEY, WILLIAM E. *Wild Bill—James Butler Hickok*. Collections of the Kansas State Historical Society, 1926–28. Topeka.

COUTANT, C. G. *History of Wyoming*. Chaplin, Spafford & Mathison, Laramie, Wyo.; 1890.

DAVIS, JEFFERSON. *Report of the Secretary of War Respecting the Use of Camels for Military Transportation*. Thirty-fourth Congress, third session; Senate Executive Document No. 63; 1857.

DAVIS, SAM P. *The History of Nevada*. The Elms Publishing Co., Reno, Nev., Los Angeles, Calif.; 1913.

DOWNEY, FAIRFAX. *Burton, Arabian Nights Adventurer*. Chas. Scribner's Sons, New York; 1931.

DRIGGS, HOWARD R. AND WILSON, E. N. *The White Indian Boy*. World Book Co., Yonkers-on-Hudson, N. Y.; 1919.

EGAN, HOWARD. *Pioneering the West*. Howard R. Egan Estate, Richmond, Utah; 1917.

GREELEY, HORACE. *An Overland Journey from New York to San Francisco*. New York; 1860.

HAFEN, LEROY R. *The Overland Mail*. Arthur H. Clark Co., Cleveland; 1926.

HANSEN, GEORGE W. *The Wild Bill-McCanless Tragedy, a Much Misrepresented Event in Nebraska History*. With an introduction by Addison E. Sheldon, State Historian. The Nebraska History Magazine, Vol. 10, No. 2, April-June, 1927. The Nebraska State Historical Society, Lincoln, Neb.

HAUCK, LOUISE PLATT. *The Pony Express Celebration.* Missouri Historical Review, Vol. 17. Columbia, Mo.; 1923.

—— *The Youngest Rider.* Lothrop, Lee & Shepard Co., Boston; 1927.

HICKMAN, BILL. *Confessions of Bill Hickman.* George H. Croffut & Co., New York; 1872.

LARIMER, WILLIAM AND WILLIAM H. H. *Reminiscences.* Printed for private circulation under the auspices of William Larimer Mellon, Pittsburgh; 1918.

LOEB, JULIUS. *The Pony Express.* American Philatelist, Fredericksburg, Md., November, 1930.

LYNCH, JEREMIAH. *A Senator of the Fifties; a Life of David C. Broderick of California.* Baker & Taylor Co., New York; 1911.

MAJORS, ALEXANDER. *Seventy Years on the Frontier;* with a preface by Buffalo Bill (William F. Cody) ; edited by Colonel Prentiss Ingraham. Rand, McNally & Co., Chicago; 1893.

NEEDHAM, H. C. AND DR. VICTOR M. BERTHOLD. *Handstamped Franks Used as Cancellations on Pony Express Letters, 1860–61, and the Pony Express Stamps and Their Use.* Reprinted from the Collectors' Club Philatelist, New York; 1927.

REID, JAMES D. *The Telegraph in America.* New York, 1874.

ROOT, FRANK A. AND CONNELLEY, W. E. *The Overland Stage to California.* Crane & Co., Topeka, Kan.; 1901.

SMILEY, JEROME C. *History of Denver.* The Times-Sun Publishing Co., Denver; 1901.

STIMSON, A. L. *History of the Express and Origin of American Railroads.* New York; 1858.

TOPONCE, ALEXANDER. *Reminiscences of Alexander Toponce, Pioneer*. Published by Mrs. Katie Toponce, Ogden, Utah; 1923.

TWAIN, MARK, *Roughing It*. Harper & Bros., New York.

TWITCHELL, RALPH E. *The Leading Facts in New Mexico History*. The Torch Press, Cedar Rapids, Ia.; 1911.

VISSCHER, WILLIAM LIGHTFOOT. *A Thrilling and Truthful History of the Pony Express*. Rand, McNally & Co., Chicago; 1908.

WILSTACH, FRANK J. *Wild Bill Hickok, the Prince of Pistoleers*. Doubleday, Page & Co., Garden City, N. Y.; 1926.

WILTSEE, ERNEST A. *The Pioneer Miner and the Pack Mule Express*. California Historical Society, San Francisco; 1931.

MISCELLANEOUS. Files of the Sacramento *Union;* San Francisco *Alta California* and *Bulletin;* St. Joseph *Weekly West;* New York *Herald* and New York *Tribune;* Salt Lake City *Deseret News*, and Kansas and Nebraska newspapers for 1860–61.

—— Documents and clippings in the Bancroft Library, Berkeley, Calif.

—— Pioneer papers of the California, Kansas, Nebraska and Nevada Historical Societies.

—— Debates on postal affairs, U. S. Congressional Globe, 1857–62.

—— Postmaster General's reports, 1857–62.

—— Special documents, U. S. Senate.

INDEX

INDEX